SONS OF THE SHAKING EARTH

SONS OF THE SHAKING EARTH

ERIC R. WOLF

 Phoenix Books

THE UNIVERSITY
OF CHICAGO PRESS

Title-page illustration. Parícutin Volcano, Michoacán, Mexico, after eruption. In the foreground, the lava-covered village of San Juan Parangaricutiro. (Courtesy of Pan American Union.)

Library of Congress Catalog Card Number: 59-12290

The University of Chicago Press, Chicago & London
The University of Toronto Press, Toronto 5, Canada

© 1959 by The University of Chicago. Published 1959
Third Impression 1962. First published as a Phoenix Book 1962
Composed and printed by The University of Chicago Press
Chicago, Illinois, U.S.A.

To My Father

Preface

This book is an attempt to trace the lifeline of a culture. In it I have striven for synthesis rather than for patient anatomy of detail. Writing as a scientist, I here offer a general statement of what anthropologists have learned about one area of the world. Three chapters deal with the geography of Middle America, with the biology of its inhabitants, with its variegated languages. Four chapters trace the prehistoric expansion of its culture; four others explore the altered rhythms of its growth after the impact of foreign conquest. But in writing this book, my aims have also been personal. Middle America has also been a personal experience; and in my writing I have attempted to convey something of the quality of this experience.

In completing this task, I derive great pleasure from acknowledging my multiple intellectual and personal debts. Hortense Powdermaker, Ruth Benedict, and Julian Steward initiated me into the mysteries of the anthropological craft; much that I have written here takes its departure from insights originally theirs. Many people have taught me about Middle America, but none so much as Pedro Armillas, who first showed me

Preface

Teotihuacán, Tajín, Xochicalco, and Tula, and my friend Ángel Palerm, with whom I shared two seasons in the field. To both of them I am indebted for many hours of pleasant company. My wife Katia has accompanied me on my Middle American journeys and throughout the travails of writing this book. But for her aid and understanding, my peregrinations would have been a great deal more tortuous. She has my love and admiration.

I am grateful to the Henry L. and Grace Doherty Charitable Foundation for supporting my Middle American apprenticeship in Mexico during 1951–52. The Institute of Research in the Social Sciences of the University of Virginia not only sent me into the field in 1956 but also underwrote the preparation of my manuscript during the two successive summers of 1957 and 1958. My heartfelt thanks go to the University, to Dr. Wilson Gee, director of the Institute, and to Miss Ruth Ritchie, who patiently typed several successive versions of this essay.

Several friends and colleagues read and commented on parts of the present volume in the course of preparation. John Buettner-Janusch proved most helpful with the chapter on physical anthropology. Floyd G. Lounsbury and A. Richard Diebold read the chapter on language and exorcised some of my more patent errors. James A. Bennyhoff reviewed the sections dealing with prehistory. Sidney W. Mintz and Peter R. Goethals commented on several of the chapters in their embryonic form, while Cármen Viqueira did me the kindness of reading the entire manuscript with a critical yet sympathetic eye. David Lowenthal gave me advice on maps, and Patrick Gallagher drew both maps and illustrations. Harold C. Conklin saved me from several embarrassing last-minute errors. I am most grateful to them for their labors on my behalf. Certainly they should not be taken to task if I have not always followed their good advice. The faults of this book are my own, as was the pleasure I derived from writing it.

Very special thanks go to Joe Seckendorf and William T. Sanders for allowing me to make use of some of their fine photographs.

All the earth is a grave and nothing escapes it;
nothing is so perfect that it does not descend to its tomb.
Rivers, rivulets, fountains and waters flow,
but never return to their joyful beginnings;
anxiously they hasten on to the vast realms of the rain god.
As they widen their banks, they also fashion
the sad urn of their burial.
Filled are the bowels of the earth with pestilential dust
once flesh and bone, once animate bodies of men
who sat upon thrones, decided cases, presided in council,
commanded armies, conquered provinces, possessed treasure,
destroyed temples,
exulted in their pride, majesty, fortune, praise and power.
Vanished are these glories, just as the fearful smoke vanishes
that belches forth from the infernal fires of Popocatepetl.
Nothing recalls them but the written page.

HUNGRY-COYOTE (NETZAHUALCOYOTL)
King of Texcoco (1431–72)

Contents

I

*The Face
of the
Land*

Where the Rockies meet the northern outliers of the Andes, Middle America rises out of the sea: its plateaus form one of the roofs of the world. Their ground still pulses with the seismic shocks that gave them birth. The great volcanoes rise above the landscape, clad in a mantle of snow as if they had relinquished their dark powers and fallen into eternal sleep. But the crust of the land is still unstable. It trembles even when asleep, and overnight a fiery monster may burst forth in a man's field, as in 1943 when Parícutin rose out of the ground and swallowed up land and crops in a sea of lava. The ancient prophets of this land spoke of five great periods of time, each destined to end in disaster. At the end of the first of these periods the sky would fall upon the earth. The second would be destroyed by storms. The third would go up in flames. The fourth would be washed away by flood. The fifth period of time is our own: it will come to an end when the world disintegrates in a cataclysmic earthquake. Thus the people of Middle America live in the mouth of the volcano. Middle America with its twin provinces Mexico and Guatemala is one of the proving grounds of humanity where men change themselves

Popocatépetl (Smoking Mountain) stands guard over the mountainous divide separating the valley of Mexico from the valley of Puebla in the central highland. (Photographed by Joseph Seckendorf.)

by changing their surroundings and labor in defiance of the perennial prophecy.

Mountains form the massive backbone of this land, and these mountains set off the three precincts of the Middle American citadel: a central highland in south-central Mexico, a southern highland in southern Mexico, and a southeastern highland in southeasternmost Mexico and Guatemala. Economically and politically, the most important of these precincts has always been the central highland. Middle America has often fallen into disunity; but when it constituted one system, it was always unified from some seat of power in the central highland. In shape, this mountain mass resembles one of the pyramids built by its early inhabitants: massive walls, an eastern and a western escarpment, thrust upward from narrow coasts into a great tableland where the snow-capped mountains with the forbidding names—Citlaltépetl, Iztaccíhuatl, and Popocatépetl—maintain their ice-bound vigil. Two rivers—the Balsas, rushing southwestward to meet the Pacific Ocean, and the Papaloapan, "River of the Butterflies," draining into the Caribbean—have eaten so deeply into its southern face that they almost pour their waters into each other in southern Puebla and northern Oaxaca.

This central pyramid contains a number of chambers, each set off from its neighbors by mountainous partitions. The central chamber is the valley of Mexico, the heartland of Middle America. Just as the central highland has traditionally dominated the periphery, so the valley of Mexico has traditionally dominated the central highland. Ultimately, all the roads of the Middle American world lead into the valley, a basin measuring 5,000 square miles and situated at 7,000 feet above sea level. Before the Pliocene its rivers poured into the Balsas to the south, but the emergence of a chain of volcanoes dammed up these waters and turned the valley into the only Middle American basin not naturally draining to the sea. The trapped waters built up to form five shallow lakes. Lake shores and mountain slopes have supported populations here since the beginning of cultivation; the land proved adaptable to all the agricultural technologies developed by men in Middle America.

3

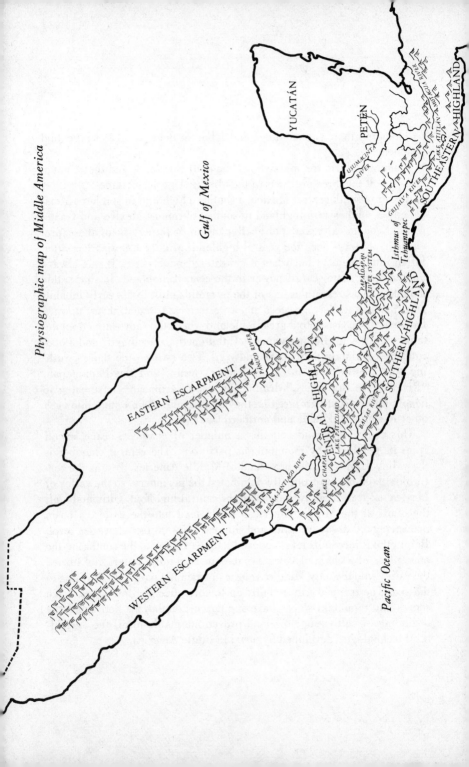

Physiographic map of Middle America

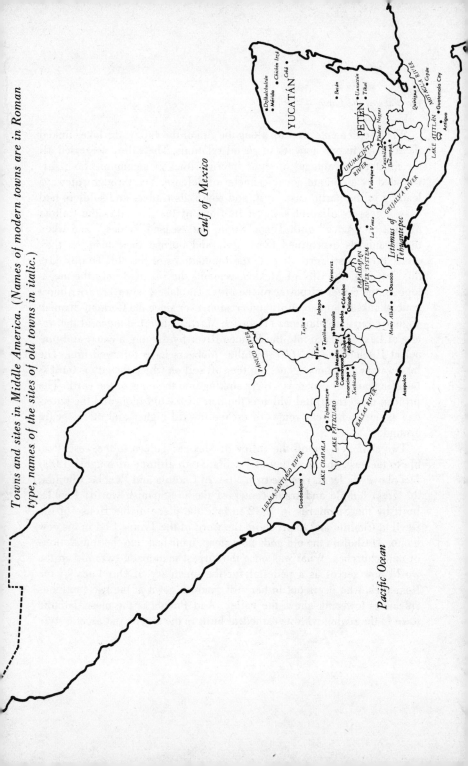

Towns and sites in Middle America. (Names of modern towns are in Roman type, names of the sites of old towns in italic.)

Gulf of Mexico

Pacific Ocean

YUCATÁN

PETÉN

Dzibilchaltún
Mérida
Chichén Itzá
Cobá

Bonlú
Uaxactún
Tikal

Quiriguá
MOTAGUA RIVER
Copán
LAKE ATITLÁN
Guatemala City
Antigua

USUMACINTA RIVER
Yaxchilán
Bonampak
Piedras Negras
GRIJALVA RIVER
Palenque
Isthmus of Tehuantepec

La Venta

Veracruz

PAPALOAPAN RIVER SYSTEM

Jalapa
Córdoba
Orizaba
Tajín
Puebla
Cholula
Monte Albán
Oaxaca

PÁNUCO RIVER

Tula
Teotihuacán
Toluca Mexico City Tlaxcala
Cuernavaca *Atzcapotzalco*
Tenancingo *Xochicalco*
Xochicalco

BALSAS RIVER

Tzintzuntzan
LAKE PÁTZCUARO
LAKE CHAPALA

LERMA-SANTIAGO RIVER

Guadalajara

Acapulco

When settlements grew up along the rim of the valley, the lakes linked them easily in one network of social relations. The valley possessed all the military advantages of short internal lines of communication, surrounded by a mountainous perimeter of defense. Yet, through gateways leading to the north, east, west, and south, its traders and soldiers had easy access to adjacent valleys. Into one of the five lakes the Colhua Mexica or "Aztec" built Tenochtitlán, the "second Venice," and when the Spaniards overturned their idols and burned their temples, they erected their new Jerusalem on the foundations of the old. To this day, this new city, the City of Mexico, remains the railroad hub, the megalopolis, the center of power of the area. The lakes, however, are almost gone, thanks to human effort and erosion, ever since the German-Spanish engineer Enrique Martínez (Heinrich Martin) diverted much of the waters of Lake Texcoco into the Pánuco River by digging a canal and tunnel at Huehuetoca in 1607–8; other pioneers have followed him. The lake waters are almost gone, but the soft soil on which the city is built is buckling, and its center is slowly sinking into the maw of the earth. The protean modern capital which is the heir of the old idols and the latter-day savior-gods seeks routes of escape toward higher and more secure ground.

Two chambers lie off the valley of Mexico: Toluca to the west, Puebla to the east. In the valley of Puebla, at an altitude of roughly 7,000 feet above sea level, rise the twin cities of Cholula and Puebla: Cholula, the great temple and trade center of the pre-Spanish world; Puebla, built by the Spaniards in 1532 to take the place of the House of the Devil at Cholula and to proclaim the word of the Triune God in his new home. At Cholula the old gods now sleep, banished into the foundations of new churches. What was once the largest man-made pyramid in the world now serves as a pedestal for the sanctuary of Our Lady of the Remedies, who peers out in her stiff Spanish gown at the two luminous volcanoes towering above the valley. And Puebla is the most Catholic town in the realm, with its cathedral built in the severe and ascetic style

6

of Juan de Herrera (1530–97), who also built the Spanish Escorial, the palace of the kings upon whose realm the sun never set.

The valley of Toluca to the west is today as dry and denuded as it was once covered with swamps and forests. The city of Toluca itself, located at 8,600 feet above sea level, is the capital of the state of Mexico and a great sprawling settlement into which the Indians of the surrounding country breathe life once a week in the great Friday market.

From the valley of Toluca we take a step down from the central precinct of the pyramid, first into the fertile plain of the Bajío, located at

Schematic diagram of the central highland. (By Patrick F. Gallagher.)

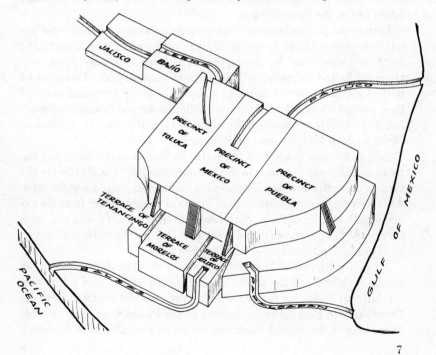

5,500–5,900 feet, then into the basin of Jalisco, down around 5,000. The course is marked out by the river Lerma. The river originates in the valley of Toluca and flows through a narrow gorge into the Bajío. Here it traverses a basin filled with black earth, past many Spanish towns that testify with ornate churches and palatial homes to the wealth of its soil and of its silver mines, when Guanajuato possessed the richest silver mine in the world. Then the Lerma reaches the lagoon of Chapala and changes its name; it leaves the lagoon as the Río Grande de Santiago. Near Guadalajara, the Lerma-Santiago breaks through the western escarpment on its road to the ocean and forms a breakneck passageway to Mexico's northwestern provinces. In the course of only 275 miles, it descends 5,000 feet to the Pacific Ocean.

Lerma and Balsas between them include a volcanic pine-covered upland, the home of the Tarascan Indians, with twin depressions in the north and east filled by the lagoon of Cuitzeo and Lake Pátzcuaro. Hemmed in and defended by their mountain country, the Tarascans of upland and lake district acquired a cultural homogeneity and unity of their own which effectively withstood both Mexica and Spanish imperialism and which is still recogizable in the social and political organization of the modern Mexican state of Michoacán.

Just as we step down from the valley of Toluca to the Bajío and the basin of Jalisco in the west, so we descend some 2,000–3,000 feet to the east, to the coffee-growing semitropical veranda of Jalapa and Orizaba. At Jalapa the Spanish merchants of Veracruz sought refuge from the endemic yellow fever of the tropical lowlands and the Gulf ports, and there they made their fortunes in the great annual fair. The coast—its forest, its savannas, and its bays—lies 4,000 feet below.

No major barrier of land and sea marks the boundary between the central highland and the north. It is increasing aridity and decreasing rainfall that divide the two regions. A great dry land stretches from the Twenty-second Parallel to the borders of the United States and beyond. At the time of the Spanish Conquest, the sedentary cultures of the center had renounced all claims to this waste. It was occupied largely by small groups of hunters and gatherers, collectively called Chichimec, or "Sons of the Dog." This term embraced groups of varied physical, cultural, and linguistic backgrounds, very differently adapted to the local circumstances of their environment. Yet all these people shared a common fate in wresting a meager living from an area that did not offer enough water for growing crops but furnished a reduced diet of wild plants and small game to its hungry inhabitants.

The Spaniards did not long stop at this divide. They crossed it, first hesitatingly, then decisively, and by 1600 were firmly settled in the "great Chichimeca." Here they established cities, mines, farms, mills. Yet though they incorporated the wasteland, they could not erase the old line of cultural division which separated the sedentary area to the south from the northern provinces. The Indian—bearer of the pre-Conquest civilizations—remained a living presence in the area to the south. In the north the Indian hunters, numerically and economically feeble, withstood the Spanish onslaught for a while, and then vanished or retreated into the inaccessible redoubts of the western escarpment. The new life on this northern frontier developed *sui generis*, and where Indians participated in its construction, they did so as frontiersmen, no longer as members of an on-going Indian culture. Frontier North and Indian South are two different worlds, with different color, smell, texture. The Mexican Republic straddles both, but the cultural gap between them continues to divide them to this day.

The central precincts lead off to the east and west; they also possess southern gateways to the hot country on the Balsas River. The valley of Mexico connects with the valley of Morelos; Toluca with the valley of Tenancingo; Puebla with the valley of Atlixco. The lush valley of Morelos lies 2,000 feet lower than the valley of Mexico; and the affluent of the capital repair to its center at Cuernavaca to rest from the pressures of life at high altitudes, just as the Mexica did before the Spanish Conquest. Similarly, the trip from Toluca leads down into a warm country drained by some of the headwaters of the Balsas. Here, at Malinalco, the Mexica carved a temple out of the living rock to commemorate their conquest of the slingshooting Matlatzinca; and here, each year, thousands of Indian pilgrims, hat in hand, descend on foot to the sanctuary of a black god worshipped in a cave, transmuted by the Conquest into the black Christ of Chalma, while at nearby Ixtápan de la Sal the inhabitants of the great cities of Mexico seek relief in sulfurous baths from the less tangible ailments of modern civilization. The valley of Atlixco, similarly, leads into warm sugar-growing country. Drained by the Nexapa, which soon changes its name to become the Balsas, it remains one of the most fertile areas of Mexico.

South of the Balsas and the Papaloapan lies the southern highland, where veritable mountains of the moon fall off in great forbidding ridges to the Pacific Ocean and the Isthmus of Tehuantepec. The Mexican balladeer sings with longing about this jagged and dissected country, but the mountains are poor and arid, and the dusty villages cling to the mountainside with the tenacity of the cactus and the prickly pear striving to survive against the odds of uncertain rainfall and denuded soils. Only in the valley of Oaxaca, in a basin located at 5,000 feet above sea level, is there enough level land to allow more plentiful crops and clustered settlements. Geological activity in Tertiary times created this valley and dammed its waters into a lake, now drained almost entirely by the river Atoyac that flows southward to the sea. But the lake is still there, just below the surface, and water can be had by digging a few inches into the ground, a boon to the irrigation farmer but also a threat to the roots of his crops. Today all the roads of this region lead to Oaxaca City (*Huaxyacac* in Nahuatl, "the spur of the acacias"), but the dead gods of the land sleep 1,300 feet above the valley floor in the sacred tombs of Monte Albán, so ancient that the real name of the site has been lost to posterity.

In the arid lowlands of the Isthmus, America appears almost to break in two; but the mountains rise once more into the cool pine-covered upland of Chiapas and, beyond, into the heart of the southeastern highland. Here a double volcanic chain—younger, steeper, and more active in the south; older, more rounded in the north—contains a series of cool, high basins. Fertile with volcanic ash and well supplied with water from many permanent streams and from heavy rains that fall between May and October, these have traditionally supplied the crops needed to support a large and dense population. Located at the foot of the Cuchumatán massif, the stronghold of traditional Indian culture, Huehuetenango collects the produce of the Indian villages in its hinterland and transmits it to Quetzaltenango, Guatemala's second largest city. Across Lake Atitlán, farther east, ply busy canoes, connecting the twelve culturally diverse communities nestling on its shores; and—on the other side of the mountains—lies the valley of Antigua, site of two ruined colonial capitals, the first wiped out by flood (1541), the second destroyed by earthquakes (1773). In 1776 the capital was again moved eastward to Guatemala City, to a valley occupied since the second millennium B.C. The new city, like the old razed by earthquakes (1917–18), again numbers 250,000 inhabitants; beyond it lies Guatemala's Orient, a relatively unpopulated hill country lying below the 5,000-foot contour.

Step by step this highland descends toward the Atlantic lowlands; great rivers wind through the country on their way to the Caribbean Sea. The Motagua rises near Lake Atitlán and flows north-northeastward into the Gulf of Honduras; on its final course it flows past the ruins of Quirigua, one of the Maya cities of the dim prehistoric past. The tropical forest has there been cleared to make room for fertile groves of banana trees. Where the Motagua flows toward the north-northeast, the Usumacinta flows north-northwestward. Two of its tributaries, the Salinas or Chixoy and the Lacantún, also have their origin near Lake Atitlán; another, the Pasión, has its source in the flat land south of Lake Petén Itzá, where the militant lords of the final period of Maya history made their last stand against the encroaching Spaniards. On the shores of the Usumacinta and its tributaries stand the ancient Maya cities of Yax-

11

chilán, Piedras Negras, and Palenque, mute witnesses to influences that traveled between the adjacent highlands and lowlands.

Toward the southeast, the highlands of Guatemala encounter no massive ecological divide of the kind which at the time of the Spanish Conquest divided agricultural Middle America from the arid wasteland to the north. The southern border of Middle American culture—running approximately along 10 degrees north latitude from Puerto Limón on the Caribbean to the Gulf of Nicoya on the Pacific—was not an environmental barrier but merely a political and economic frontier. It marked the maximum perimeter of expansion reached by Middle American settlers and traders pushing down through the narrow neck of land toward South America. The centrifugal pull of political allegiances divided the region of this cultural frontier among Guatemala, Honduras, and El Salvador.

Although the bulk of Middle America is mountainous, along the Pacific shore and along the Gulf the highlands are edged by coasts—two coasts as different as the two oceans on which they fringe. The Gulf coast is relatively broad: it measures 45 miles at its widest point; the west coast, only a dozen miles at its widest, is narrow. The west coast is hot and arid; the east coast is rainy. On the east coast, rains average between 50 and 118 inches per year, some areas receiving even more. On the west coast, in contrast, there is little rain, and fate, in one of the ironies that plague this land, has also made it nearly impossible to draw water from the rivers into the thirsty fields. The rivers of this coast fall down to the sea from great heights. They often run dry in the dry season; but when the snows melt upland, or heavy rainfall beats on the upland reaches of the Pacific watershed, they swell with water and malevolence and flood the country. On the east coast, however, where rainfall is more than sufficient for human purposes, the problem is too much water rather than too little. Like the Papaloapan, the rivers here are turgid with water, long, and slow-moving, winding now this way, now that way, often inundating the country about them, their periodic floods long one of Mexico's sorrows.

12

Only in two areas is the rainy belt of the east coast interrupted by other climates. In central Veracruz, an arid wedge penetrates the tropical rain forest near the ruins of Cempoala. Here "the plain groans in solitude, delivered over to that sun," and irrigation was needed to allow human beings to live in concentrated settlements. And, again, northwestern Yucatán is dry bush, a country with long, waterless winters and little annual rainfall. There water runs deep underground, and people make their homes where the waters penetrate to the surface in natural wells, called *cenotes* (in Yucatecan-Spanish adaptation of the Maya word *dz'onot*). Further south, where *cenotes* are increasingly rare, water is obtained mainly from small dolines filled with rainwater or from numerous small lakes, many of which have never been explored or named.

Rainfall increases as one travels toward the south (18 inches of rainfall a year at Progreso, 35 at Mérida, 48 at Valladolid, 83 at Belize), until each increment of water delivered to the land recreates the conditions of the tropical rain forest. This forest separates the peninsula of Yucatán from its Middle American base; so dense and impassable does it become that, as far as communication is concerned, the peninsula is almost an island.

A belt of hot swampy jungle and grassland, crossed by slow, winding rivers like the Coatzacoalcos, the Grijalva, and the Candelaria extends from southern Veracruz to Campeche. Here it rains for nine months out of the year; rainfall for the nine-month period averages between 75 and 100 inches. The rivers periodically flood their banks. Even in pre-Hispanic times, this country never supported a dense population: estimates put the pre-Conquest population at 30,000. The Indians rather prized it for its precious yield of cacao and for its numerous inlets and lagoons linking southern Veracruz with the Maya-speakers in a series of portages and ports of call.

The belt of moist forest continues inland, until it reaches the mountains that rise toward the uplands of Chiapas and Guatemala. Here and

Tropical rain forest, like this stand in northeastern Chiapas, Mexico, covers much of the Gulf coast and the base of the peninsula of Yucatán. (Courtesy of American Museum of Natural History.)

there the forest is interspersed with swamplands, impassable in the rainy season, as well as with grasslands. The grasslands are especially characteristic of areas with deep but clayey and unproductive soil, like Campeche and the central Petén, south of Lake Petén. This whole jungle country was the core area of the ancient Maya. Here they built their great ceremonial centers. It is not easy to imagine a more difficult setting for the development of life in cities; the tropical rain forest is not a propitious environment for the rise of civilization. Tropical soils are rarely rich in the minerals that make for productive farming, and clearing of the forest cover admits rain water, which quickly leaches the nutritious elements from the exposed soils. We have not yet discovered how the Maya could reconcile such quick exhaustion of arable soils with long-term, stable city life, though we shall discuss some possible hypotheses when we come to speak of the Maya civilization.

Nature has not made it easy for men in Middle America. So much of the land is mountainous, and wherever there are mountains men must cling precariously to patches of cultivable soil, in the face of runoffs and erosion. Altitude spells cold and sudden frosts, capable of ruining a man's crops from one day to the next. All too often mountain ranges capture rain-bearing clouds and hold them fast, leaving the leeward slopes and the flat country beyond parched for lack of moisture to water the crops. The eastern escarpment constitutes Middle America's major rain barrier. On its windward side, toward the Caribbean and the Atlantic, lies the warm and moist country of the Gulf with its heavy tropical rains and soils that tire quickly and recover but slowly. On its leeward, inland side begins the great dry country which extends, with occasional interruptions, to the far-off Pacific coast. There rains fall only in summer, and the farmer can raise but one crop a year watered by the seasonal rainfall (*temporal*).

In this country, water has become the prime need of men and plants. Hundreds of place names like Apan ("on the water"), Atetelco ("water upon rock"), Apipilhuasco ("water slowly trickling") play endlessly

15

upon the same theme of necessity and deprivation. A water hole, a canal, can here mean the difference between plenty and utter lack, and water sources have been fought over and defended with great rancor and jealousy. In other parts of the world, favored by more gradual slopes and open spaces, human societies have overcome the challenges of aridity through the construction of great irrigation works. To this end they have accepted the burdens of highly centralized governments and stringent social controls. In Egypt, Mesopotamia, China, and Peru, men have massed labor and resources to impound water in artificial lakes or to guide its flow in artificial rivers, and have paid, as Karl Wittfogel has shown, the price of tyranny and despotism for the success of their collective effort.

Irrigation has also been important in Middle America; everywhere canals and small dams perform the task of storing and channeling water to the dry fields, to secure that first crop against dry spells, to help grow the second crop on otherwise sterile land. But the very lay of the land inhibited the growth of large-scale irrigation, and thus of the all-dominant, overweening hydraulic state. There are no great bodies of water, only a rivulet here and there. Except in the lowlands where irrigation is not needed, there are no great, permanent, slow-moving rivers that could be held back or diverted easily through massed effort; all too often streams of water tumble precipitously from the steep mountains, too fast to be tapped except in occasional feeder canals. There are no great wide-open spaces that could be saturated with water from one canal; too often mountains protrude to shut off one irrigated valley from its neighbors. Everywhere the patches of irrigated land are visible, like cool green islands against a background of drab and arid soil, but to this day irrigation has remained essentially localized, insular, in a world of uncertain rainfall. Even today, when modern farmers are mastering the Great Chichimeca, the dry north beyond the Twenty-second Parallel, with gasoline pump and modern hydraulic technology, an aerial view of the country reveals only occasional oases in a landscape where a customary sight is still the figure of a man on horseback, raising a lonely flag of dust on a far-distant horizon.

Hard as the country is to live in, it is rarely uniform. The dissected surface of the land harbors a multitude of islands, each with its special variation of rainfall, its direction of prevailing winds, its patches of cultivable soil, its streams, its irrigated oases. The mountains which govern the shape of the land also turn the country into a mosaic of climatic conditions. A valley may experience a warm, temperate, sunny climate; its surrounding slopes may feel the foggy breath of the cold mountains. Bleak desert may ring an irrigated garden; mountain barriers may shield a subtropical pocket from frost or cold. A chain of mountains may deny rain to the land in its shadow, precipitate water on the country beyond. In summer it may rain furiously in one spot, while farmers a mere mile away catch only a few scarce drops upon their outstretched hands. Cool uplands may border on warm tropical lowlands: with spectacular suddenness pines may give way to the foliage of lush bananas.

Such environmental diversity early made for social cohesion: where each pocket produced its own variety of products, the products of one pocket could easily be exchanged for the products of another. Each valley even constitutes a separate ecological system: the valley floor, the hillsides, the mountain tops each produce goods which are not raised or made in the other. Thus in the vicinity of Texcoco, in the valley of Mexico, for example, the lake shore produces maize; the piedmont, fruit and flowers; the high ground, century-plant beer and charcoal. In similar ways goods flow from lowland to highland, from subregion to subregion, from region to region. Characteristically, the exchanges are never direct but take place in towns, towns that serve as market center and ceremonial center at the same time, where men come to buy and sell and also to burn incense before the altar of their gods or to convert their cash into entertainment. Each valley forms such a planetary system in which a number of villages, located at different altitudes and capitalizing on the variations of their environment, move like moons around a planet, in the field of force of a town on the valley floor. Perched on the flank of a great mountain, centered upon its lonely whitewashed church, surrounded by its fields of maize, an Indian village in Mexico or Guatemala can seem infinitely isolated and self-sufficient. Yet the impression is deceptive: for nearly three thousand years Middle American communities have formed the warp and woof of larger Middle American worlds.

As the villages in a valley converge upon a valley town, so the valley towns converge upon a regional capital. So also may two regions be pulled toward a town strategically located at their juncture. Thus the local community forms part of an ever widening network of relations, reaching toward ever wider external connections. The relationships of economic exchange, mediated through markets which link village to valley town, valley town to regional capital, translate the centrifugal tendencies of the environment into centripetal, cohesive patterns. Where nature pulls toward disunity, men have wrought unity in diversity through human means.

But Middle American history has thrown up still other forces working toward ever widening cohesion. Traditionally such forces have had their origins in areas favored over their hinterland with relatively abundant land, crops, and means of transportation, areas capable of generating more energy than could be used up within each area itself. Such areas are key areas of social development, nodal points of growth, which pull other areas into fields of force. In Middle America, such areas have been, at one time or another, the valley of Mexico, the frontier marches between the settled world of the cultivators and the nomadic world of the food collectors in Hidalgo, the region of Cholula and Puebla and nearby Tlaxcala, the basin of Lake Pátzcuaro, the Bajío, the basin of Jalisco, Morelos, pockets in the mountains of the southern highland, the valley of Oaxaca, the basins of highland Guatemala, the Petén, northern

Yucatán, southern Veracruz, and Tabasco. The most enduring of these has been the valley of Mexico.

From such areas have proceeded all movements toward the integration of Middle America, in its ancient and modern forms. Thus Teotihuacán spread its influence from the valley of Mexico throughout Middle America during the first millennium A.D. Thus the armies of Tula and Tenochtitlán moved from the valley or its vicinity to conquer wide areas of Middle America during the first half of the second millennium of our era. Thus the Spaniards attempted to govern their New Spain from Mexico City for the period of their three centuries of colonial rule during the sixteenth, seventeenth, and eighteenth centuries. Thus independence from Spain produced a brief period of Middle American political integration in the early decades of the nineteenth century, until the structure again fell apart in political chaos. Thus today the two republics, Mexico and Guatemala, from their respective capitals in the valley of Mexico and in the basin of Guatemala strive to organize their countries into centripetal galactic systems to contain the ever present centrifugal tendencies toward localism and regional isolation.

These areas have repeatedly spurred the movement toward political integration, because they alone could generate time and again the energy needed for more complex social development. Always they are areas in which, given an adequate technology, men could consistently produce a social surplus, sufficiently large not only to increase population but also to widen the division of labor of their societies.

A society which can divert some of its members from the food quest into full-time specialization can at the same time free skills and knowledge from the narrow confines of the individual household and speed their development in a multitude of crafts and occupations. Inevitably, in the development of human societies, such a growth of economic surplus and diversification of labor are accompanied by still a third phenomenon: the rise of the full-time political specialist, to co-ordinate the increased efforts of an increasingly diversified population and to arbitrate the disputes of its newly formed interest groups. Inevitably, also, such political specialization constitutes a turning point in the lives of most societies; for the functions of co-ordination and arbitration spell power, and power is translatable into special liens on goods and services. Perhaps, as Franz Oppenheimer recognized long ago, there is no inherent reason why such services should be rewarded more heavily than those of other skilled specialists. Yet, inevitably, where political specialists have assumed the task of concentrating and reallocating the surplus to other members of their society, they have concentrated both wealth and the power that goes with wealth in their own hands and for their own purposes.

When an area becomes the setting of such multiple growth, it begins to draw the villages and towns of its periphery like a magnet. Its growing population offers an ever increasing market of ready consumers for the produce of the countryside; its craft specialists need raw materials to convert into finished products; its elite, hungry for surpluses, begins to look beyond the confines of its domain to other domains. Power exercised within the society grows into political and military power exercised against the outside. Through widening conquest and widening trade, the solar system of the favored area becomes a galaxy, absorbing the constellations of villages and towns beyond its limits, building a super-regional ecology under the aegis of the growing state. But the process is also reversible. The cohesion of such a galaxy depends ultimately on the pull of its center; if the key area weakens in its power of attraction, the satellite systems slip again from their orbits around it and resume their independent courses. In this way galaxies again yield to solar systems, until another key area can generate power for a new metabolic cycle of integration. Thus, upon the face of this land, human societies have grown and declined in continuous pulsations, first widening their scope, then retreating again, in continuous tension between expansion and decay.

II

*Generations
of
Adam*

Middle America is not only a region of astonishing geographical diversity; it is also protean in its biological diversity. In one narrow area of its southeastern highland occur more kinds of maize and more kinds of birds than in the entire United States. As with plants and birds, so it is with human beings. Middle America has been a great meeting ground of men, a laboratory for the production of human varieties. Here American Indian, Mediterranean whites, and African Negroes all encountered each other and recognized their common humanity by producing common offspring.

American Indians, or Amerinds, were first in this land. They entered the New World around 25,000 B.C., crossing from Siberia to Alaska. Much has been written about the physical characteristics of these early Americans. Some scholars have thought that all Indians were representatives of one physical type, like Ales Hrdlička's "American Indian homotype," and that all variations upon the theme set by the first type were later and transitory modifications produced by the New World environment. Today, however, we no longer defend any notion of a prehistoric

Monroe doctrine barring entry to a variety of physical types from Asia. It seems probable that people came across Bering Strait in several waves, some perhaps as early as 25,000 B.C., others as late as the time of Christ. On the basis of dated skeletal finds the earlier immigrants seem to have been less Mongoloid than the later arrivals; that is, they bore less resemblance to the Chinese, Koreans, Tungus, or Mongols of northern Asia than later comers.

These earlier people were rather small, with long flat-sided heads that bore rather heavy ridges above the brows. In this they resemble a population which was once common in Asia and Europe and which has left descendants in the marginal areas of the Old World, such as among the natives of Australia or among the "hairy" Ainus of northern Japan. Birdsell calls these people "Amurians" and sees in them a root population which gave rise to a number of pigment phases of modern man. Among the later Amurian variants, with yellowish pigmentation, is the Mongoloid, with his fairly large face, smooth forehead, prominent cheekbones, moderate projection and flatness of the upper jaw, flat and broad nose, shovel-shaped incisor teeth, epicanthic eyefold, padding of the face with fatty tissues, small chin, straight black hair, dark eyes, and scant body hair. It is probable that this new variant of man with his broad, flat, padded, and hairless face represents a special adaptation to cold, specially selected over time by the dry cold of northern Asia. Yet few Amerinds show all of these "specialized" Mongoloid features. Amerinds often have coppery skins rather than yellowish ones, wavy hair as often as straight hair, deep-set eyeballs and eyes without Mongoloid eyefolds, pronounced convex noses and foreheads strongly marked by rims of bones. In all these characteristics, they more clearly approximate the archaic Amurian than the cold-adapted Mongoloid. It thus seems possible that Amerinds represent a hybrid of Amurians with Mongoloids who had not yet developed all the strategic features of the later specialized Mongoloid variant. This would explain both their differences from the specialized Mongoloid, as well as their generic family resemblance to him.

The distribution of blood groups among Amerinds points to the same conclusion. Of the Asiatic Mongoloids 20 to 40 per cent possess blood type B, but B is wholly absent in the aboriginal population of the Americas. It may well be that the Amerinds left Asia before B became widespread; or that the small migrant groups of Amerinds which broke off from the parent population carried accidentally less B than their parental mass, and that these small percentages of B-carriers were eliminated in the New World because natural selection favored O and A over B under the new conditions. Certainly the Amerinds remained unaffected by the great movement of people in the Old World which distributed B to many parts of the hemisphere where no B had existed in the past. At the present time, Middle America shows a blood group distribution of roughly 85 per cent O and 15 per cent A on its northern frontier, 100 per cent O in its southern reaches. Nor was this blood group distribution seriously upset later by the Spanish Conquest and consequent hybridization of the Amerind with Mediterranean whites. For Spain, like the New World, was marginal to the Eurasiatic-African land mass, and remained comparatively free of accretions of B, which on the Iberian Peninsula occurs only in low frequencies of 5–11 per cent.

The first Americans in this New World discovered from Asia were hunters of big game. Present-day hunters of big game that moves in herds also travel in groups, each group usually comprising several families; we may assume that the early Americans, too, possessed some such larger persisting social unit. Fanning out from their beachhead in Alaska, they followed their quarry southward. Some 600 generations and 18,000 years later (around 7000 B.C.) they reached the southern-most tip of South America, some 11,000 miles away from their point of entry into the New World. In the course of this slow expansion (18.3 miles per generation) their hereditary characteristics probably underwent considerable change.

Some of these changes were due to mutations, random changes in the complex molecules or genes which govern the appearance of characteristics in living organisms. Such mutations seem to occur in man at the rate of 1:50,000–100,000; some certainly occurred in the course of 18,000 years. Mutations had little chance of affecting large populations, however, since the constituent social groups were small and widely dispersed and the carriers of new mutations could shuffle their hereditary potentialities only with a restricted number of possible mating partners within their immediate geographic range. But mutations within relatively isolated groups undoubtedly increased the variability of the Amerind stock in the New World, thus accentuating further any genetic variability which the Amerinds had brought with them as part of their Asiatic legacy.

This variability due to differential mutations must have been reinforced by a process especially important in small populations that do not have much opportunity to shuffle their genes within large breeding populations. Because of the operations of chance, a daughter population is never a complete sample of the genetic makeup of the parent group from which it splits off. There is always a chance that such a daughter group will carry either more or less of any given set of genes than its parent. We can easily assume such a split-off or hiving-off of a daughter population from its parent group every second or third generation (a not unreasonable estimate for populations of large game-hunters). As a result, groups that varied in the distribution of genes from their parent groups came into existence every second or third generation, or at least two to three hundred times during the southward march toward Tierra del Fuego.

If mutations and drift played an important part in establishing the early genetic variability of Amerind groups in the New World, interbreeding between groups grew more and more important as the population became sedentary and grew both in size and density. The genetic variability of a group of individuals is necessarily limited by the size

24

of the population with which they habitually breed. A man's hereditary equipment is really no more than an individual share temporarily withdrawn from the genetic storehouse of the group to which he belongs. If the group is isolated and small, its storehouse of hereditary equipment will be limited. If the group grows in size, and receives shipments of new equipment from the outside, it also enlarges its ability to produce new kinds of individuals. The early hunters formed small groups with limited range in their choice of mates. These groups were thus physically homogeneous, with strongly segregated stores of genetic equipment. With the growth of population, breeding populations enlarged and merged. This undoubtedly broke down small-group boundaries, spread and shuffled genetic equipment widely. The result of more extensive pooling of divergent hereditary resources must have been increased variability of individuals.

Upon these populations produced by mutation, drift, and genetic recombination, the forces of natural selection were continuously operative. Even a small selective advantage of one gene over another would immediately increase the chances of its survival and hasten its spread at the expense of the less advantageous trait. There is increasing evidence, for instance, that matings between human males and females with certain incompatible blood types will fail to produce viable offspring. This may hold true not only for blood types but for many other genetic features in man. In each of the immigrant Amerind groups, therefore, some individuals would fail to reproduce, while others, exchanging different genes, would father the next generation. Each generation would witness a repetition of this process, until some genetic combinations had been eliminated entirely from the genetic storehouse of the group and had been replaced by others which proved fruitful and capable of indefinite multiplication.

Similar mechanisms may have been at work also in selection under various environmental conditions. Two strategic dimensions of the animal body in adapting to gross differences in heat or cold are body mass

25

and body surface. The larger the body surface relative to body mass, the greater the ability of the body to eliminate heat and to permit cooling. The smaller the body surface relative to body mass, the greater the ability of the body to retain heat and to resist cooling. Adaptation to heat or cold therefore involves changes in the relation of body mass to body surface. These changes may operate in two directions: the animal body may increase its body mass relative to its body surface by growing in sheer size; conversely, it may decrease its body mass relative to its body surface by growing smaller. In very general terms this means that hot latitudes will tend to favor small or slender populations, cold latitudes large or stocky organisms. This has been demonstrated for the distribution of body size in the American puma; and recently Marshall Newman has applied this rule to the racial anthropology of the aboriginal New World.

By and large, the smaller people with broad heads, broad faces, and broad noses inhabit the lower latitudes. As you go northward or southward from the equator, stature increases, extremities elongate, and faces, noses, and head shapes grow longer. This is true also of Middle America. The smallest people in Middle America are found in the south, in the lower latitudes (Maya, Tzotzil-Tzeltal, Mazatec), the tallest in northern Mexico (Pima, Pápago, Yaqui). The southerners possess rather short legs, people like the Yaqui in the north rather long legs. Southern Middle Americans like the Maya, Chinantec, and Huave are broadheaded, while northerners like the Tarahumara, Pima, Pápago, and Yaqui are long-headed.

The Middle American picture is, however, still further complicated by altitude. Much of Middle America lies in the highlands, where the effects of tropical heat and sunlight during the day are counteracted by cold during the night, as well as by diminished barometric pressure and oxygen pressure and by increased ultraviolet radiation. The incidence of cold in such an area may modify the stature of people in the direction of small size and stockiness by stimulating the adrenals during the

26

process of growth, while a decrease in oxygen-intake may put a premium on the development of massive chests and lungs. Other effects may be due to increased organismic stress at high altitudes. If Mongoloid characteristics indeed originated as a result of selection under conditions of extreme dry cold, they would prove highly adaptable to this new high-altitude environment.

With these general factors in mind, we may arrive at a very tentative picture of Amerind differentiation in Middle America. The first immigrants were probably non-Mongoloid longheads who survive today largely in the marginal areas of the western escarpment (Tarahumara, Pima, Pápago, Yaqui), perhaps among the Otomí and among the Tzeltal-Tzotzil speakers of the Chiapas highlands. They were followed by later immigrants of increasing Mongoloid physical cast. These in turn differentiated into several highland-adapted groups, generally with broad and medium heads, short legs, deep chests, and stocky build, and into lowland-adapted small broadheads. The lowland population seems in turn to have produced two widespread variants: a rather gracile, small-boned, broad-nosed, and broad-headed type such as one can find among the Totonac and Huastec of Veracruz, and a small, thick-bodied, extremely broad-headed type with high curved noses characteristic of the Maya-speakers who combine these features with a rather high incidence of Mongoloid eyefold.

The existence of still another physical type is suggested by the artistic representations belonging to the so-called Olmec tradition. The type depicted has infantile features with strongly everted lips, is often obese, or shows symptoms of dwarfism, acromegaly, androplasia, or hunchback. Skeletal finds from the Olmec site of Cerro de las Mesas do not, however, give evidence of these features. It is therefore reasonable to suppose that the physical characteristics appearing in art may have been chosen as symbolic representations of aspects of the supernatural; symptoms of disease may have been seized upon by the artist to lend special power to his work. The hunchback is a common supernatural being in these

Left, *Porphyry mask from Teayo, Veracruz, Mexico, carved in the Mexica manner during the fourteenth or fifteenth century A.D., showing the facial features of a physical type common in the central highland.* Center, *Clay head, 7 inches high, modeled in the pre-Hispanic art style of central Veracruz, Mexico, showing the facial features of the gracile, small-boned, lowland-adapted physical type.* Right, *Clay figurine head from Tabasco, southern Gulf coast, Mexico, showing the broad-headed physical type with the high curved nose and epicanthic eyefold so commonly found among Maya-speakers.* (*Courtesy of American Museum of Natural History.*)

latitudes, as are the little people of the forest, who may have been artistically represented as dwarfs. Also, the feline features of many Olmec figures are representations of the jaguar, not realistic pictures of real people.

To this differentiated heritage of Amerind physical characteristics, the invading Spaniards added their own storehouse of white Mediterranean genetic traits. The basic population of Spain is another archaic population of brunet Mediterraneans, akin to the North African Berbers. It is mesocephalic, orthognathous, narrow-nosed, narrow-faced, small in stature, and brunet. This basic population has maintained itself despite repeated invasions of the country from the eastern Mediterranean by Megalith builders, Phoenicians, Jews, and Arabs, and from the northern margins of Europe by Celts, Goths, and Vandals. It contains no population element like the stocky and broad-headed Alpine, so common in other parts of Europe. This absence of Alpines, together with the blood

28

group distribution discussed above, shows that Spain remained marginal within the larger European area.

It has long been argued that the Spanish immigrants to the New World came mostly from the steppe country of Extremadura and the plains of Andalusia. Recent investigations, however, have shown that the immigrants were drawn from all parts of Spain. During the sixteenth century, the core of emigration lay in a broad belt of country running from the Basque provinces in the north through León, Castile, and Extremadura to western Andalusia. Later, the contribution of Andalusia and Extremadura declined, while emigration increased from the mountainous provinces of the north and northwest. Men predominated in the emigration, but women also came, often called by the colonial authorities as part of their program of colonization. The total number of Spaniards who migrated to Middle America has been estimated at 300,000.

With the Spaniard came another element of population, the African slave. Roughly 250,000 were imported into Mexico during the three centuries of the slave trade. Most of them were settled along the Gulf coast or on the Pacific coast, but many also went to work in the cattle ranches of the highlands and in the mines. No part of Middle America is without Negro admixture, although the physical evidence of this admixture has probably been submerged. It is most evident to this day on the coast of Veracruz, along the Gulf of Honduras and on the Pacific coasts of Guerrero and Oaxaca. Yet some 10 per cent of the highly marginal Otomí population of the highland show Negroid characteristics, probably owing to the presence of Negro slaves employed in neighboring mines. Similarly, a Negro element played an important role— together with Zapotec-speaking Indians, Spaniards, and later immigrants from northern Europe—in the formation of the handsome population of Tehuantepec, famed throughout Middle America for the beauty of its women.

Thanks to the work of Gonzalo Aguirre Beltrán, we know that most of the Negroes imported into Middle America came from west-central

Generations of Adam

Africa. This is an area inhabited by a stocky, muscular, barrel-chested, and long-headed population. Characteristically, this type possesses rather long extremities in comparison with the length of the trunk. In Middle America, such a population probably reinforced the tendency toward stocky body-build present in the highland-adapted Amerind, while at the same time elongating his rather short limbs. African longheadedness probably also modified the Amerind type toward greater dolichocephaly, to the despair of the physical anthropologist who has often classified Middle American longheads as survivals of an old Amerind population of pre-Mongoloid characteristics. Finally, African influence also acted to maintain the established distribution of the major blood groups. Like Spain, Africa had remained relatively untouched by migrations of people bearing blood type B from its Asiatic fountainhead.

Negroes were not the only slaves imported into Middle America. Small numbers of Indians, Burmese, Siamese, Indonesians, and Filipinos were also brought in to serve in a similar capacity. The degree of their influence on the human biology of Middle America is unknown, but seems to have been slight. Concentrated in small numbers in major cities, their genetic contribution was soon dispersed in the larger gene pool of the area.

In appraising the relative genetic contributions of the three major parent populations, we must consider their numerical relationship. If the Amerinds had maintained their pre-Conquest level of population, 300,000 Spaniards and 250,000 African Negroes could probably not have affected the Amerind gene pool appreciably. One of the immediate consequences of the Conquest, however, was a catastrophic decline of the Indian population. We shall have occasion to analyze some of the factors involved in this decline in chapter ix. At the moment, let us simply take note of the fact that probably more than two-thirds of the Indian population died between 1519 and 1650. To measure the depth of this holocaust, we must know something about the pre-Conquest population. This is a much-discussed subject.

Skeptical of exaggerated estimates, many scholars have refused to trust Spanish estimates made at the time of the decline and have put the pre-Conquest Indian population total no higher than four and a half million. The most conservative of these conservative estimates is probably that made by Alfred Kroeber, who set the figure at three million. Recent careful studies of the Spanish records have shown, however, that there is no need to distrust those most careful of all bureaucratic observers. Modern estimates using these records for their basis of departure confidently assert population totals running from nine million for all of Mexico to eleven million for Mexico north of the Isthmus of Tehuantepec alone. These recent estimates thus tend to support the informed judgment of the German scholar Karl Sapper, who put the total population of Middle America before the Conquest at between twelve and fifteen million as early as 1924. If we use this figure, then more than six-sevenths of the pre-Conquest population was liquidated in the wake of the Conquest between 1519 and 1650. This means, in terms of our present discussion, that the genes introduced by Europeans and Africans entered an Indian gene pool much reduced in size and viability. As a result, it can be asserted with confidence that there are no more "pure-blooded" Indians in Middle America. All Indians are the heirs of a process of genetic interchange with Europeans and Africans, just as all Europeans and Africans have been involved in genetic exchanges with Indians. As a result, all are hybrid; all are, to use the Middle American word, "mestizos." At the same time they differ in the degrees to which their genetic equipment contains contributions from each of the other groups.

It is difficult, if not impossible, to arrive at adequate measurements of the different degrees of admixture. This is due in large part to deficient census-taking, both past and present. Even if the census-takers had been trained and reliable observers, comparison of the different censuses would still founder on the hard fact that each used different criteria for separating Indians from non-Indians. Thus we are thrown back on guesswork. Guessing on the basis of the returns for the Spanish census of 1793, we can say that at the end of the eighteenth century Indians and Indo-mestizos (mestizos in whose outward appearance Indian physical characteristics dominate) made up 70 per cent of the Middle American population. Afro-mestizos (or mestizos in whom Negroid characteristics were dominant) accounted for 10 per cent. Whites and Euro-mestizos (mestizos in whom European physical characteristics were dominant) accounted for 20 per cent.

The period between 1793 and the present has in all probability diminished still further these somewhat hard-and-fast differences and greatly strengthened a mestizo physical type or range of physical types as such, in contrast to more Amerind or Europoid variants. This type possesses features of all three parent stocks, but in characteristic combination. The mestizo of the central highland and the Gulf coast is definitely taller than his Indian parent; he approaches the average height of the Peninsular Spaniard. Both Indian and Spanish parent groups possessed heads of similar shapes; the mestizo does not differ appreciably from them. Generally, the mestizo combines the Indian's broad face, greater breadth of nose, and somewhat narrower forehead with the higher head vault, the longer face, the longer nose, and the narrower mandible of the Spaniard. In Yucatán, the mestizo type is influenced both by the smaller stature of the Maya-speaking parent stock—when this group is compared with other Amerinds—and by its tendency toward extreme broadheadedness. Yet here, as elsewhere, the mestizo type remains appreciably taller and less broad-headed than the Indian. In the tendency toward tallness, as well as in the retention of the stocky trunk, the African element may have played its contributing part.

In all cases studied, such hybrid types show signs of vigorous health. Contrary to some prophets of doom, there is no evidence that race mixture has deleterious effects; mixed offspring are at least as fit biologically as their parents, and they may even be more so. We must certainly guard against the purveyors of cracker-barrel anthropology who trace

32

the rise or decay of a civilization to changes in the measurements of people's skulls or to variations in their pigmentation. Biology is not directly translatable into culture; the ability to possess and develop culture is not a function of the length of one's nose or the vault of one's skull. There is no short-term relationship between physical differences and differences in culture. At the same time, there exists a long-range relationship. A species incapable of variation can operate only within narrow limits, and any change that upsets these limits also threatens its biological survival. A species, like ours, which is capable of great variability also greatly increases its chances of survival, all the more so if it can speed its variability further through crossbreeding of its constituent subspecies. For such a species does not stake its survival on a narrow range of chance; its resources answer many challenges. In our racial and individual variability lies the best hope of mankind—its inherent plasticity. Some areas of the world are veritable staging grounds of our biological mobilization. Middle America is one such area.

III

*Confusion
of
Tongues*

Middle America is a mosaic of geographical environments and of human physical types. It is also a mosaic of human languages. A recent catalogue of the indigenous languages of Latin America records some 260 languages for the area between the northern border of Mexico and the southern border of Guatemala. In this veritable Tower of Babel most of the languages are mutually unintelligible. The cultivation of maize is known everywhere. But the word for maize in Nahuatl is *centli;* in Zapotec it is *žuba;* in Chontal, *kosak;* in Zoque, *mok;* in Mam, *xál;* in Yucatec Maya, *nál.* The word for black is *yopalli* in Nahuatl, *nayàzéz* in Zapotec, *yak* in Zoque, *kyeq,* in Mam, *ēk* in Yucatec Maya; the word for white, *istaak* in Nahuatl, *nakiči* in Zapotec, *pópo* in Zoque, *saq* in Mam, *zak* in Yucatec Maya. Often inhabitants of neighboring villages cannot communicate with one another unless they learn a lingua franca, a third language which permits them to converse across the barrier of their mother tongues. In some parts of Middle America, therefore, people may grow up speaking two or more entirely unrelated languages. In the Huastec-speaking zone of northern Veracruz, for instance, many

Indians speak Huastec at home, Nahuatl in the market place, and Spanish when they want to communicate with officials or outsiders. In the Isthmus of Tehuantepec, people switch with ease from Zapotec to Spanish, though the two languages are no more related than Bantu and Norwegian.

Each of these languages is a vehicle of communication, organized to allow men to define common understandings through the arrangement of sounds into words and word order. Different languages make use of different sounds and different arrangements. Some languages, like Nahuatl or Maya or German, are polysynthetic: they build meaning by building up long and composite words. Other languages are analytic, like Chinese and—increasingly—English: they build meaning by arranging short words in careful sequence.

But the mold of language never sets; it is ever changing; and to the student of culture, this fact of change in language is all-important, for it allows him to use the study of language to probe the past. Languages are spoken by people. It follows that if two languages can be shown to be related, we may also suppose that the two peoples speaking these related languages were once upon a time involved with each other. Perhaps they were once one people and shared the same language, the same system of expressing meaning. In such cases, it may be possible to reconstruct the ancestral language common to both. Or, perhaps they were not related genetically but came to share a common language through contact, in the course of some shared experience. In either case, similarities in sounds, grammar, and vocabulary illuminate the past and permit us to throw light on some of its secrets.

Morris Swadesh has recently added an important instrument to our inventory of techniques for mapping the linguistic past: the technique of glottochronology. He discovered that one part of every language tends to change at a constant rate. This is the "basic" or "non-cultural" vocabulary, a set of words that refer to phenomena which tend to be constant in pan-human experience, regardless of cultural variation, such as

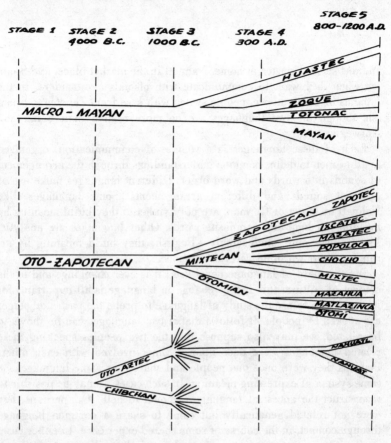

STAGE 1

STAGE 2
4000 B.C.

STAGE 3
1000 B.C.

STAGE 4
300 A.D.

STAGE 5
800-1200 A.D.

MACRO - MAYAN

HUASTEC
ZOQUE
TOTONAC
MAYAN

OTO-ZAPOTECAN

ZAPOTECAN

ZAPOTEC
IXCATEC
MAZATEC
POPOLOCA
CHOCHO

MIXTECAN

MIXTEC

OTOMIAN

MAZAHUA
MATLAZINCA
OTOMI

UTO-AZTEC

NAHUATL
NAHUAT

CHIBCHAN

Language streams. (Chart by Patrick F. Gallagher.)

designations for the sun, the moon, and the stars; for night and day; for parts of the body. By comparing such word lists from different languages, it becomes possible not only to say whether or not they are related but also to infer how long they have existed as separate entities. If 74 per cent of this basic vocabulary is still shared between two languages, then, according to Swadesh's findings, at least 1,000 years

36

must have gone by since the time of their separation. After 2,000 years of separation, the two word lists will still show 74 per cent of 74 per cent, or 55 per cent. After 3,000 years of separation, the word lists will agree in 74 per cent of 55 per cent, or 40.7 per cent of the terms. It is possible to achieve a fair measure of certainty up to an elapsed time of 10,000 years; beyond this time period, relationships grow shadowy.

These linguistic techniques help us to unravel the Middle American past. Chart 1 shows the main streams of language and their variations over time, while Maps A, B, C, and D depict the same processes in space. Map A shows us linguistic conditions around the year 5000 B.C., when an uninterrupted belt of related dialects stretched from northwestern Mexico to Colombia. This continuum of related dialects was broken around 4000 B.C. into two divisions: a northern division, commonly called Uto-Aztecan, and a southern division, called Chibchan. The groups which were responsible for this geographical separation were probably the Oto-Zapotecan-speakers—expanding from a core area around the headwaters of the Balsas River—and the Macro-Mayan speakers, who spread through the lowlands of the Gulf of Mexico and the Caribbean Sea and into the southeastern highlands (Map B). The Chibchan-speakers were driven southward beyond the confines of Middle America; some Chibchan languages are bunched up today along the narrow land bridge to South America.

Between 4000 and 1000 B.C., all these parent tongues underwent considerable differentiation (Map C). The Uto-Aztecan division split into a number of daughter languages, of which Nahua proved the most important in Middle American history. The area in which Nahua achieved its diagnostic characteristics lay outside the core area of the central highland, probably along the foothills of the western escarpment extending to the north of Jalisco. Oto-Zapotecan differentiated into Otomian, Mixtecan, and Zapotecan. Mixtecan and Zapotecan acquired tonemes, that is, they began to indicate differences in meaning by raising or lowering pitch, a feature which is absent from Otomian. The area of

37

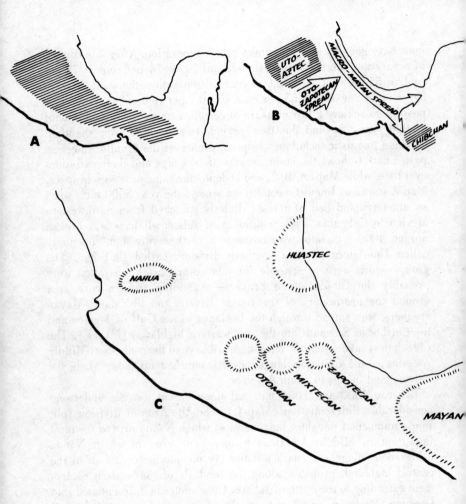

MAPS A AND B (above, left and right).—*Language differentiation around 4000 B.C.* MAP C (below).—*Language differentiation 4000–1000 B.C.* (Maps by Patrick F. Gallagher.)

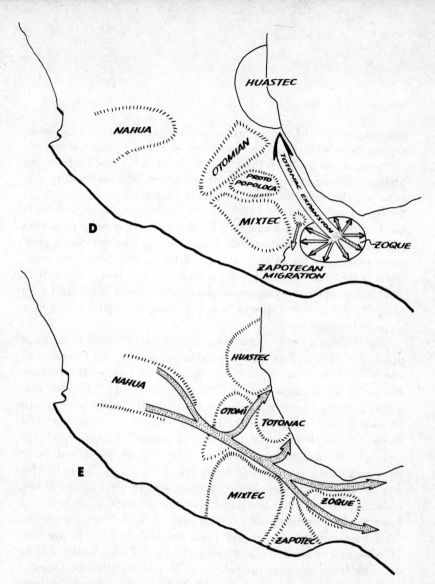

MAP D (above).—*Language differentiation and spread about A.D. 300.* MAP E (below).—*Language differentiation and spread A.D. 800–1200.* (*Maps by Patrick F. Gallagher.*)

characterization of Otomian lay probably in the vicinity of the snow-capped Nevado de Toluca in the valley of Toluca; this area contains the greatest diversity of Otomian languages today and is therefore probably the oldest area of Otomian settlement. Mixtecan and its dialects probably achieved definition in the vicinity of the headwaters of the Balsas and spread southward into the southern highlands and northward into the valleys of Mexico and Puebla. The area in which Zapotecan achieved its special characteristics is unknown; I believe that a good case can be made for an area of origin in the eastern escarpment somewhere in the triangle formed by the modern towns of Tehuacán, Acatlán, and Ojitlán. Macro-Mayan, extended along the shores of the Gulf, also began to differentiate. Huastec was beginning to acquire shape as a separate language.

Map D shows us still another later stage in the unfolding of the same processes. By A.D. 300, two Macro-Mayan languages—Totonac and Zoque—had begun to expand, driving a wedge between the Huastec and the Maya languages proper. This penetration cut off Huastec altogether from its parent tongue and set it definitely on the path toward its own linguistic development. In their expansion the Totonac and Zoque—or people on whom they exerted pressure in turn—probably dislodged the Zapotec-speakers from their area of origin and drove them across the mountains into the valley of Oaxaca. Mixtecan had begun to differentiate into Mixtec proper and Protopopoloca. Mixtec maintained its essential unity and split into a series of dialects; but Protopopoloca broke up into several quite distinct languages. At the same time, all these languages expanded still further: Mixtec into Morelos, eastern Guerrero, and western Oaxaca; Protopopoloca and its daughter languages over the valleys of Mexico and Puebla. Otomian spread north and northeastward until Otomí-speakers established contact with Huastec-speakers along the crest of the eastern escarpment. The Nahua-speakers had begun to send outliers into the central area, but the bulk of them still remained confined to the Middle American periphery.

Map E shows us the irruption between A.D. 800 and 1200 of Nahua-speakers into the area. This irruption seems to have taken the form of two great waves, an earlier wave around 800 and a later wave after 1100. The earlier wave, among other traits, lacked the characteristic *tl* sound of the later comers. Thus, for instance, the Pochutec dialect of Nahua (spoken in Pochutla, Oaxaca) and the Mecapayan dialect of Nahua (spoken in Veracruz) both say *tet* or *tot* where later Mexica calls a stone *tetl*. To mark this difference between older and more recent Nahua dialects, linguists call the first Nahuat, the second Nahuatl. Nahuat dialects are today found on the periphery of Middle America, Nahuatl in its center. Nahuatl became the dominant language of the Mexica state. As such it both preceded and followed their banners of conquest. It became a lingua franca, a language of politics and trade. It carried prestige, and many people gave up their native languages and adopted Nahuatl. Thus, for instance, many groups of Popoluca in Veracruz had adopted Nahuatl by the sixteenth century: first the men, and only later the women, just as today these same Nahuamized Popoluca are learning Spanish; the men first, for the women still cling conservatively to their adopted Nahua. To groups who could not speak Nahua, the Nahua applied contemptuous epithets which have remained to serve as their official designations to this day—epithets such as *chontal* ("foreigner"), *popoluca* or *popoloca* ("unintelligible"), *totonac* ("rustic"). Thus we find today linguistically quite unrelated groups called Chontal (in Tabasco and Oaxaca), Popoluca (in Puebla, Veracruz, and Guatemala), Totonac (in Veracruz, but also in sixteenth-century Spanish reports from Jalisco and Oaxaca), to the confusion of the investigator. Nahua names have also become the standard designations of other populations, such as the Mixtec (from *mixtlán*, "cloud land"), the Zapotec (after the zapote tree, *Achras Zapota*), and the Otomí (apparently from Nahuatl *totomitl*, "man who wings birds with arrows"). The Mixtec call

themselves *ñusabi*; the Zapotec, *di'z*, with a suffix designating the territory they inhabit; the Otomí, *nhyū*.

In time, the Nahua also developed a polished and sophisticated "aca-
demic" dialect which was adopted by ruling groups everywhere; the
rulers of the Mixtec, for instance, spoke both Mixtec and this polished
Nahuatl. The home of sophisticated Nahuatl was Texcoco, at the time
of the Conquest the intellectual capital of the Mexica domain. Not only
did its court develop polished Nahuatl, however; its king also composed
poems in refined Otomí.

The Nahua thrust was most successful in the valleys of Mexico and
Puebla, in Morelos and Atlixco, on the terrace overlooking the Gulf
coast and in the Gulf lowlands. Here 822,000 Nahua-speakers survive
to this day. Nahua-speakers reached Yucatán and the southeastern
highlands. They brought with them their specialized vocabulary of military and political terms for a fortified and walled town, for the tight-
fitted jacket worn by soldiers, for shield, for banner, for palace, lord,
and commoner. But they never seriously modified the prevailing linguistic picture. Here and there we find islands of Nahua-speakers, called
pipil or rulers, but they are always surrounded by a sea of Maya-
speakers. It is possible that some of the ruling groups among both the
highland and the lowland Maya after A.D. 900 were of Nahua derivation,
but if this is so they quickly lost their linguistic identity among the
people they ruled. These continued to speak Maya; and the map of
Maya languages and dialects shows no major breaks or interruptions.

The Maya languages grade imperceptibly into one another; Maya-
speaking groups which live close together geographically also speak
similar languages; as distance between groups increases, so does the
divergence in the languages which they speak. This would seem to indicate that Maya-speakers have been in the area for a long time and that
the basic Maya-speaking population has remained relatively undisturbed, in spite of repeated invasions and social upheavals. Had these
upheavals displaced large groups of people or introduced new groups

42

in significant numbers from the outside, we should hardly find so gradual a picture of linguistic differentiation. Similarly, the physical type depicted on Maya monuments remained remarkably stable throughout the course of Maya history. Thus it is more than likely that both the people who planned and supervised the building of the great cities of the Petén and Yucatán and the men who labored in their construction spoke one of the various Maya dialects.

In 1519 Middle America witnessed the coming of the Spaniards, who brought with them to the New World their Romance language, historically the linguistic legacy of Roman rule in Spain. The Roman Empire yielded to pressures from without and within, but the population of the Peninsula continued to speak its Iberian Latin dialects in the face of conquest and occupation by Vandal, Goth, and Arab. When the Christian principalities of the Spanish north rallied to drive out the Arab invaders again, one of the north Spanish dialects, Castilian, spoken in the narrow confines of the kingdom of Oviedo in the Cantabrian Mountains, became the idiom of the Reconquest. As the Reconquest led to the political consolidation and hegemony of the kingdom of Castile, this dialect of the northern marches became the language of the new Spanish state. The year 1492 marked the victory of the Spanish armies over the Arabs in Spain and the expansion of Castile overseas, into the New World beyond the Atlantic. But 1492 also marked the appearance of the first Castilian grammar, the *Gramática de la lengua castellana*, by Antonio de Nebrija (1444–1532), written with the express purpose of acquainting future subject populations speaking other languages with the new language of command.

Today, the overwhelming majority of people in both Mexico and Guatemala speak only Spanish; this majority includes 85 per cent of all Mexicans, 60 per cent of all Guatemalans. In Mexico about half the remaining population is bilingual; that is, they speak Spanish as well as their mother tongue, one or another of the autochthonous Indian languages.

When we plot the Indian-speaking area on a map, we find that the speakers of autochthonous languages survive in a series of islands, of lesser or greater extent; these islands of Indian speech are most common in the eastern portion of the central highlands, in the southern and southeastern highlands, on the northern Gulf coast, on the southern Gulf coast, and in Yucatán. Only a few islands of native speech remain in the western half of the central highlands. These include some 44,000 speakers of Tarascan, a language which has no immediate relatives in Middle America. Swadesh has recently grouped it with Macro-Mayan in a Penutioid phylum, a large stock of languages which extends from Tsimshian in British Columbia to Aymara in Bolivia and which supposedly differentiated between 8000 and 5600 B.C. But the immediate origin of Tarascan remains unknown.

Even within the major areas of autochthonous speech, Spanish-speakers and the speakers of native languages are distributed in rather checkerboard and irregular fashion. In only a few areas do the speakers of native languages constitute more than 60 per cent of the total population. Such is the case in the northern valley of Toluca and in Hidalgo (Otomí, 209,000; Mazahua, 79,000); in northern Veracruz and southern San Luis Potosí (Totonac, 136,000; Huastec, 54,000); in Oaxaca and portions of neighboring states (Mixtec, 271,000; Zapotec, 248,000; Chinantec, 43,700; Mazatec, 116,000); in northeastern Chiapas (Tzeltal, 77,000; Tzotzil, 86,000); in Yucatán (Maya, 283,000), and in the Guatemalan highlands, especially above the 1,000-foot line (Quiché, 442,000; Cakchiquel, 329,000; Mam, 272,000; Kekchi, 246,000). Everywhere there are islands of Spanish speech interspersed among the speakers of autochthonous languages. Everywhere, too, Spanish has affected the native languages, phonetically, grammatically, and in their vocabularies. In the long run, the Indian languages are perhaps slated for extinction. In Mexico, Alanís Patiño has estimated that if the present rate of linguistic shift from native languages to Spanish continues, all Mexican native languages will have disappeared in another 110 years.

The Conquest of the New World was carried out in the name of the kings of Castile, and the idiom in which the Spaniards claimed possession of the Indies and their inhabitants was Castilian. The conquerors came from all parts of Spain; they brought with them the gamut of Spanish dialects spoken in the Peninsula. But, since all understood Castilian, Castilian became the common medium of communication of the Conquest; the other dialects were relegated to a place of secondary importance. Nor did the conquerors settle in the New World according to their provenience in the mother country. Conquest and settlement thus at first restricted the range of variation in language, as in other aspects of culture (see chap. viii). Yet this initial standardization soon gave way to renewed differentiation, this time on New World soil.

Not very long ago it was still the custom to ascribe the differences between the dialects of Spanish spoken in the New World and those spoken in the Old World to the influence of Andalusian migrants, on the mistaken basis that most of the conquerors came from the Spanish province of Andalusia. In fact, the conquerors came from all over Spain, and no one Spanish region can be held responsible for the linguistic differential between the Spanish of the two hemispheres. It would seem, rather, that sixteenth-century Spanish was undergoing all sorts of internal changes everywhere. For instance, the twin phenomena of *yeismo* (the substitution of *y* for *ll*) and *seseo* (the substitution of *s* for Spanish *c*) appeared simultaneously in scattered parts of the Peninsula as well as in the New World.

As the Conquest progressed, moreover, the wide-open spaces of the New World exerted a centrifugal pull on the unifying Castilian of the conquerors. The cities, dominated by a new elite of lawyers, officials, priests, merchants, and absentee landowners, strove to maintain a tradition of Castilian literacy. They thought of themselves as Spaniards *in* America but not *of* America and clung self-consciously to the verbal formulas of court life in the metropolis to demonstrate their continued identification with the fate of the mother country. But in the countryside, out of reach of the schoolmen, changes due to shifts within Spanish it-self—and due also to Indian influence—produced a series of colonial Spanish dialects. Nahuatl sentence melody invaded Mexican Spanish; Maya sentence melody influenced the Spanish spoken in Yucatán. Some 5,000 Nahuatl words—like *metate* (from Nahuatl *metlatl,* "quern"), *chiquihuite* (from Nahuatl *chiquihuitl,* "basket"), *tepescuingle* (from Nahuatl *escuintli,* "little dog"; in Mexican Spanish, "little boy")—came into everyday use among speakers of Mexican Spanish. In Yuca-tán, on the other hand, Spanish speakers began to make use of about 300 Maya words, until a Yucatecan could use a Maya word like *poch* ("eager") in a Spanish phrase such as *estoy poch de un vestido como el tuyo* ("I'd just love to have a dress like yours") or a word like *hochobear* (from the Maya *hoch'ob,* "to covet a meal to which one has not been invited"). As the Indians learned the new colonial dialects, they in turn developed new variants of Spanish. Linguists sometimes refer to these new linguistic media as "substandard Spanish," a term which does them little justice. They certainly do not conform to the rules laid down by formal bodies of scholarly specialists regarding the use and abuse of Castilian; but they did and do mediate linguistically in the cultural encounter between conquered and conquerors.

Nor is Middle American Spanish at a standstill today. More recently, it has received the impress of French and English, notably of the English dialects spoken in the United States. The eighteenth and nineteenth centuries witnessed the introduction into Middle American Spanish of some 850 Gallicisms, the small change of polite conversation of a period when French was the language of diplomats and literati in the Euro-American world, and wealthy Middle Americans sent their children to be polished in Paris. The twentieth century marks the appearance of such words as *jonrón* ("home run"), *hamburguesa* ("hamburger"), *overol* ("overall"), *couche* ("couch"), *líder* ("leader"), *supervisar* ("to supervise"), *mecanizar* ("to mechanize"), *eradicación* ("eradica-tion"), *rehabilitación* ("rehabilitation"), symbolic of the growing in-

46

fluence of Anglo-American culture south of the Rio Grande. A recent dictionary of such Americanisms in Middle American Spanish lists 1,200 words, a gold mine for the cultural historian of the future, who will infer from such linguistic detritus the direction of the flow of culture in our time.

IV

Rise
of the
Seed-Planters

Men first entered the New World in the Upper Pleistocene (27,000 years ago), across Bering Strait, at the northwesternmost corner of Alaska. Today the Strait is covered by water; then it was probably still spanned by a land bridge. The great northern glaciers—which at one time extended as far south as Illinois—had begun to recede, but they still held in their grip enough of the world's water supply to lower the surface of the sea significantly below present levels. The first immigrants to America were hunters, in pursuit of food. Equipped with darts tipped with projectile points and spear-throwers to lend added strength to their throwing arm, they followed in the wake of wild mammoth, horse, and llama. We have seen that it did not take these hunters long to reach the tip of South America. Around 7000 B.C. they were feasting on wild horses in southern Chile.

The presence of these men is also attested in Middle America. Huge bone-beds, containing the remains of mammoth, llama, bison, and wild horses, have been discovered at Tequixquiac, just north of the valley of Mexico. Among the unquestionable human artifacts which have come to light in this animal graveyard are a chalcedony graver, a point carved from the tibia of a bison, and a vertebra of a species of extinct llama carved in the shape of a coyote. The carved vertebra comes from a geologic layer dated Terminal Pleistocene, probably around 11000 B.C. The same date was assigned to the remains of a human skeleton, excavated near the town of Tepexpan, close to the western outskirts of Mexico City. Unfortunately, the skeleton itself was not associated with the remains of prehistoric animals, though the layer in which it was found is heavily shot through with fossil bones of mammoth. Its dating therefore must remain problematical. But more recent finds have definitely established the presence of man in the valley of Mexico during the Late Pleistocene. In 1952 and 1954, human projectile points were found in association with mammoth remains at Santa Isabel Iztapan, close to Tepexpan. The points show distinct similarities to game-hunter projectile points encountered in North America.

The big-game hunters were not, however, the only settlers in Middle America. In the southwestern United States archeologists have discovered remains of people of quite a different cultural orientation. Instead of relying on large game, they hunted small game and obtained most of their food from wild plants and their seed. Still today, Indians in the arid Southwest use one or another tree-borne fruit that can be stored easily and for a long period of time: piñon, mesquite, or acorns. Archeologically, these people left behind their querns and mullers, the grinding platforms and the milling stones, on which they ground their plant food into a palatable meal. These seed-gatherers appear to have lived between 15000 and 2500 B.C. For some eight thousand years they lived alongside the hunters of large game but essentially independent of them. Around 7500 B.C. environmental conditions began to favor their chances of survival, while lessening the survival opportunities of the big-game hunters. This date marks the onset of a great change in climate. Over a wide area extending from Utah to the southern highland of Middle America large tracts of grassland became waste desert; large game and plants requiring a lot of water gave way to small game and desert-adapted plants. The seed-gatherers survived, because their hardy basic staple survived. The big-game hunters disappeared, as their food supply declined and finally vanished.

Like all living organisms, the game hunters and their game depend, ultimately, on plants. To live and to survive, organisms require fuel—energy. The ultimate source of energy is the sun. To tap this energy, we must as yet rely on plants; plants are the only organisms capable of synthesizing significant amounts of organic material in the photosynthetic process. We can also eat animals and animal products, but animals in turn depend on plant food for their energy supply. Plant food is thus the strategic element in the chain of life, and man's chances for survival hang upon his success in obtaining that food. The big-game hunters lost the battle for survival; the seed-gatherers won it.

Seed-gathering proved more viable also in another way. Around 6000 B.C. some seed-gatherer somewhere began to interfere successfully in the planting, germination, and fruition of wild plants. Anthropologists have long recognized this technological achievement as a milestone in the evolution of human culture. V. Gordon Childe, the British archeologist, speaks of it as the first major revolution in man's existence. It is certainly a major step toward giving man greater control of his environment, toward making him its master rather than its slave. For a hunter and gatherer of wild food is a slave to his food supply: if his game or wild food crop is abundant, he may live the life of a savage Riley; if it decreases or vanishes, he may face extinction with it. In controlling the growth and maturation of plants and animals, man still makes use of natural processes. But he assumes some of the functions of nature himself, replacing the natural controls over plant maturation and growth with his own.

The origins of cultivation in Middle America, as in the entire New World, are still shrouded in mystery, though we are getting closer to an understanding of its beginnings. Many different disciplines contribute to

50

this search. The archeologist digs for material objects which would indicate the presence or absence of cultivation and looks for plant remains which are now—thanks to the C-14 method—datable. The linguist attempts to trace the presence or the absence of terms denoting cultivation and cultivated plants in the reconstructed vocabularies of extinct and reconstructed languages. Similarities and differences in the names of plants from one language to another may also tell him how the plants diffused from one linguistic group to another. The botanist attempts to define the ancestors and the relatives of the present cultivated varieties and to trace their distribution, as well as the distribution of the cultigens. Frequently, he will seek to define the area in which they achieved their greatest diversity, on the hypothesis that such diversity occurs where the plant has been cultivated for the longest period of time.

To date, the earliest evidence for plant domestication in the Middle American area does not come from Middle America proper but from its northern periphery, from New Mexico in the northwest and from Tamaulipas in the northeast. There is also a promise of more to come from the valley of Mexico, where in 1958 Helmut de Terra and Arturo Romano located a burial associated with grinding stones and mullers, traceable perhaps to an early seed-gathering population and dated tentatively at between 8000 and 6000 B.C. Such finds will close the gap which now exists between the disappearance of the big-game hunters around 7000 B.C. and appearance of the first full-fledged farmers around 1500 B.C. Until then, however, we are still largely reduced to guesswork on the basis of such meager information as we now possess.

Taking our departure from such uncertain bases, we would say that New World cultivation developed practically independently of agriculture in the Old World. Its techniques and its cultivated plants both differ sufficiently from those of the Old World to make this statement more than probable. Within the body of New World cultivation, we find essentially two divergent traditions. The first of these is found largely to the south of Middle America. It was based on vegetative reproduction,

51

that is, reproduction through cuttings. The crops which belong to this tradition of cultivation yield mostly starches and sugar and are low in proteins and fats. The chief of these is a root crop, manioc (*Manihot utilissima:* Nahuatl, *quauhcámotl;* Maya, *tsin*) which has been cultivated so long that it has nearly lost its ability to set seed. The older maniocs are sweet and non-poisonous. They are distributed more widely than the bitter or poisonous variety grown in the Caribbean and in Brazil but unknown in Middle America, in Colombia, and along the Pacific drainage of South America. Another such crop is the sweet potato (*Ipomoea batatas:* Nahuatl, *camotli;* Maya, *iz;* Spanish, *batata*). For some time scientists thought that this food complex once dominated also the Gulf coast in Middle America, largely because querns and griddles, characteristically associated with maize-processing, are absent from early archeological deposits in the coastal area. But this is based on a misconception. Maize can be eaten without grinding, and griddles are used to prepare dishes other than maize. All evidence goes to show that even on the Gulf coast vegetative reproduction always remained of secondary importance.

Middle American cultivation belongs basically to the other major tradition of New World cultivation, to the tradition based on seed-planting. This complex does not involve setting out cuttings: each year seed is harvested, stored, selected for desirable qualities, and resown. It is notable that seed-planting remained dominant even on the coastal lowlands where the tuber complex might have achieved greater importance. Nor was Middle America lacking in wild plants which could be reproduced through cuttings; such plants (like *camotes del cerro*) are still collected wild and sold in the market place, but they are not cultivated. The seed-planting tradition probably had an origin wholly different from the tradition based on vegetative cuttings. Its inventors were probably the same hardy seed-gatherers who outlived and outlasted the more dramatic big-game hunters after the great climatic change of 7500 B.C.

Several factors may have predisposed them to such an invention. They used seeds, and after the climate grew increasingly arid they probably began to concentrate their existence around certain well-watered and favored spots where wild seed crops appeared with regularity, even when other areas failed. This semi-sedentary existence attracted plants in turn. Many of the plants used later in cultivation were once common weeds which—attracted by human refuse—grew up around habitation sites. Weeds and men were bound together by mutual advantages: human beings provided the disturbed soils in which these plants could grow; the plants provided seeds which men required for their diet. We know that plants throw up new varieties all the time. Many of them die out, often because they cannot find room in the environment, some unoccupied niche where they might take root and flourish. Human habitation sites, however, represent a radical change in the environment, new niches with new opportunities for plant adaptation and growth. Similarly, men burned over the land to speed the taking of game, and burned-over ground furnished a similar ecological haven.

Nor are men the only agents in plant growth and dispersal. Rivers often change their courses, eat into mountainsides, and deposit the acquired sediment, thus furnishing environmental opportunities for plants seeking a new home. Once such plants develop, men can contribute to their propagation by aiding their geographic spread. Old varieties get an opportunity to meet new variants with which they can exchange hereditary characteristics. Thus new offspring are born, possessed of the great vigor which usually comes with hybridization. This process continues even today, when cultivated plants are often hybridized with weeds to produce new and hardier offspring.

Some of the earliest weeds selected for increased attention and cultivation may have been plants like amaranth and chenopodium, which are improved relatives of the common pigweed of farm and field. Amaranth (*Amaranthus lescarpus* and *A. cruentus*: Nahuatl, *huauhtli*; Maya, *xtez*; Spanish, *bledo*) seems to have been especially important, up to the time of the Spanish Conquest. The annual food tribute of the Mexica state consisted of 200,000 bushels of amaranth, compared with 280,000 bushels of maize and 230,000 bushels of beans. In pollen profiles from the valley of Mexico, corresponding in time to the beginnings of cultivation, a marked rise in amaranth pollen precedes the rise in maize pollen. The Spaniards forbade its cultivation, because it was heavily associated with ritual practices; this association would again suggest a certain antiquity. Needless to say, they did not succeed in stamping it out. It is still grown as a minor adjunct to peasant diet throughout Middle America. Similarly, chenopodium (*Chenopodium Nuttalliae* Safford: Nahuatl, *cuauhzontli, epazote; Maya, lucum xiu*) is still cultivated, eaten, or used in folk medicine. It is closely related to the Andean quinoa and may even be the same plant. In the Andes, quinoa is characteristically a high-altitude plant which takes the place of maize in the higher mountains and is either ground into a meal or fermented into beer (*chicha*).

By 1400 B.C. cultivation was no longer peripheral to Middle America but an integral aspect of its existence. Looking at the scattered relics of these full-fledged cultivators, we are conscious of the big gap which separates them from their pioneering ancestors. They were fully sedentary; they lived in villages; fragments of burned clay, bearing the imprint of sticks or poles, tell us that their houses were made of wattle, daubed with clay or mud and probably thatched with reeds or straw, in the manner of Indian huts or *jacales* (Nahuatl, *xacalli*) to this day. By this time, they possessed maize and squash, and a little later they added the bean, thus completing the trinitarian basis of the Middle American diet. Their equipment for processing maize was the same as that of any modern Indian household: the stone quern or *metate* (Nahuatl, *metlatl*) on which maize was ground to a meal, the stone muller or *mano* (Nahuatl, *metlapil*, or "son of the metate"), the circular clay griddle or *comal* (Nahuatl, *comalli*) on which maize cakes were baked over the fire. In the highlands of Guatemala they stored their crops in rectangular and bottle-shaped pits, which they filled afterward with trash and often used to bury their

54

The early seed-planters probably built wattle-and-daub houses thatched with reeds or straw, much like those shown in this picture of a Nahuatl-speaking village in Morelos, Mexico. Note the round granary common to a number of buildings and the stone fences dividing one lot from another. (Courtesy of American Museum of Natural History.)

dead. Deer bones and bird bones are numerous, tell-tale remnants of food obtained with dart points made of obsidian and carved with stone and bone scrapers. Where people lived near lakes, as in the valley of Mexico, or along rivers, as in northern Veracruz, fish provided a vital source of protein.

The main tools employed in cultivation were the stone ax and probably the wooden digging stick, its point treated in the fire. The wooden digging stick or *coa* is still in use today. Most people probably still made their other tools as they needed them, but a concentrated group of obsidian workshops with large refuse pits from highland Guatemala shows that specialization had set in at least in this one important region. A simple kind of pottery was made and traded to adjacent localities. Cloth was woven; a fragment of cotton cloth mixed with apocynum fiber has been found in the valley of Mexico. The cotton (*Gossypium hirsutum* L.: Maya, *tamán*; Nahuatl, *izcatl*) must have come from the lowlands, since cotton will not grow in the altitude of Mexico City. Perhaps it came from Morelos or from northern Veracruz. Snails and shells were traded inland from the coastal country, from the Pacific shore first, later from the Atlantic. Salt was probably an important item of trade, vital to people who were beginning to rely increasingly on a plant-derived diet.

When people died, they were interred in scattered graves and given offerings to accompany them on their journey. These offerings do not vary greatly from grave to grave; they indicate a rough equality of wealth and power among the dead. At the same time, some men were buried with companions—either members of their family or perhaps servants whose involuntary death provided aid for their master in the world of the spirits. In such multiple burials, the male occupied the central position. Perhaps people were interred near their house, or even under the floors of their house, as was the custom in much of Middle America in later days. At any rate, the unity of the community was not yet symbolized by grouping the village dead into a common burial ground.

Plentiful everywhere (but in the lowland Maya area after about 500 B.C.) are small clay figurines which represent women, women with swelling thighs and heavy breasts, or women with narrow hips and braided hair of a type called "pretty lady" by the archeologist. Holding one of these little works of art in the palm of our hand—they are rarely longer than three or four inches—we can only wonder about their meaning. Are they portraits of individuals who once walked the earth? They are indeed strongly individualized, as if the artist had been trying to capture in clay the features of some person he knew. Are they representative of some form of erotic art? Their nudity, together with the careful exaggeration of their generative organs and the secondary characteristics of their sex would lend support to this view. Yet, by and large, there is little erotic art among American Indians (Peruvian Mochica art of A.D. 600–900 is the striking exception), and what is erotic art to a modern beholder may simply be conventional stylization to the native artist. Do the figurines then embody some general concept of fertility,

56

A millennium before Christ, seed-planters in the valley of Mexico made female figurines of clay, such as the one shown, now in the American Museum of Natural History. Note the turban, earrings, and breast pendant. (After Vaillant; drawing by Patrick F. Gallagher.)

magically expressed in their emphasized organs of reproduction? Many archeologists incline to this view, but the individualized faces of the figurines speak rather against it. We should expect a generalized concept to find expression in more stereotyped form.

The same objection can be raised against the idea that the figurines depict a "corn mother," a female generative principle which makes the corn grow, as a "rice mother" is thought to be responsible for the growth of rice throughout Southeast Asia. Are they perhaps representations of ancestors who bring fertility and happiness to the living, just as the kachina dolls of the Hopi and Zuñi Indians of our Southwest represent the collective rain-giving supernatural ancestors of the tribe? But the kachina cult is not attested before the thirteenth or fourteenth century among the southwestern Pueblos, and, anyway, why would all the ancestors depicted be females? Are we dealing with a culture in which descent through females provided the main organizing principle of social life? This is not impossible; women carry the burden of agriculture among many simple farmers and are the strategic sex in the production of food for such a society. Under such circumstances, property in houses, goods, and crops frequently passes in the female line. Yet the evidence of the figurines is contradicted here by the central position of the male in those burials which contain multiple occupants. In Guatemala, however, we also find figurines of monkeys, animals later associated with the deities of the dance and fertility.

We have no systematic knowledge of the ways in which these early farmers grew their crops, but the major system of cultivation was probably slash-and-burn farming, still practiced in many parts of Middle America today. Tourists traveling along the Pan-American Highway into northern Veracruz in the summertime can see fields cultivated in this manner without getting out of their cars. Under this system, fields are carved out of the forest by cutting back and burning off the vegetative cover. Occupation of a field is temporary. After the first two years, yields usually decrease sharply. The modern Totonac and the Yucatec Maya abandon their cultivated clearings after two years; the Huastec after two to three years. The farmer will then cut and burn over another strip of forest or brush land to obtain a new clearing; and he will repeat this process every two years until his initial clearing has reverted to forest and regained its fertility. He may then return to the point of origin in his circuit. It is important to recognize that yields may be very high during the brief period of years that a field is under cultivation. In Tepoztlán, a modern Nahuatl-speaking village in Morelos, yields from slash-and-burn clearings run on an average twice as high as those obtained on land plowed year after year; among the modern Totonac yields run 100:1 per unit of seed put into the ground, and a farmer can obtain two crops a year.

One limiting factor in this kind of cultivation is, however, the availability of land. As long as the farmer has access to new land, he can maintain his yield; when his access to land is restricted, he may have to farm his old clearings before they regain their fertility, and his yields will suffer accordingly. It follows that a man needs a rather large area of land to produce at a constant rate of productivity year after year. Among the modern Totonac of the Gulf coast a family of five members

58

Slash-and-burn farming is still widely practiced in Middle America.
This picture shows a Huastec-speaking farmer clearing land along the
Pan American Highway, near Tamazunchale, San Luis Potosí, Mexico,
in late August, 1956. (Photograph by Eric R. Wolf.)

needs thirty acres to feed itself on the basis of such field-forest rotation
without declining yields; among the Maya of Yucatán a family of the
same size may need as much as seventy-two acres. Lack of land may
ultimately cause a population to abandon this system of cultivation; but
as long as land is available, its advantages outweigh its disadvantages.
We know from other areas of the world that people have even abandoned
sedentary agriculture based on careful terracing if presented with new
land frontiers. On the other hand, the disadvantages of the system may
be heavily increased by any means that limits the amount of available
land. A Dutch scholar has even worked out a mathematical formula
expressing the amount of land which must be taken from a slash-and-
burn population to force them to work on European-owned plantations.

The system is thus ultimately predicated on a very lavish use of natural resources, on a situation in which only a few men use a great deal of land. It thus contributes to low population densities: men must live apart if they are to feed themselves today and their increasing generations tomorrow. At the same time, the system is strongly centrifugal. It inhibits tendencies toward population concentration, as well as the reach and effectiveness of secular and sacred rulers. The inherent mobility of its component units would make it rather unlikely that a strong state based on tribute and labor drafts could arise under such circumstances. Just such an unlikely combination of circumstances has been alleged for the ancient Maya of the Theocratic period (900 B.C.–A.D. 900). There are only two logical possibilities under which a Maya-like system could arise with such a system of cultivation as we have been discussing here. One possibility is that Maya society, with its priestly centers, stabilized itself through the use of some other system of cultivation, yet unknown. The other possibility is that the Maya priestly center was the product of population increase and increased occupation of the land, that it served as the centralized control needed to allocate land and to regulate shifts in cultivation. Both possibilities are present, and we shall return to both later.

Another system of cultivation which may have originated early is the two-field system familiar to economic and social historians from accounts of medieval Europe. In this system, one field is planted in crops, while the other is left fallow one or two years until it regains its former fertility. This can be done only where climatic conditions do not completely destroy the mineral content of the soil after tillage. In Middle America this system has been described for the highland Totonac and for the Tarascan area. In all cases, it is associated with permanent residence of the cultivator in a house, with the use of a kitchen garden. Among the highland Totonac only 6.25 acres are needed to feed one family each year, and such a family needs only 16.25 acres to maintain productivity. This is in sharp contrast with the figures reported for the

60

lowland Totonac, who carry on slash-and-burn farming. Under the two-field system associated with a permanent kitchen garden, then, many more people can live off the same amount of land than in slash-and-burn cultivation. Where a slash-and-burn community of 100 families of 5 members each needs 7,200 acres in northern Yucatán, only 1,625 acres are required to feed a similar community among the highland Totonac with the two-field system.

From the beginning of cultivation, Middle American farmers opened fields on the hillsides and the slopes of mountains in preference to cultivating the valley floors. In many areas, this preference was due to the mountainous nature of the terrain: there were simply not enough level lands to cultivate. Often, however, the valley soils look better than they are in reality. They may be covered with silt, sand, and gravel but recently washed down from the heights by mountain streams and torrential rains and insufficiently weathered to offer good nutriment for plants. Frequently such sterile deposits cover highly productive soils and render them unusable for agricultural purposes. Yet even good and easily available valley soils presented serious obstacles to primitive farmers: their pointed wooden digging sticks frequently could not destroy the web of grass roots in the soil. Not until the Spaniards introduced the plow did some of the plain areas become accessible to cultivation. The lighter soils of the hillsides did not represent such a barrier. At the same time, hillside farming has a positive advantage: frost hazards are less severe along the lower slopes than they are along the floors of valley basins, a fact of which modern Indian cultivators are keenly aware.

Slash-and-burn clearing and hillside farming had, however, unrecognized side-effects which acted in turn to make food production less viable. As a cultivator, man controls his environment, and yet he may in the very process, all unknowingly, unleash environmental forces which threaten his survival. The ax and the torch of the cultivator cut back the forest but opened the way to invasion of the former forest floor by tough competitive grasses. Such an invasion by grass is a menace to the tropical cultivator. Forest floors after burning are soft and easily worked and fertile because of the soluble minerals contained in the ashes; but grass creates a tough network of rhizomes and roots which is very difficult to uproot without iron tools. Grassland, in turn, may reduce rainfall: it reflects the rays of the sun and evaporates moisture, while stands of forest bind water and reduce evaporation.

In the uplands of Middle America, cultivation also set free other forces which men are still fighting to contain. Mountains are precarious repositories of cultivable soils; gravity and the flow of water speed the soil on its way to lower altitudes. Soil is a temporary product, a stage in the process of dissolution that carries rocks and minerals to the sea. Plants feed upon this process of dissolution; it is essential to them. Yet if man is to survive, he must regulate its speed and intensity. When he cuts down the trees that stand guard over the deposits of soil in the mountains, he also undercuts his chances of survival. Today, deserted villages, barrens thickly sown with potsherds that bespeak the dense settlement of past eras, canals and terraces laid out many feet above present water levels, provide mute testimony to a process which began four thousand years ago or more. The modern Indian who lets the dry soil of his meager field run through his hand to test its moisture and organic content sees in his dry land the sign that the present world is approaching its appointed ruin. He, however, is but the heir of men who first ravaged the crust of the earth in the hope of increasing their chances of survival, their own and also that of their sons.

By 900 B.C., the Middle American diet had in all probability achieved the standardized form which it still possesses today. It rests essentially on the consumption of plant food, in contrast to the diets of Europe and North America, which combine the consumption of cereals with meat-eating and milk-drinking. Domesticated animals, however, played and still play a very minor role in the Middle American diet. In pre-Hispanic times, small dogs were raised and fattened for eating; together with the turkey (Nahuatl, *totolli;* Maya, *tso;* today called *guajolote* in Middle

62

American Spanish after the Nahuatl *uexólotl,* "male turkey") they constituted the only inhabitants of the barnyard. The people of the lowlands, like the Maya and the Totonac of the Gulf, kept bees, and the Maya mixed fermented honey with the bark of the balche tree (*Lonchocarpus longistylus* Pittier) to make a fermented drink, but the highland people obtained part of their supply of sugar from the sweet juice of the century plant. There were none of the many burden-carrying food animals of the Old World which played such a vital role by lending mobility in transportation and warfare to masses of men. In Middle America burdens were always carried by men, and troops moved on foot, until the Spanish Conquest presented the Indians with the spectacle of armed centaurs whose nostrils breathed hot metal and fire.

If the Middle American diet indeed began with the pigweeds, its mainstay became the staple combination of maize, beans, and squash, sometimes called the Trinity of the American Indian. The earliest evidence for cultivated maize (*Zea mays:* Nahuatl, *centli;* Maya, *ixim*) comes from Bat Cave in New Mexico, where layers dated as early as 4000 B.C. yielded a maize with cobs the size of strawberries which united the characteristics of both popcorn and podcorn. Similar kinds of maize have come to light in southeastern Tamaulipas, where they are dated at 3000 B.C. Yet it is clear that maize has existed in Middle America as a wild weed since Pleistocene times; pollen of wild maize has been found in the valley of Mexico to a depth of some 200 feet. Somewhere in Middle America—though we still do not know where—some group of seed-planters must have domesticated this weed. At some later time, probably in the southeastern highland of Guatemala and Chiapas, the domesticated maize plant hybridized with a weed called *teocentli,* itself a hybrid between maize and a weed called *Tripsacum.* From here it spread into South America, but it arrived late—after the system based on cuttings had a secure hold—and always remained a secondary food. Its earliest appearance in Peru is dated at 900–700 B.C.; its use as food was as corn on the cob—low in efficiency when compared to the Middle American manner of using it—or as the basis for maize beer (*chicha*).

The plant is possessed of an astonishing variability and is extraordinarily adaptable to different environments. It grows at altitudes ranging from sea level to 12,700 feet at Lake Titicaca in the high Andes; in regions with short summers and cool climates, as well as in deserts with an annual precipitation of less than 8 inches. In Middle America, maize kernels are toasted, ground into a meal, and eaten either dry or as a gruel (modern Mexican, *pinole*; Nahuatl, *pinolli*; Maya, *kah*); or mixed and left to stand in a lime solution, later finely ground, patted into round cakes, and cooked rapidly on a griddle to make tortillas (Nahuatl, *tlaxcalli*; Maya, *uah*). The tortilla can be eaten as such, or wrapped around meat, beans, and chili to make tamales or tacos. Tortilla dough can be mixed with water to make *pozole* (Nahuatl, *pozolli*; Maya, *keyem*) or cooked slightly with an added flavoring of some sort to make *atole* (Nahuatl, *atolli*; Maya, *za*). It is safe to say that at least 75 per cent of the daily energy intake of people in Middle America today is based on maize prepared in one of these several guises.

The second member of the Trinity of American seed plants is the bean, high in proteins and fat content, usually eaten boiled. Again, the center of distribution of most New World beans seems to be in Middle America, but the different species are adapted to quite different climatic conditions. Thus the common kidney bean (*Phaseolus vulgaris*: Nahuatl, *ayacotl*; Maya, *buul*; Spanish, *frijol*) which forms a mainstay of Mexican diet, is mainly an upland bean which does not prosper in lowlands or at very high altitudes. The tepary bean (*Phaseolus acutifolius*, var.) is a desert-adapted plant. The lima bean (*Phaseolus lunatus*: Maya, *ibé*; Spanish, *frijol*) is a hot-country crop, usually found in tropics with a marked dry season, and only rarely encountered above 4,000 feet. The earliest Middle American evidence of the bean comes from southeastern Tamaulipas, dated at 2500 B.C. Yet while some of the earliest known farming communities in the valley of Mexico possessed maize, about 1350 B.C., they did not get beans until somewhat later. This would mean that at one time they lacked a most important source of protein to supplement the carbohydrates furnished by maize.

Ralph Linton argues persuasively that any group of people must control an adequate source of protein to maintain stable life. Hunters and gatherers can obtain proteins by hunting game or wild fowl, or by fishing. Cultivators, on the other hand, find it increasingly difficult to fill their protein quota if they do not also possess domesticated animals. Middle America, as all America before Columbus, possessed only a scant number of domesticated animals, when compared with the large inventory of such animals in the Old World. The bean may therefore have been an important strategic addition to the developing diet of the Middle American farmer.

The third major type of plant included in the American Trinity are the squashes and pumpkins (*Cucurbita:* Spanish, *calabaza;* Nahuatl, *ayotli;* Maya, *kum*) and the gourds (*Lagenaria siceraria:* Spanish, *calabaza;* Nahuatl, *tecomatl;* Maya, *bux, lek*). These are among the oldest agricultural remains found, both in southeastern Tamaulipas and in Peru in South America; in both places, they preceded beans and maize. They were undoubtedly first protected and then cultivated for their oily, protein-bearing seeds rather than for their flesh; the seeds still form an important part of the Middle American diet. Flowers and leaves are also eaten. The wild varieties have no flesh; human control, however, has produced a wide range of large starchy and sugary varieties.

An inevitable companion of the Middle American meal is the chili pepper (*Capsicum annuum* L., and *C. frutescens* L.: Nahuatl, *chilli;* Maya, *ic;* Mexican Spanish, *chile*). It occurs in innumerable varieties; the areas of greatest diversification—Middle America and Brazil—may also be the areas where the species originated. Some varieties are eaten raw, some in sauces. They are a valuable source of vitamins and serve as an aid in the digestion of foodstuffs high in cellulose. Another necessary addition to such a diet is salt. Meat-eaters and milk-drinkers do not seem to need salt in the same amounts as plant-eaters, who seem to crave added quantities of sodium chloride. Salt deposits thus played a strategic role in Middle American historical development. The valley of Mexico was especially blessed in that salt could be obtained from its saline lakes by evaporation. Elsewhere it had to be transported overland or across the sea: the salt trade was an important factor in linking the Gulf coast of Mexico with Yucatán from early times.

So standardized is this diet and so invariable its adherence to maize, squash, beans, and chili that many observers have concluded that it must produce serious dietary deficiencies. Meat-eaters and milk-drinkers are, however, apt to pass uninformed judgments on the dietary norms of other cultures. Middle American Indians ate and still eat many foods in addition to the above, foods which may not suit the palates of people whose tastes derive from a tradition of animal husbandry coupled with grain agriculture. Laboratory analysis has discovered considerable quantities of protein, vitamins, and minerals in such Middle American foods as *axayacatl*, a highland moth, and its eggs (*ahuauhtli*), a very elegant caviar; in *malva*, a wild highland plant which tastes like spinach; in cactus (*nopal*); in sesame and squash seeds; in peanuts and piñon nuts; in the red-and-white worms that infest the century plant; in the iguana, the large lizard of the tropical lowlands that tastes like frogs' legs, and its roe; in turtles, snakes, triatomas (*chumil*), rats, and many other occasional additions to the daily diet. Furthermore, in the highlands, the Indians also drink considerable quantities of pulque (Nahuatl, *octli*), the fermented and unfiltered juice of the century plant (*Agave atrovirens*: Nahuatl, *metl*), which possesses an alcohol content of from 3 to 5 per cent. In many areas, the drink provides significant daily amounts of minerals and of vitamins C and B. Often confined in pre-Conquest times to nobles or old people and taboo to commoners or to the young and able-bodied, pulque is today drunk by everyone. Discoveries of scrapers used to increase the flow of juice from the heart of the century plant have been made at Teotihuacán; the use of pulque is thus at least as old as the Theocratic period and very probably much older.

In the second half of the second millennium B.C., then, we witness throughout Middle America the growth of a life centered upon villages maintained by farmers with simple tools, bent upon winning the basic crops of a standardized diet from the earth, and with an approach to the powers of the supernatural that seems to involve some projection of the female generative principle into the world of the sacred. Ties between communities are still tenuous; they are based on occasional commercial contacts, and the communities are not yet subordinate to an authority which has its seat outside their limits. These seed-planters are thus still primitive farmers, not yet peasants in the strict sense of the word, because a peasantry is no longer an isolated segment of society, sufficient unto itself; it is a functional part of a larger social whole, in which the society has become dichotomized into a center of power and control and a rural hinterland of dependent cultivators. Such a society comprises three levels of organization: the individual household; the community which embraces the individual households; and the emergent state which embraces the communities and dictates to them.

Until 900 B.C., however, there was no sign of this last phenomenon. The community was the autonomous unit of social life; and the growth of ties beyond its limits was still to come. And when we look at this unit in long-term perspective, we find that in Middle America it was never obliterated. The simple inventory of farm tools and kitchen equipment,

Stone querns (metates) *and mullers* (manos) *have remained essentially the same from the time of the early seed-planters to the present.*

the tasks of farming, the religious concepts geared to the cycle of planting and harvesting, the style of life centered upon the community of one's birth—these have remained basic and stable until today. Empires and conquests sweep over the land, cities arise, new gods announce salvation, but in the dusty streets of the little villages a humble kind of life persists, and rises again to the surface when the fury of conquest is stilled, when the cities crumble into ashes, and when the new gods are cast into oblivion. In the rhythm of Middle American development we recognize phases of great metabolic construction, followed by catabolic processes which gnaw at the foundations of temples and citadels until they collapse of their own weight or vanish in a fury of burning and destruction. Yet until today the community of cultivators has retained its capacity to turn in upon itself and to maintain its integrity in the face of doubt and disaster—until today and perhaps not much longer, because the modern world is engaged in severing once and for all the ties which bind people into local unity, in committing them to complete participation in the Great Society. This is a one-way street, along which there is no return. The Middle American world has survived many destructions; our present cycle of time is now approaching its nadir.

V

Villages
and
Holy Towns

Around 900 B.C. the egalitarian life of the simple farming community yields to increased complexity. The number and range of cultivated plants has increased; hunting is less important. Surpluses are larger and more dependable and need no longer be plowed back to meet needs of elementary subsistence; cultivation and its yields seem more assured. It was thus possible for groups of men to develop a lien on the disposal of that surplus, to employ it for ends which transcended subsistence. If it is true that man does not live by bread alone, he must first attend to gaining the daily bread that keeps him alive. Yet no human society restricts its purposes to the pursuit of the food quest; as soon as this basic need is met, it raises it sights and strives to transcend its earth-bound limitations.

This striving is evident in several ways in the tangible remains which the early Middle Americans left behind them. There is evidence of increased specialization and trade: pots are no longer made only for the home; they are also made for export. Shells, jade, turquoise are imported and exported. There are growing differences in burial offerings.

A man is buried at Kaminaljuyú in a mound 20 feet high, and set to rest surrounded by 400 pots, jade, marble greenstone vessels, jade-incrusted masks, pyrite mirrors, and ornaments of shell or bone. Another is interred without these marks of distinction. A social gulf yawns between the two members of the same society, a gulf which continues to separate them on their last journey and will continue to divide them in their after-life. In the valley of Mexico and elsewhere, we now find male figurines as well as female ones, many of them engaged in secular tasks: playing ball, holding dogs, or holding babies.

Here we get our first glimpse of men set off from their fellows in appearance as well as in prerogatives. They are shown wearing masks over their faces, breastplates, cloaks, anklets, bracelets, hats; and only people so dressed are shown in the company of one or two female companions, or seated on a four-legged bench. Although these masked men are not yet stereotyped—details of dress and appearance differ from individual to individual—they are probably the first representatives of a social type which is to dominate Middle American society for close to two millenniums. This man is the priest, set off from common humanity by dress, deportment, and skills, as well as by his vision of the universe and his dedication to the realization of this vision. In another way, 900 B.C. marks his emergence in Middle American society. To this date belong the first large-scale constructions built for a religious purpose—the prototypes of the burial mounds and temple platforms—which will provide the stage upon which these new specialists will enact their social role.

The development of differentiation between priest and common believer, hieratic intellectual and earth-bound peasant, is accompanied in many parts of Middle America by the spread of a distinctive art style, usually called Olmec by archeologists. The origin of this style, the cultural characteristics of its carriers, and the depth and continuity of its influence are the subjects of much exciting speculation. The greatest Olmec site is at La Venta, a great ceremonial precinct erected on an

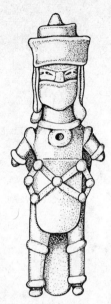

This clay figurine of a masked man from Tlatilco in the valley of Mexico indicates the emergence of full-time religious specialists around the year 900 B.C. (After Piña Chan; drawing by Patrick F. Gallagher.)

island in the middle of a mangrove swamp in northern Tabasco, on the Gulf coast. But Olmec style objects come from as far north as Tlatilco in the valley of Mexico, as far west as Guerrero, as far south as Costa Rica. Some of its works are dated at 900 B.C., but at the type site of La Venta the art style persisted until 400 B.C. Elsewhere, it may even have lasted longer. The features of this art style are highly distinctive, easily recognizable no matter where its manifestations may be found. Two of these features stand out strongly: a delight in carved jade and an obsession with the jaguar, an animal which these people represented in a multitude of forms. No other people has equaled the Olmec artists in their skilful use of jade, nor in the quantity of jade objects which they left in their sacred caches at La Venta or at Cerro de las Mesas. And no other Middle American artistic tradition has been so possessed by the feline form. The Olmec carved the jaguar into ceremonial axes and altars; the teeth, spots, and claws of the animal are depicted on pottery, ear plugs, and masks. Jaguar incisors are ground in jade. Human heads are marked with the tattoo mark of the jaguar; men are shown wearing jaguar skins; and human faces, centered upon jaguar-like mouths, acquire the features of the feline face.

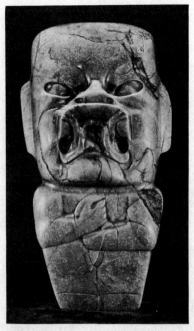

This anthropomorphic ax of blue-gray jadeite, 11 inches high, probably comes originally from Oaxaca, Mexico. It is an excellent example of the Olmec art style, combining, as it does, the features of a baby face with the diagnostic traits of the jaguar. (Courtesy of American Museum of Natural History.)

We can only guess at the meaning which jade and the jaguar possessed for these eager idolaters. In Middle American religious tradition, the jaguar is associated with the god of rain and fertility, who was called Tlaloc among the Nahuatl-speakers, "He Who Makes the Plants Spring Up." One of Tlaloc's guises is the earth-god, who dwells in caves and mountains and possesses the "heart of the land." The jaguar is thus a symbol for the power that controls the heart of the land. But in the complex symbolic language of the area, caves and mountains also denote settlements and towns; and I incline to the view that the jaguar symbol is a symbol of domination not only over the sacred orifices of the earth but also over their human counterparts. Jaguar jaws are often found in Maya graves; thrones carved in the likeness of the jaguar are depicted in sculptured representations in the Maya area; headdresses portraying the jaguar adorn the Maya priests and rulers; and jaguar features mark the faces of gods as well as of men.

Jade was the most precious stone of Middle American lapidary art. Twenty-five centuries later, at the time of the Spanish Conquest of Middle America, when a noble died among the Mexica of the valley of Mexico or in Yucatán, a piece of jade was put into the man's mouth upon burial to represent his heart; a commoner received only a common green stone. The same use of jade is attested for Kaminaljuyú by A.D. 300. Again, we have a link between object used and nobility, uncommon status, domination, and rulership. These hints lead us to interpret the Olmec art style as the outward manifestation of a religious cult which also possessed strong political overtones. We get a view of new, rapacious deities; and this cult is linked to novel differences between men and men, associated with distinctions in function and in power. The Olmec art style spread so widely and exerted such lasting influence because it underlined the new lines of cleavage within the social order.

The change from food-gathering to the control of domesticated animals and plants involved a major change in technology, the harnessing to human ends of major new sources of energy. Was the growing complexity of the new ceremonial societies based on similar shift in technology, or was it due rather to more efficient exploitation of potentialities already implicit in the older, corn-planter pattern? In the Old World, the shift from the egalitarian farming societies of the Neolithic to the class-structured, urban societies of the Bronze Age involved both a heavy increase in productivity through the introduction and intensification of irrigation and the growth of new patterns of organization enforced by new ruling groups. We cannot be sure which of these phenomena came first. Some

scholars believe that irrigation farming created the need for more efficient organization and co-ordination in the construction and maintenance
of dams, dikes, and canals and in the supervision of workers who built
and repaired these waterworks. Irrigation farming also produced the
agricultural surpluses that fed both the laborers and the new organizers
of production. Other scholars favor the opposite view and hold that the
new patterns of organization came first and made the new productive
enterprises possible.

Similar questions must occur to us when we ask ourselves how the new
temple centers were provisioned. Some of them were probably mere cathedral towns, permanently inhabited only by a small group of religious
caretakers but visited by the population of the surrounding countryside
on certain holy days. Many of the centers of the tropical forest in the
area of the Petén seem to have been of this type. Other centers, however, were clearly cities. One such city was the central Mexican metropolis of Teotihuacán.

Sanders has estimated the population of Teotihuacán at a minimum
of 50,000 inhabitants, with the possibility that it may have been as high
as 120,000. To support such a population on the basis of the two-field
system would require roughly between 150,000 and 400,000 acres, not
counting an equal number of acres to sustain the producing population.

On the basis of such logical considerations alone, we may assume that
a city of this size relied on systems of cultivation in addition to or in lieu
of slash-and-burn and two-field cultivation. Is there evidence for any
such systems? Four such systems are known, and all are demonstrably
pre-Hispanic. The first is terracing. Terracing with stone retaining walls
to keep hillsides from eroding and preventing the free runoff of rain
water is certainly pre-Hispanic; it may be older than the Theocratic
cultures. Another system makes use of humid bottom lands (*tierra de
jugo*). We may assume that this also was in use from early corn-planter
times. A third system is today restricted to a small and ever shrinking
area in the southeastern part of the valley of Mexico. Here cultivation

74

takes place on *chinampas*, often called "floating" gardens, probably because they do not float. A chinampa is a platform built up of layers of mud alternating with layers of aquatic plants, built out into the lake but usually firmly anchored to the shore by the roots of an *ahuehuete* tree (member of the genus *Taxodium*). A chinampa is enormously productive, often permitting harvests up to three times a year. Plants are grown in seedbeds and transplanted to the chinampa after each harvest, so that production is practically continuous. For centuries, the chinampa villages on Lake Chalco and Lake Xochimilco supplied the larger centers of the basin of Mexico with primary foods and vegetable products. Even as late as 1900, the great market of Mexico City was supplied by hollow-log canoes which punted up the great Canal de la Viga, today dry and desolate. The drying-up of the lagoons has almost caused the disappearance of the chinampas.

To date no one has yet excavated a "fossil" chinampa. We do not know how old this system of cultivation is but we may make several educated guesses. Chinampa cultivation requires fresh water, and was thus

Pre-Hispanic agricultural terraces still in use in the valley of Tenancingo, Mexico, photographed in 1942. (Courtesy of Geographical Review.)

Chinampas along Lake Xochimilco, valley of Mexico. (From Elisabeth Schilling, Die "schwimmenden Gärten" von Xochimilco [Schriften des Geographischen Instituts der Universität Kiel, Vol. IX, 1939]. By permission of the Geographisches Institut der Universität Kiel.)

possible on a significant scale only when men had achieved control of salt-water flooding on the valley lakes through the construction of dikes. Such a dike existed at the time of the Conquest, but it may not have been the first one. The location of a major early Theocratic center like Cuicuilco close to the shores of the fresh-water lake is rather suggestive. Perhaps such early construction work was undertaken during one of the dry spells of the late seed-planter period. If so, it is not impossible that some of the changes in the level of the lake were caused not by natural desiccation or other climatic factors but by men. At any rate, we cannot be certain that chinampas existed before the middle of the fourteenth century, when the Colhua Mexica or Aztecs first reached the valley of Mexico and began to build chinampas. The Colhua Mexica were then barbarians from the northern frontier; it is most unlikely that they originated the idea. Probably they borrowed the method from the older established populations of the valley. Still, we are thrown back on educated guessing until an enterprising scientist lays bare the earliest chinampa.

We are similarly in the dark about the fourth system, irrigation. Irrigation certainly existed at the time of the Spanish Conquest. We possess a list of over four hundred communities with irrigation for this period,

76

and some studies of irrigation works of attested pre-Hispanic origin. However, the earliest assured date for an irrigation canal is no older than the period immediately after the fall of Teotihuacán. There is some evidence of possible irrigation ditches near Cuicuilco, but, faint and not properly stratigraphic, it does not yet meet the criteria of scientific acceptance. Irrigation may have been practiced early. It was practiced in Arizona as early as the Theocratic period. But again we shall be merely guessing about its presence in the valley of Mexico until we have more certain data.

What is true of the valley of Mexico holds true for all other regions of Middle America, including the Petén. If we assume that the Maya of the Petén possessed only slash-and-burn cultivation, how then do we explain the numerous ceremonial centers of the area? Slash-and-burn cultivation usually implies a scattered population, a population unwilling to pay homage to a center of control. How did the Maya priests accom-

Flood-water irrigation in the valley of Teotihuacán, Mexico, May, 1955. Note the high rate of water retention. (Photograph by William T. Sanders.)

plish this feat, not once but many times, not for a brief period but for well over eight hundred years? It is more than likely that the Maya, too, possessed some system of intensive cultivation, supplementary to their slash-and-burn practices, which allowed them to maintain stable centers of control, while at the same time controlling an ever shifting peasantry. Perhaps it was a system of chinampas, or a related system, which made use of the many lakes and swamps of the Petén. Perhaps it is this which is symbolized in their ever recurrent use of the water-lily motif in art and religious representation. It is also possible that the Petén Maya imported part of their food from the highlands. In the ancient prophetic Books of the Hidden Prophet, written down after the Spanish Conquest in Maya phonology on European paper, there occurs a prophecy which might certainly make us think so. In the year 5 Ahau, says the prophet, there will be a drought, "but its burden of hunger will not be very heavy, because the water in the canals will yield up food there on the other side of the mountain, on the other side of the rocky hills." Some day we shall have the answers to these various problems. Until then, we are faced merely with logical contradictions and a vacuum of evidence.

If we cannot yet point with assurance to an ascertained body of facts which would show that the Theocratic period was ushered in by a set of technological changes, we can be certain that the organization of society had undergone a major change. The dominant figure of this new social order was the religious specialist, its center of power the ceremonial center. The center was a sacred precinct, divorced from the everyday routine tasks of the cultivator and set off from his huts. Within this precinct, the special apparatus was housed through which supernatural energy was concentrated, stored, and distributed to common men. This machinery was in the hands of uncommon men, priest-rulers, whose special training and esoteric knowledge allowed them to approach the deity and to transmit its will. These specialists wore the symbols of divinity, the mask of the jaguar or the feathers of the quetzal bird, and they spoke with the voice of gods. But they were not only devotees of the supernatural; they

78

were also devotees of power, power over men. In them, society had developed a body not only of full-time religious practitioners but also of specialists in organization, capable of exacting labor and tribute as well as worship from the mass of men. Such rule has been called theocratic; under it the power to rule and the power of religion are one. Ultimately, then, the social order is but an aspect of the universal order. If gods work to keep men in their place, and men labor to keep the gods in their heaven, the balance of society is properly maintained.

All early states were based on the combination of supernatural terror and secular power: the kings of China, Mesopotamia, Egypt, or Peru were sons of heaven or children of the sun, responsible in their exalted position to uphold the balance of the universe. They stood before their awed subjects in the splendor and terror of their godhood, but they also showered upon their subjects the benefits of peace and of a well-ordered social life, which was but an aspect of the well-ordered universe.

Painted murals and pottery of the Theocratic period show priests but seldom warriors. The leading figure of the society dominated by the ceremonial center is the full-time servant of the gods on whose mediation between supernatural and human beings the welfare of man depends. He is the steward of his gods on earth, their representative on earth. While he lives, he wears their symbols; when he is buried, these symbols are buried with him. In the name of the gods, he marshals labor to erect the gigantic pyramids, and in the name of the gods he exacts obedience from the men whom he controls.

Compared to the later Militarist period (A.D. 750–1519), there seems to have been little warfare, though it was not entirely absent. The only evidence of military power from Teotihuacán is a mural representing a warrior. He carries a spear, but the spear is decorated with plumes; his arrows are sheathed in protective balls. The glyphs of Monte Albán probably refer to towns defeated and conquered some time around the beginning of the Christian Era. Representations of men armed with clubs are fairly common in Olmec art. I am also inclined to think that the

Warrior, bearing arrows tipped with cotton balls. Mural painting, Teopancaxco, Teotihuacán, Mexico. (From Walter Krickeberg, Altmexikanische Kulturen *[Berlin: Safari Verlag, 1956].)*

representations of heads hanging from the belts of Maya figures on stelae are not innocent decorative items but human trophy heads. Bound prisoners appear on Maya stelae, and human sacrifice seems to have been quite general, though the victims were mostly children and not adults, as in later times. The spear point found in the grave of a priest of Teotihuacán, moreover, may serve to remind us that coercion need not be directed only against foreign enemies; it can also be practiced against one's own people. Still, the Theocratic period seems to have differed from the later Militaristic both in the amount and in the kind of warfare practiced. The power of the priesthood was probably primarily ideologi-

80

cal, though the spear, the club, and the arrow may never have been entirely absent from the scene.

The new specialists also possessed economic functions. Some of these functions were allied to their religious activities. Malinowski has shown us how the performance of magical rites can aid in the organization and timing of economic activities. The new priesthoods controlled the religious calendar which told people when to clear new land for planting, when to plant, when to weed, and when to harvest. Religious ceremonies were held to further the tasks of cultivation. The earliest representation of such a ceremony that has come down to us is probably the curious relief from a stone quarry in Jonacatepec, Morelos. The relief depicts three priests in Olmec style regalia; they hold spades in the air, while a fourth showers the land with his own seed from his erect penis. The priests of Tlaloc at Teotihuacán cast seed and water from their open hands; a personage wearing jaguar headgear is shown, in a Maya codex, planting corn with a planting stick. If irrigation was in use in Theocratic times, we may assume that the priesthood played a major role in its organization and in the distribution of the surpluses it produced. Where slash-and-burn cultivation was practiced, the priesthood probably played a part in allocating land to farmers and in regulating circulation upon the land, so that fertility could be maintained at high levels. Finally, it is possible that the temples served as deposits for seed from which the next year's crop was raised.

The priests did not, however, serve only as administrators and organizers of agricultural effort. As servitors of their gods they also administered the many goods made as offerings to the deities. The temple centers became veritable storehouses of the gods, where costly produce accumulated in the service of the supernatural. Thus at Teotihuacán, we find shells imported from the two coasts, precious stones from Guerrero, rubber balls from the southern Gulf, mica from Oaxaca, feathers from the southern lands of the quetzal bird, and cotton from Morelos or from Veracruz. At Uaxactún, finds of obsidian, flint, grinding platforms and

81

mullers of granite and lava, jade, marble vases, shells from both oceans, and quetzal feathers bespeak continuous trade in the service of the gods. We find Maya Tzakol pottery, polychrome with geometric designs, at Teotihuacán; the fine Teotihuacán cylindrical tripod vessels, with the conical tops, everywhere. Thin orange ware, a specially fine trade ware, probably from southern Puebla, has been found as far north as Colima and as far south as Copán.

It is likely that the trade expeditions which traveled from one center to another were sponsored by the priests or were protected by them. Acosta Saignés has made the interesting suggestion that the professional traders of later Militarist Mesoamerica, the Pochteca, represent an old kinship group, with strong ties to the coastal regions of the Gulf. It may be that such intermediaries were the carriers of this trade in luxury goods from center to center. At the same time, there undoubtedly existed another kind of market, a popular market, in the shadow of the temples in which the peasantry around the ceremonial center brought their goods to the center of the gods either regularly, on a weekly basis, or more irregularly, in the course of pilgrimages. Permanent markets appear to have

Priest sprinkling water from a staff. Mural painting, Atetelco, Teotihuacán, Mexico. (From Pedro Armillas, "Teotihuacán, Tula y los Toltecas," Runa, III (1950), Plate XIIIa. By permission of Runa, Buenos Aires.)

existed at Teotihuacán; in the Maya centers people probably came to weekly markets in the great squares. Still today, the Indian markets of Middle America are intimately linked with the centers of worship. The Indian comes to town to sell his goods; but he comes also to seek supernatural favors in the gold-incrusted dwelling place of his saints.

But the priests not only stored goods and sponsored trade. Like the ecclesiastical lords of medieval Europe, they probably employed craftsmen on their own behalf who produced on order to satisfy the requirements of cult and priestly display. One such group was perhaps the Amanteca, the kinship group of feather-workers, who later worked for the Mexica of Tenochtitlán. Their traditional association with Atzcapotzalco, where people from Teotihuacán sought refuge when that city was undergoing its final period of decline, makes it more than likely that they represent bearers of the older Teotihuacán tradition.

The center of this new order was always the temple precinct. In Middle America, as in other parts of the world, the temple precinct and its monuments were conceived as magically one with the supernatural world. Each precinct was oriented to the axes of the universe: north to south, as at La Venta and Monte Albán; or 17 degrees south of east, as at Teotihuacán, where the axis was in line with the point where the sun sets on the day of transit through its zenith, a day which also marked the beginning of the rainy season; or in relation to the solstices and the equinoxes, as at Uaxactún. The tiers of the temple pyramids were equated symbolically with the tiers of the universe, the pyramid itself with the mountain of the sky which the sun had to climb and descend to complete its daily circuit. Or a temple was but a magical replica of a world navel, as the great temple of Tenochtitlán, which was identified with the mythical Mountain of the Snakes where Hummingbird-on-the-Left leapt from the womb of his monster mother to slay the moon and the stars.

Within their replicas of the universal order, the priesthood labored in the daily rebuilding of order and consistency in the universe. In simple groups that must rely on hunting and gathering for their food supply and that lack permanent priesthoods, there are always individuals whose conceptual cast of mind leads them to grapple intellectually with the consistencies and inconsistencies of the world around them. The process remains individual and non-cumulative, however, until there develops a body of specialists who see this intellectual labor as their duty and are rewarded by society for their efforts on its behalf. In Middle America, this effort at systematization, at making the universe routine and predictable, is evident in the abandonment of the traditional cult of the figurines or in its conventionalization; in the growing definition of a series of gods with specialized dominions; and in the development of priestly writing and of a calendar.

Figurines suddenly disappear in southern Mesoamerica over a wide area—in the Guatemalan highlands, in the Petén, in British Honduras. Elsewhere, to the north, figurines are sharply conventionalized and standardized by means of molds. The common folk are thus robbed of their ability to portray their deities or supernatural principles on their own. In contrast, the art of the tombs and temples acquires great rigor, severity, and austerity, in contrast to the more exuberant art of the folk.

Instead of the protean range of figures, a pantheon of gods emerges. The chief of these is He Who Makes the Plants Spring Up (Tlaloc), the god of rain and fertility. The Nahuatl-speakers called him Tlaloc; the Otomí, Muye; the Zapotec, Cocijo; the Mixtec, Dzaui; the Totonac, Tajín; the Maya of Yucatán, Chac; the Quiché of highland Guatemala, Tohil. In murals found at Teotihuacán he is depicted rising from the sea, with blessed rain dripping from his hands. His face is masked; the quetzal bird—symbol of rulership—spreads its wings above his head. Priests and servants stand on his left and right, sing his praises and pour out jewels and streams of seed. Men and butterflies disport themselves

---

Feathered serpents, Tlaloc masks and symbolic snails and sea shells decorate the wall of a structure later completely covered by another. The "Citadel," Teotihuacán, Mexico. (Courtesy of Pan American Sanitary Bureau.)

among the corn and flowers which grow along the shores of his watery paradise. Tlaloc's image appears as far south as Copán, in certain standardized associations with art forms symbolizing his several aspects. As jaguar, he represents the lord of the land who has claim to the earth, and its political and religious domination. As serpent, his undulating feathers represent the growing vegetation. The owl symbolizes his association with rainfall. In the esoteric sophisticated hieratic style which developed, these symbols could be combined as jaguar-serpents or serpent-butterflies to express in symbolic shorthand certain attributes of the deity.

Other gods, less important than Tlaloc, include a god of fire hunched under a bowl, a legacy of earlier times; a fat god who seems to have come from the Gulf coast and in later periods disappeared without a trace; a bat god, especially notable in the south among the Zapotec; and a masked personage who may be an ancestral form of Our Lord the Flayed One, in whose honor men were later—in the Militaristic period— sacrificed by flaying. If this interpretation is correct, human sacrifice probably existed at Teotihuacán. Self-torture in penance or in honor of the gods is also indicated by little incense burners shaped like candlestick holders, in which probably burned a mixture of copal gum and blood.

One of the great priestly accomplishments was the Mesoamerican calendar. All religions are interested in binding time. They gear the life-cycle of the individual to the recurrent rituals of society, and they synchronize this social time with the march of cosmic time. As the individual merges his life-span with that of society, he gains the security of knowing that his life will be lived in a rhythm which was there before he was born and will be there when he is gone. But even societies contemplate the infinite silence of cosmic space with fear and uncertainty. Calendar systems serve to bind this cosmic time, to domesticate it, as religion domesticates other aspects of the universe, and men derive comfort in visualizing the passage of cosmic time reduced to the mere se-

The realm of Tlaloc (Tlalocan). Mural painting, Tepantitla, Teotihuacán, Mexico. Above, Tlaloc rises from stylized waves, heavy with marine animals, to drip water upon the world from two outstretched hands. His face is covered with a bird mask, his head decorated with quetzal feathers. Below, the dead chase butterflies and play in the waters tumbling from the Sacred Mountain of the Dead. Flowers issuing from their mouths denote speech or song. (From Gisèle Freund, Mexique Précolombien *[Neuchâtel and Paris: Éditions Ides et Calendes, 1954].)*

quence of cycles of social time. Different societies have possessed different cultural views of time. Some have pictured an original golden age desecrated by a single act, followed by a time of sin and guilt, which will end only when celestial trumpets announce a final judgment. Other societies have seen new cycles of time ever widening out in a continuous expansion of time. Middle American civilization was possessed by its own vision of time, in which the universe is not one but many, and in which each world, each universe, has its own allotted span of time that must inevitably end in catastrophe. When one universe collapses in flood or fire, another universe is born, though it too must come to a violent end.

The Middle American calendar system is the expression of this view of time. We do not know how it originated. The basic pattern may have been provided by a farmer's calendar, invented to measure agricultural time or the lapse of time between depletion and renewed fertility of land. Such a basic pattern may have been complicated by a magical concern associating numbers like two with a concept of cosmic duality; or four with the directions or with worlds created in the past; or five with evil caused by lack of measure and restraint. Such magical numerology may have been at the root of an original lunar count. Whatever the origins of the Middle American calendric system, it measures both recurrent social time and recurrent individual fate. It sets the time for celebrations and spiritual crises; it also allows the religious specialist to divine the future of men by interpreting the signs of days and their associated numbers.

The basic count (Nahuatl, *tonalpohualli*; Maya, *tzolkin*) combines 13 numbers and 20 signs like crocodile, wind, house, lizard, or snake into a count of 260 days. This calendar was clearly known to the priests of Teotihuacán and Monte Albán. Among the Nahuatl-speakers, Mixtec, Otomí, Huastec, Totonac, and Maya, this count was geared into a second count, a solar year of 365 days, composed of 18 months of 20 days each, plus 5 evil days at the year's end. The same combination of day number and day sign occurred in both counts every 52 years. Such a recurrent event the Mexica of the fourteenth and fifteenth centuries called *xiuhmolpilli,* a year knot or bundle. They felt that every 52 years the universe reached a cosmic crisis which threatened its survival, and men waited with bated breath to see the sun rise again in the continuation of a new cycle that might yet guarantee life to mankind for another 52 years.

In the southern part of the valley of Puebla (Tehuacán, Teotitlán del Camino) and in the Maya area, the priests carried the counts still further into a Venus year of 584 days. According to this count, the *tonalpohualli,* the solar year and the Venus year coincided at the end of every two 52-year cycles in another period of great supernatural crisis.

The lowland Maya appear to have taken these calendric calculations further than anyone else in Middle America. Only they seem to have developed a fixed starting point for their system, set at 3133 B.C. The date is clearly imaginary; the calendar itself probably originated around 500 B.C. Time was reckoned in ascending units (20 *kins* or days = 1 *uinal;* 18 *uinals* = 1 *tun;* 20 *tuns* = 1 *katun;* 20 *katuns* = 1 *baktun*). This reckoning was basic to the so-called Long Count practiced during most of the Theocratic period. Toward the end of the period, dates were abbreviated in a short count, which fixed the date accurately within a given lapse of time but which leaves us today wondering where the lapse of time belongs in relation to past or future lapses of time, just as a date written today as '58 could refer to 1958, 1858, or 1058.

Hand in hand with calendric calculations went the development of writing. Bars and dots for numerals were used by the Olmec, the inhabitants of Monte Albán, and the Maya-speakers of the Petén. The Teotihuacanos, Monte Albán, and the Theocratic Maya also made use of pictorial symbols to designate days and months. The oldest glyphs dealing with some sort of information which is not purely calendric appear on the Olmec Tuxtla statuette which bears a date of A.D. 162. The oldest phonetic elements in Middle American script seem to come from Monte Albán (Monte Albán II) where names of places were represented by additions of symbolic representations bearing phonetic value, in a manner later used by the Colhua Mexica. While we can read the calendric information on the Theocratic monuments, we are still largely unable to interpret the accompanying glyphs. Glyphs which may represent dates, and therefore the names of individual persons who were named after the day on which they were born, like "1 Reed," or "2 Rabbit," also appear on a number of objects associated with the Theocratic period. It is not impossible that such objects represent the first signs of clear-cut private property in luxury objects.

The priestly rulers also gave expression to their new power and the power of their gods in art. This art is often called "Classic." The term "Classic" is a stylistic term; it indicates that during this period there was not only a florescence of society but also a florescence in the forms of expression employed by this society. It is ultimately a term that refers to a culmination, a fruition of art forms; and indeed the Mesoamerican Theocratic period is such a period of culmination and fruition. Yet artistic style is inherently difficult to express in words, just as it is very difficult to evaluate. It is all too easy to let oneself be guided by Occidental notions of fulfilment in art, and to associate Classic florescence with sobriety and purity of line, while ascribing decadence to a love for riotous expression. Mesoamerican priestly art possessed at least two great artistic styles which we could call the Mexican and the Maya. The Mexican style came to fruition primarily in the central and southern highland; the Maya style dominated the rain-forest cities of the Petén. The Mexican style is geometric, monumental. The Maya style, on the other hand, loves riotous movements, luxuriant form, flamboyance. Both styles are equally Classic. Yet their difference denotes in all probability a wide divergence in basic values and feeling-tones.

The great contrast between these two styles is most apparent in public architecture. The Theocratic Mexican pyramids of Cuicuilco, Teotihuacán, Monte Albán, and Cholula emphasize horizontal lines. They are man-made mountains of superimposed tiers, rising slowly and ponderously toward the ceremonial hut at the summit, gigantic platforms for a celebration of the contact between man and the supernatural. The Theo-

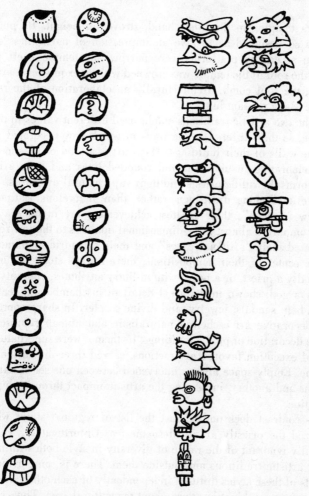

*Day glyphs of the Maya (left) and Mexica (right) illustrate a tradition
of counting time and writing which had its beginning in Theocratic times.*

cratic Maya temple, on the other hand, strove for height. Its public façade was so designed as to give an impression of narrowness and height. The ascending platforms were narrow, the temple itself was small, and the roof of the temple was crowned with an exquisitely carved false front, the roof comb, architecturally an elaboration of the roof-crest on the Maya peasant hut.

Just as the two artistic traditions emphasized different values in their architecture, so they differed in the ways in which they decorated and adorned the walls of their buildings. Maya art is a kind of plastic calligraphy celebrating in undulant and rounded lines and a luxurious wealth of forms the ruling priests and their supernatural overlords. The Maya were marvelous draftsmen rather than marvelous sculptors. They "drew in stone"; their greatest achievement lay in the way in which they imparted almost three-dimensional qualities to the low relief that decorated their "artificial caves" and their calendric monuments. And at the center of their compositions, there always stood a human figure, usually a priest, or a priest with military attributes, and only exceptionally a god, shown in the great detail of his flamboyant feather headdress, belt, sandals, jewelry, and divine scepter. In sharp contrast, Mexican decorative art eschewed naturalistic and human representations in the decoration of public buildings. Its themes were supernatural; its mode of execution favored abstractions, carved three-dimensionally out of stone. Empty space always intervened between one set of carved abstractions and another, increasing the artistic impact through rhythm and repetition.

But this contrast does not exhaust the list of regional styles which characterized the priestly art in Mesoamerica. Unfortunately, we are still woefully ignorant of the range of diversity in style both within the two major artistic traditions and outside them. There is some evidence that aspects of these styles diffused independently of each other and are found in various combinations throughout the cultural area. Thus, some of the decoration of the temples at Monte Albán are Mayoid, as is the

92

manner of decoration on the late Theocratic–early Militarist pyramid at Xochicalco. Tajín, in the lowlands of Veracruz, bears the imprint both of the Maya and of the Mexican art styles. It may simply be that we do not as yet have a full range of artistic representations from all parts of Middle America. Yet the contrast between highland and Petén is so notable that it seems to correspond to an actual difference in style of life between these two areas.

It is also important to realize that the contrast embraces primarily public art and cannot be extended so easily to art forms which were not for public consumption. The murals of Teotihuacán are as free-flowing, realistic, and human in scale as the outside of the Teotihuacán temples are hieratic, abstract, and supernaturally oriented. Zapotec funeral urns, while depicting deities with their manifold attributes, are lively and man-oriented, while the complex of the tombs and temples of Monte Albán are impressive, impersonal, and austere.

The biggest and most influential center of Theocratic times appears to have been Teotihuacán, situated in a rather dry valley 25 miles northeast of Mexico City. Teotihuacán means "house of the gods." This designation can be interpreted in two ways. It may simply refer to a place of worship; or it may signify the place where the lords of the people woke from the dream of life and became gods. Sahagún, the Franciscan friar to whom we owe such a great deal of our knowledge of pre-Hispanic Middle America, tells an ancient tale according to which, "From Tamoanchan they travelled to offer sacrifices at the town called Teutihoacan, where they built two mountains in honor of the sun and the moon, and in this town those who were to reign over the others were elected, for which it was called Teutiocan, which means Veitoacan, or the place where they made signs. There the most important lords were buried."

The city may well have been the largest settlement in Middle America. It grew from a size of 700 acres before A.D. 350 to 2,000 acres in another three centuries. On aerial photographs, the densely settled area within the city limits shows up clearly in contrast with the open fields of the surrounding countryside. The oldest dated remains at the site are assigned to the time of Christ, though the Pyramid of the Moon—the second largest pyramid of the site, measuring 495 by 405 feet at the base and 140 feet in height—is probably older. The big temples were built or rebuilt several times between the time of Christ and A.D. 250. Teotihuacán was finally destroyed and abandoned around A.D. 800. The fury of destruction is recorded for posterity in a thick gray layer of ash which shows that the city was put to the torch.

The settlement pattern is laid out along a main axis, 60 yards wide, formed by the Avenue of the Dead. It takes its origin at the Pyramid of the Moon, runs past the Pyramid of the Sun and the temple precinct of the Feathered Serpent; most of the civic and religious buildings are located along it, as are the wealthy residential buildings. Small streets lead off the avenue into the popular quarters of the city where people lived in crowded quarters separated by small courtyards and alleyways. Each quarter seems to have had its own religious center, suggesting that the pattern of main center, satellite centers, and dependent communities is very ancient in Middle America. Large open squares west and north of the big pyramids were probably markets. The main avenue and its buildings were drained through an underground drainage system which carried rain water and waste off to a nearby river.

The big pyramids themselves represent mute testimonies of a social system which harnessed the labor of its members for gigantic religious constructions. The Pyramid of the Sun, 689 feet by 689 feet at the base and 210 feet high, contains about 1,300,000 cubic yards of earth. Its construction must have absorbed the labor of 10,000 people for 20 years.

Across the divide in the valley of Puebla rises another man-made mountain, the pyramid of Cholula. Its beginnings predate the Theocratic period; its core is a pyramid 55.5–58.8 feet high and covering 9.88 acres. The walls of this early structure were painted red, black, and yellow with representations of mythological insects. Four reconstructions and superimpositions by people closely related to the inhabitants of

94

The Pyramid of the Sun at Teotihuacán, Mexico. A small, perishable structure with a high straw roof once crowned the summit. (Courtesy of Compañía Mexicana Aerofoto, S.A.)

Teotihuacán brought the pyramid to its present size: 181 feet high and nearly 40 acres in extent, it is larger than the pyramid by which Cheops assured his immortality. The surfaces of the final structure were painted with dark rectangles. According to a tradition collected by the Spaniards the temple was dedicated to the worship of the god "9 Rain," probably a local incarnation of the Teotihuacán Tlaloc.

Who built Teotihuacán and Cholula? The builders probably did not belong to a single linguistic group. On the contrary, we may suppose that such large centers dominated an area inhabited by a number of different cultural and linguistic groups. Various sources identify the builders of Teotihuacán and Cholula with a group called Olmeca-Xicalanca. The Indian historian Chimalpain calls these Olmeca-Xicalanca *quiahuiztecos*, or "people of the rain," the Nahuatl cognate for the name by which the Mixtec call themselves—Ñusabi. It is increasingly likely that these Olmeca-Xicalanca were a Chocho-Popoloca or Mixtec-speaking group.

Beyond Cholula, Teotihuacán influence is associated with two other major centers. One of these, Kaminaljuyú, lies in the southeastern highlands, on the southwestern outskirts of Guatemala City. The other, Tajín, rises from the tropical rain forest, near the town of Papantla, in northern Veracruz. Kaminaljuyú has a history going back to the beginnings of seed-planting. By 500 B.C. it had achieved a peak of prosperity and population, a commercial influence, which it was never to experience again. Around A.D. 400 it was invaded and occupied by a group of people who brought with them Teotihuacán patterns of such faithfulness and completeness that we can easily assume they came from the main metropolis itself. The newcomers built a strongly nucleated ceremonial center and ball courts in an acropolis arrangement reminiscent of the Maya lowlands and took over control of trade relations within the region. Toward the end of their occupation, however, they seem to have severed connections with their mother city, and around A.D. 900 they abandoned the site in the face of military pressures which they could not withstand.

The center at Tajín seems to have been constructed some time around A.D. 600. Its core is formed by a pyramid, 82 feet high and 115 feet at the base; it differs from all other known Mesoamerican structures in that its surface is honeycombed with niches. These may be purely ornamental, or may represent symbolically the caves that harbor the "heart of the land." The surrounding site has been excavated only partially; much of it still lies under the tough tropical forest cover. Its strong Teotihuacán affiliations make it likely that Tajín was a colony of Teotihuacán satellites in the tropical lowlands. It was abandoned in A.D. 1200, in the wake of the disturbances which followed on the destruction of the Theocratic world. Yet the local population continued to live in its vicinity, undisturbed by the fate of the political and religious nucleus. Surface sherds of all periods litter the surrounding countryside.

Teotihuacán influence, as measured by kinds of pottery and styles of mural decoration, also reached the great ceremonial center of Monte Albán in the valley of Oaxaca, where city-builders had carved a man-

96

made platform, 3,117 feet long and 1,476 feet wide, out of the living rock, because they were not content to use the natural contour of the mountain. Here, 1,300 feet above the surrounding valley floor, they built great courtyards, surrounded by stairways and pyramids, tombs and courts, a great ceremonial complex perfectly oriented in space along a north-south axis. Westheim says that this architectural attempt "is basically and from its very beginning a departure from nature. The men who built it not only did not respect the lay of the land; they rejected it, they saw it as a part of chaos on which man must impose order." The function of this great ceremonial center remains a mystery. The large number of tombs suggests that the headmen of many communities lie entombed there. No source of water has been found to allow us to imagine how the inhabitants of the mountain assuaged their thirst. Perhaps they were the masters of a social system so tightly organized that they could rely on systematic deliveries of food and water from the three surrounding valleys.

This social system probably also retained some autonomy in the face of Teotihuacán influence. Teotihuacán influence is stylistic, not basic. The men depicted in the paintings, the day signs associated with their names, are not those of Teotihuacán. And in the elaboration of its burial urns, many of them realistic portraits of the persons laid to rest, Theocratic Monte Albán also achieves a style of its own, independent of contact with centers beyond. It would seem that Teotihuacán influence was directed mainly toward the east and southeast, leaving Monte Albán and its satellite centers off to one side. Perhaps Monte Albán lay off the main trade routes and routes of expansion and did not have to be brought under the domination of Tlaloc.

Contemporary with these highland and lowland Mexican sites are the Theocratic Maya sites of the tropical forest. The area in which Maya culture found its initial characterization is the north-central Petén, in which dense forest alternates with open savannas. The two main sites in this area are Tikal, probably the largest site in the Petén, and Uaxactún, perhaps the oldest. Tikal, "where the voices of the departed are heard," is situated in limestone country, 700 feet above sea level, on the shores of a lake now converted into a swamp. Its central precinct covers about a square mile; its core is formed by six great pyramids, the highest in the Maya area. Beyond the central precinct, suburbs extend for 2 to 3 miles in all directions. Its total population in A.D. 600 has been estimated at 100,000. Uaxactún, a few miles north of Tikal, is the site of the oldest Maya temple, the oldest dated monument in the Maya area, and the first site on which the appearance of the corbeled vault has been noted. The temple, called E-VII-sub, rescued from the depths of temple E-VII, which had covered it, was 27 feet high, faced with stucco, and provided with a ceremonial stairway flanked by huge masks representing the jaguar god. Four postholes on top mark the former location of a small sanctuary made of perishable materials. Stela 9, the oldest carved monolith in the Maya area, bears a date which corresponds to A.D. 328; the corbeled vaults are dated A.D. 278. The ceremonial district here was surrounded by settlement clusters. A survey carried out in 1937 revealed seventy-eight house mounds within a third of a mile around the ceremonial center. In both of these towns, the outlying settlements were connected to the ceremonial precinct by broad roads. Recent aerial photographs made in the course of explorations for oil have further revealed a great road in the northern part of the Petén area.

The cities of the central Petén seem to bear relationship to the settlements recently excavated in British Honduras. There settlements follow the course of the Belize River; house mounds cluster along the alluvial terraces in groups as small as five or six or as large as three hundred. Each of the clusters of a dozen or more houses maintained a small ceremonial center, while larger centers, such as Baking Pot or Benque Viejo, probably linked several settlement clusters.

Traveling westward across savannas and jungles, we encounter the cities of the Usumacinta River. Yaxchilán, together with its dependency of Bonampak, lies closest to the Petén. Piedras Negras occupies an inter-

Model of Temple IV at Tikal, Guatemala. Note the narrow base, the high silhouette, the small ceremonial chamber, the elaborate roof comb. (Courtesy of American Museum of Natural History.)

mediate position, while Palenque is the northwesternmost of the Usumacinta towns. In these cities, Maya sculpture and stucco-work reached its zenith. At the same time, they show traits which are non-Maya, which recall rather the highlands of Mexico. Piedras Negras is especially aberrant, in its reluctance to make use of the corbeled vault at the beginning of the Maya Classic; in its representation of human sacrifice, absent elsewhere in the Classic Maya area. And at Bonampak, Giles Healey encountered murals of enormous fluid power, depicting a raid and the ceremonial disposal of prisoners long before these customs were in general vogue in other parts of the Maya area.

Such highland ties we find also at Copán, the second largest Maya city in western Honduras. It lies in a fertile and well-watered valley, 1,800 feet above sea level, on the banks of the Copán River. Its acropolis, built under the direction of a group of Maya priests and their followers who immigrated sometime near the beginning of the ninth cycle of Maya calendar series, covers 12 acres. The large amount of utilitarian ware scattered in and about this area suggests that the residences of the common people lay in the shadow of the central ceremonial precinct. During its development, Copán was the scientific center of the Maya world. The astronomers of Copán worked out the length of the tropical year, first used or developed the eclipse tables, and worked out a calendar correction formula more accurate than our Gregorian leap year, all toward the end of the seventh century A.D. Two altars commemorate the meetings of this Copán Academy of Sciences: they show the assembled scientists facing toward a central date. Thompson suggests that the scientists came from all parts of the Maya domain. A figure wearing the ceremonial headdress of a bat may have come from the Chiapas mountains to represent the Bat People (Tzotzil) at this scientific meeting. Certainly, shortly after the calendar reform at Copán, other centers accepted the innovation with an alacrity not commonly exhibited by rival bodies of professionals. But then this period around 700 may have witnessed not only the unification of the calendar but also some form of political unification.

At the same time, new art forms, symbols of rulership, spread from the periphery of the Maya area across the entire Maya land; among these are the formal plumed headdress, the fringed sandal, the cuff-like wristlet, beaded plumes, and the manikin scepter. At Copán we find many representations of the Mexican Tlaloc. Are we dealing with a movement of political consolidation that had its origins outside the Maya area, even though it made use of traditional Maya forms? But near the

100

end of the Classic period, Copán is abandoned suddenly. One day the town bustles with activity; the next day priests and commoners alike pack up and leave, and abandon their temples and houses to the jungle and to the jaguar.

Usually not included among major Maya centers, because they lagged behind the others in the refinement of their art, are Calakmul, Cobá, and Dzibilchaltún. Calakmul, in southern Campeche, possesses with its 103 stelae more time markers than any other Maya site, though it lacks other monuments of artistic merit. Cobá has the earliest Long Count date in northeastern Yucatán; its beginnings date back to A.D. 623. It lies amidst five small lakes, the largest of which is a mile long. Sixteen known causeways, each 15 feet wide, connected the town itself with outlying centers. The longest, over 60 miles long, linked Cobá with Yaxuna, not far from Chichén Itzá. Like other Theocratic Maya centers, both these towns are located in the tropical rain forest. Dzibilchaltún, however, near modern Mérida, lies in the dry bush country so characteristic of northwestern Yucatán. Only now under excavation, it may well turn out to be the largest of all known Maya centers. Its size has been estimated at 20 square miles, 10 square miles of which was densely packed with temples and house platforms. Moreover, it was inhabited continuously from 1500 B.C. to the time of the Spanish Conquest. The continued study of its remains may well throw an entirely new light on the Theocratic period in the whole Maya-speaking area.

VI

*Coming
of the
Warriors*

When a painter depicted jaguars and coyotes on the walls of a building complex called Atetelco, on the southwestern outskirts of Teotihuacán, a feeling of impending crisis and doom must already have been in the air. For the theme of the murals no longer fits the pattern of Teotihuacán art. The appearance of predatory beasts within the confines of Teotihuacán marks the coming of a new style of life, borne by new peoples who— until then restricted to the borders of civilization—stand suddenly within its precinct. We find the same procession of wild beasts at Tula, the city of the new warrior orders who inherited the legacy of Teotihuacán by the sword.

Shortly after the murals of Atetelco were painted, around A.D. 800, Teotihuacán burned down: the black layer of charcoal and burned brick is clearly visible in the stratigraphy of the city. Was the city attacked from outside and burned by conquerors from the north? Or did it fall prey to an internal conflict, which divided rulers from rulers and rulers from the ruled? Refugees from Teotihuacán continued an epigonal Teotihuacán settlement at Atzcapotzalco across the lake; but the great

102

Jaguar (above) and coyote (below) from a mural painting at Atetelco, Teotihuacán, Mexico. The appearance of these predatory animals in Teotihuacán art presage the irruption of Militarist groups into Middle America. (From Pedro Armillas, "Teotihuacán, Tula y los Toltecas," Runa, III [1950], Plate XV a and b. By permission of Runa, Buenos Aires.)

metropolis was abandoned to the winds of time. Soon after, a group of newcomers buried their dead in its ruins. As goods to accompany the bodies on their last road, they left vessels of a new kind of pottery, called Mazápan, typically associated with the people of Tula, soon to rise to prominence in the frontier area of Hidalgo.

At the same time, the priests at Monte Albán abandoned their ceremonial precincts and their tombs, and departed. A similar phenomenon took place in the Petén. In 790 nineteen cities erected calendric markers to commemorate the beginning of a new cycle of time; by 889, only three marked the following cycle in the same fashion. A jade gorget from southern Quintana Roo bears the last known date of the Maya Long Count. The date is 909. In some towns, as at Copán, "the priests appear simply to have packed up and left," says Longyear. Elsewhere, as at Piedras Negras, broken thrones suggest that there was violence. Everywhere, however, the centers are deserted and the temples decay. Silence descends on the jungle. When the first Spaniards reached Tikal and Yaxchilán in 1696, the two towns had been dead for 700 years.

The years between 750 and 900 thus shook the old world order to its foundations. New peoples appear on the scene, bearing with them new ways of ordering society and new visions of their place in the universe. The difference between the old order and the new order is profound. What were the causes of this shift in ways of life?

Causation is probably never simple, and we can do away with some simple explanations without difficulty. A rash of earthquakes or a spread of malaria have been suggested as possible explanations, but there is neither geological evidence of earthquakes violent enough to account for a similar change all over Middle America nor medical evidence of malaria in the New World before 1492. More deserving are hypotheses which explain the fall of the Theocratic order as the result of an increasingly unfavorable ecological balance. Thus Cook explains the fall of Teotihuacán as due to a rising population pressing more and more heavily on the soils which supplied its food; resultant erosion served

104

to remove valuable soils from continued production. At such a time, the construction program of the metropolis would have wiped out all economic reserves, leading to internal dissension as well as inability to withstand assaults from the outside. A parallel argument applies to the abandonment of the Maya towns. The slash-and-burn cultivation of the Maya resulted not only in a destruction of the forest but in a spread of grassland into the burned clearings which the Maya with their stone tools could not prevent. As usable land declined, therefore, the agricultural base of Maya civilization became too weak to support the weight of the parasitic ceremonial centers.

These arguments are weighty, though it may be doubted whether such factors operated alone or even in the manner postulated. As we have seen, it is rather doubtful whether both Teotihuacanos and Maya relied wholly on extensive cultivation. If they also possessed some sort of intensive cultivation, the arguments adduced involve only the extensive component of Theocratic ecology, not its intensive component. Furthermore, the deficiencies of slash-and-burn cultivation may permit us to understand the general ecological limitations of Theocratic civilization; this does not mean that they were operative in every particular instance. They do not explain, for instance, why Teotihuacán settlement remained stable throughout the whole period and did not shift with decreasing use of the soil, or why Copán was suddenly abandoned, even though it is located in a valley so fertile that soil exhaustion seems nearly impossible, or why savannas are common in the Petén but ruins are not usually located near them. The ecological explanations set the stage for further explanations, but they do not suffice: we must also take account of a shift in the internal structure of Theocratic society.

First of all we must realize that the collapse of the old temple centers was not complete. Cholula in the valley of Puebla and Cobá and Dzibalchultún in Yucatán were never destroyed. Cholula experienced a change of masters, but achieved renown in the Militarist period. Indeed, it probably benefited directly from the destruction of Teotihuacán; perhaps it had a hand in it. With its rival gone, Cholula greatly expanded its influence over eastern and southern Mexico, though it never challenged the direct heirs of Teotihuacán in the valley of Mexico and in the frontier march of Hidalgo.

Each age bears its own mark, and yet each age is also merely a bridge between what is past and what is still to be. The Theocratic societies of Middle America are strongly characterized, and yet they were but transitions between the simpler village societies that preceded them and the Militarist societies that replaced them. Every society is a battlefield between its own past and its future; it was such a conflict that opened fissures in the Theocratic edifice.

The basic source of power of the priesthood that ruled the holy towns was apparently power over men's minds and power over goods gained in the service of the gods. But there is an inherent limitation to purely ideological power, and this limitation must have been apparent from the first. One case of conflict, based on divergent interests, can shatter the uniform adherence to a godhead, and then the priests must not only advise and reprimand but also judge, condemn, and carry out their sentence. But one such conflict may breed others, and the economy of naked power is persuasive: it quickly breeds more naked power. The Theocratic society had brought together holy town and hinterland, priest, trader, artisan, and peasant, men who spoke different languages, stranger and citizen. In unifying, it had also sown the inevitable seeds of internal dissension and the possibility of revolt, and with these dissensions it created—again inevitably—the need for that form of warfare between rulers and ruled which we call the state. Finally, the flames of revolt and the violence of repression left the old gods impotent and brought to power the gods of war and human sacrifice. This process may be reflected in the destruction of the great dais at Piedras Negras, deliberately smashed. It may be reflected in the shattered stelae of Tikal, later reerected by pious hands. It may be reflected also in the reconstruction of the so-called Citadel at Teotihuacán, where the sculptured representa-

Quetzalcoatl, the Shining Serpent, salient deity of the Militarist period.
Note jaguar skin hat and stylized alligator mouth, worn by him in his guise
as Ehecatl, God of the Winds. (From the pre-Hispanic Codex Borbonicus.)

tions of the Feathered Earth Serpent on the central temple were covered over with a mundane, utilitarian facing which removed the older religious symbols from public view.

The web of Theocratic society contained another fatal flaw: a built-in imbalance between holy town and hinterland, between city and provinces. Ultimately, the towns grew wealthy and splendid, because the countryside labored and produced. Not that some of the wealth of the centers did not flow back into the rural area. Some benefits must be returned to the ruled in any complex society; the jade objects found by Gordon R. Willey and his co-workers in the grave of a Maya peasant in the Belize Valley in British Honduras clearly show that this held true also in Middle America. Undoubtedly the Theocratic society forged its own chain of command with the final links in the villages and hamlets; some men in the countryside must have acted as messengers of the gods and received rewards commensurate with the utility of their services. The growing gap between center and hinterland was not based on an absolute enrichment of the center while the countryside remained absolutely impoverished. Both grew in their involvement with each other; but the centers grew more quickly, more opulently, and—more obviously.

Such disparity in growth may produce more conflicts than the absolute exploitation of one community by another. For a measure of prosperity which is yet confronted with the image of an ever more opulent prosperity in its midst breeds not only envy but also the desire to lay hands on the surplus for one's own purposes. Revolt occurs not when men's faces are ground into the dust; rather, it explodes during a period of rising hope, at the point of sudden realization that only the traditional controls of the social order stand between men and the achievement of still greater hopes. In complex societies, this confrontation of hope with the denial of hope pits rulers against ruled, rich against poor, and hinterland and periphery against core area and center. The periphery suffers by comparison while the center grows bloated with wealth and power. Yet it is also at the periphery that the controls of government and

108

religion tend to be at their weakest; it is here that the forces of dissatis-faction can easily gain both strength and organization. Here the pull of the center and its ability to compel people to its will are at a minimum. Theocratic society witnessed this rebellion of the periphery against the center. The fissures opened up in three major regions: along the western margin of the Petén; along the southern border of the central highland; and in the northern marches that held the frontier against the hunters and gatherers beyond.

The earliest fortified site in Middle America is Becán, a city in Campeche encircled by a dry moat. In time it belongs to the second half of the Theocratic period; geographically it lies close to one of the rivers which feed into the Candelaria. Its position is significant, because it is so close to the later Militarist trade state of Acalán, situated on the main route between the Gulf of Mexico and the Gulf of Honduras. Our first clear-cut evidence of warfare from the Maya region appears in the Usumacinta Valley—around Palenque, Piedras Negras, and Yaxchilán. There we find the first representations of warrior figures on public monu-ments, and the great murals at Bonampak speak to us of raids and captive-taking around the end of the Theocratic period. Unusually strong Mexican influences appear on the upper Usumacinta, especially at the town of Seibal. These data all point in the same direction. Warfare first makes its appearance on the western frontier of the Maya Petén, not in its heartland.

If we look at the map we see another phenomenon: the fact that war-fare along this periphery could easily have blocked off trade and other contacts between the highlands of Chiapas and the Gulf lowlands on the one hand and the centers of Maya civilization on the other. This impres-sion finds added support in recent studies of the distributions of different kinds of pottery in the Maya Theocratic period. Toward the end of this period, political and trade barriers interrupted the traditional movement of pottery between east and west. Moreover, the Teotihuacán outpost of Kaminaljuyú in the Guatemalan highlands loses its contacts with the

109

A raid. Mural painting, Bonampak, Chiapas, Mexico, end of the eighth century A.D. The war leader, clad in jaguar tunic and equipped with stabbing spear, grasps an enemy by the hair in the gesture symbolizing capture. (From J. Eric S. Thompson, The Rise and Fall of Maya Civilization *[Norman: University of Oklahoma Press, 1954]. By permission of University of Oklahoma Press.)*

metropolis and becomes merely another regional center. As warfare spreads in the highlands, too, people begin to abandon the valley sites and to move up into the hills where they can fortify themselves adequately against surprise attacks. Perhaps it was a major shift in trade routes from the highlands to the Gulf lowlands and attendant shifts in political controls which caused the Petén cities to be abandoned. Perhaps the Petén cities could no longer count on food deliveries from the highlands. Whatever the direct causes, they precipitated a major upset in the fabric of Maya society. The theocratic rulers lost their grip; the stela cult came to an end.

Now it cannot be emphasized too strongly that the end of the stela cult does not mean that settled populations everywhere just disappeared. We know that the priests abandoned Copán, but a heavy population remained in the area until the time of the Spaniards. After Uaxactún was abandoned, people still came to bury their dead in the silent city. But certainly the power of the cities was broken. Culture retreated into the countryside, until warrior groups from the north and west once again gathered the population into nucleated settlements. The new military states developed along the old trade routes: the lowland states of Yucatán lay north of the route across the peninsula; the highland states divided among themselves the heritage of Kaminaljuyú. Between them the Petén lay silent and abandoned. Perhaps the Quiché legend of how Hunahpu and Xbalemque descend from the highlands into the depth of the underworld of Xibalba to wrest control from the rulers of the land in a series of ceremonial ball games refers to a historical event or a series of historical events in which the highland lords took over the vestiges of Petén power.

About the same time, a major fortified site appears in dry and arid southern Morelos, at Xochicalco. Xochicalco was a fortress town covering 620 acres. Built on a steep terraced hill, it was defended by a series of walls and moats. The peasantry which supported the lords of the fortress lived and farmed down below in the plain. Xochicalco was probably built toward the end of the Theocratic period, perhaps by Mixtec-speakers. There is good reason to suppose that it proved to be a pivot of militarist expansion from the southern periphery of the central highland into the southern highland.

Without doubt the largest Militarist site—still only partially excavated—was Tula, in Hidalgo. For a long time, references to Tollán in the written sources were identified with Teotihuacán. Yet as early as 1880, Desiré Charnay had drawn attention to the Atlas-type figures of Tula, Hidalgo, and their warrior characteristics. In 1938, Wigberto Jiménez Moreno was able to identify place names associated with Tollán

The fortress of Xochicalco, Morelos, Mexico, located on a steep terraced hilltop, defended by walls and moats, one of the earliest Militarist sites. (Courtesy of Compañía Mexicana Aerofoto, S.A.)

in the old sources in the immediate vicinity of Tula; and in 1940 Jorge R. Acosta began excavations in the Toltec capital. It now seems likely that Tula, rather than Teotihuacán, was the prototypical Tollán. The Mexica traced the name Tollán to *tollin*, i.e., "reed," and translated the name as "Place of Reeds," but it is more likely that the name signified "metropolis," a meaning which is retained in the modern Otomí name for Tula—Mamenhi.

The core of Tula consisted of an enormous courtyard surrounded by temples and palaces. Excavations show that the main temple, which probably served the cult of the sun, was systematically destroyed by the people who later conquered Tula, in 1168. The same fate befell the Temple of the Morning Star, though it preserved the marvelous friezes of walking jaguars alternating with eagles feeding on human hearts, as well as the sculptured representations of warriors crowned with eagle feathers, wearing square ear-plugs, breastplates in the shape of stylized butterflies, knee bands and wristlets, and sandals decorated with the feathered serpent, and bearing spear-throwers and curved swords. On one side the temple was surrounded by a great hall of pillars; on another by monumental sculptured walls. Two ball courts were also discovered. We do not know a great deal about the housing amenities of this city, although a building complex discovered by Charnay in 1880 some 3–7 miles from the center of the city shows that houses consisted of rooms connected by small passageways, with stuccoed floors and walls. Overlooking the city from the nearby Cerro de la Malinche—called Coatepetl or Snake Hill in ancient times—is a relief carved into rock depicting One Reed Our Lord Servant, steward on earth of the god Feathered Serpent, together with the glyph corresponding to the year 8 Flint or A.D. 980. Ruins are visible on all nearby hills, but to date remain unsurveyed and unstudied.

The location of Tula is itself significant. Just as Xochicalco in the south, so Tula in the north lies on the periphery of the valley of Mexico, on the outskirts of Teotihuacán and its influence. It lies in the Teotlálpan,

The core of Tula, Hidalgo, Mexico. The Temple of the Morning Star rises in the center. Rows of pillars are all that remain of extensive halls. To the left lies the open ball court. (Courtesy of Compañia Mexicana Aerofoto, S.A.)

the Country of the Gods, the mountainous barrier north of the valley. At the time of the coming of the Spaniards, in the sixteenth century, this was the frontier region where agriculture and settled life stopped and hunting and gathering and a nomadic existence began, the Great Chichimeca, populated by food-gathering tribelets of varying linguistic affiliation. This location on the frontier played a large part in the development of Tula.

Nor was this frontier a simple and unchanging line which divided cultivated fields on the one side from xerophytic bush on the other. Rather, it was a large and changing zone which was sometimes under the control of food-gatherers, sometimes under the control of cultivators. Whether the balance of control passed to one or the other side depended largely on whether the zone maintained connections with bases outside or not. At the time of the Spanish Conquest, these connections had been severed. But this was not always so. There are indications that cultivation once extended much further north. On the Pacific coast, cultivation and life in settled communities reached up as far as the Sinaloa River. In earlier times, part of the Bajío—later overrun by the Chichimec—were farmed by cultivators. A narrow tongue of cultivators extended through Zacatecas and Durango to the present boundary of the state of Chihuahua. This tongue follows the foothills of the western escarpment, bordering on desert to the east. The pivotal center of this zone seems to have been La Quemada, a fortified hilltop site southwest of the city of Zacatecas. La Quemada combines the features of a fortified temple center with pyramids, ball court, and walled courtyard. Even farther north, at Chalchihuites, lies a smaller unfortified site, a sort of outlier of the Quemada stronghold. Sixty-five miles north of Chalchihuites lie other small ceremonial centers surrounded by hamlets of sedentary cultivators,

---

Eagles feeding on human hearts, and jaguars, decorate a wall of the Temple of the Morning Star at Tula. (From Pedro Armillas, "Teotihuacán, Tula y los Toltecas," Runa, III [1950], Plate XI. By permission of Runa, Buenos Aires.)

until the known zone of cultivator settlement ends at Zape, where the hot steppe begins. An attenuated form of the Quemada complex is represented at Loma San Gabriel on the Chihuahua-Durango border.

These cultures met other sedentary cultivators coming down from the Rio Grande. The closest ties of this complex are with Tula and the Tula pattern. It is dated at A.D. 900–1350. But an earlier date is not excluded. It may date back to the flowering of Teotihuacán. The picture is similar in the northeast. Here too, there is evidence of cultivators living in hamlets centered upon small ceremonial centers in southwestern Tamaulipas and the Sierra of Tamaulipas about A.D. 300–900 and again later, after an intermediate break. There are sources which mention irrigation agriculture as far north as Meztitlán.

In all this area, Tula influence was predominant. It maintained the strongholds of La Quemada and Chalchihuites; it pervaded sites from Nayarit to the Sinaloa River. If it is more uncertain to the east, we can nevertheless say that Tula mediation would explain many of the long-recognized similarities in culture between the cultures of Nayarit, the Otomí and Huastec.

Again, the separate pieces of the puzzle begin to shape a coherent picture. Tula developed on the outskirts of Teotihuacán civilization, not near its center. Perhaps it began as one of the outposts of that metropolis in an area which was arid and where rainfall was scant. Irrigation and terracing here became categorical imperatives, while they may have remained optional in more favored areas. The need for irrigation produced a group of controllers who in turn acquired the means of control over people through control of their water supply. The new rulers may have clothed themselves in the pomp and circumstance of theocratic rule, but—in contrast to the Theocratic centers—their religious function is much less obvious than their military role. It is their role as soldiers that is most visible, and it is as soldiers also that they spread their culture patterns to people beyond the frontier. Some hunters and gatherers may indeed have settled down and become cultivators; some took up military

116

service along the frontier and became auxiliaries along this northern "wall." Some, like the people who later came to be called Mexica or Aztec, did both: in the services of Tula they learned to cultivate the earth and also to bear arms as mercenaries, twin lessons of civilization which they later turned to their own advantage.

None of this is to say that Tula domination of the northern frontier produced a stable and viable expansion of agriculture toward the north. After A.D. 1100 we see cultivators receding before hunters and gatherers throughout the entire arid north, from Utah to the borders of the Teotlálpan. Even only occasional nomadic attacks could render cultivation unprofitable in precarious areas, and most of the islands of cultivation in the arid corridor between the escarpments were precarious. Islands of greater strength like La Quemada may have survived for a while, but when Tula later collapsed, toward the end of the twelfth century A.D., the kingpin was removed from the system, and outpost after outpost collapsed, never to be rebuilt. When the Mexica inherited the ruins of Tula and of its political influence, they did not venture again into the northern wastes. Instead, they followed the traditional lines of expansion to the south, into the lands of jade, cacao, and precious feathers.

But the experience along the borders of settled life marked Tula strongly, and through Tula the entire Militaristic period. No longer are religious loyalty and trade the main forces making for social cohesion. Warfare and military expansion on the one hand, intensive agriculture and the appropriation of surpluses through tribute payments on the other, are the hallmarks of this new period. Where the network of controls during Theocratic times was loosely knit, the new era drew tight the strands of power. The processes which had begun during the Theocratic period thus reached their fruition. The new societies had solved a basic problem of their constitution, only to be faced with another of their own making.

These new military powers embraced many different linguistic and cultural groups. The legends of Middle America speak of some as

117

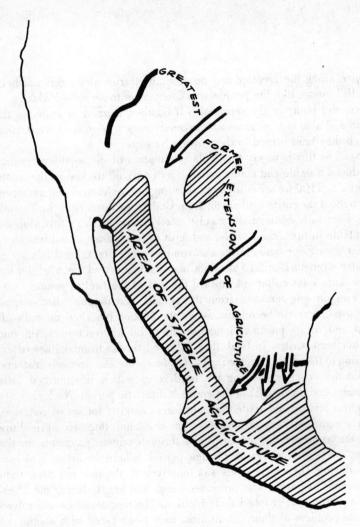

The retreat of agriculture and the advance of hunters and gatherers after A.D. 900. (Map by Patrick F. Gallagher.)

Tolteca, of others as *Chichimeca*, of still others as *Tolteca-Chichimeca*. Often these terms carry a double or a triple meaning. "Toltec" can refer to the inhabitants or the descendants of a city called Tollán. It can also mean craftsman and, in a wider sense, a person involved in city life and in civic society. "Chichimec," on the other hand, means literally "descendants of the dog," and was used in one sense to refer to the hungry nomads who inhabited the wide-open spaces north of the cultivated fields, the hunters and gatherers who used the bow and arrow, dressed in deer skins, and ate their meat raw. In contrast to "Toltec," it thus referred to people who had not accepted settled life and tight governmental controls. But the term possessed yet another meaning. As Toltec power spread into the arid north, it erased the simple dividing line between civilized folk and savages. Groups of hunters moved into the orbit of civilization and took up service with Toltec garrisons. This new role as mercenaries or auxiliaries allowed them to cultivate the arts of war and of the hunt, while accepting few of the responsibilities of statecraft and orderly urban existence. The Toltec state could contain their war-like energies as long as it was strong. But as its grip on the controls of government weakened, the mercenary soldiery began to seize power on their own behalf. It was these upstart rulers who used the term "Chichimec" in its second sense, asserting with it proudly and arrogantly their right to rule by force of arms and underlining through its use their warrior freedom and their superiority over their peasant subjects.

In contrast, all those who used the term "Toltec" for themselves indicated through this usage some bond of legitimate association with the precincts of civilization, and thus some claim to the civilized inheritance. Yet there is no need to suppose that all such claims were legitimate. There is indeed no reason to suppose that all Toltec mentioned in the genealogies and migration legends of Middle America originated in the same place or at the same time, or belonged to the same social and political system. We have already seen how Mesoamerican culture used cosmological symbols to interpret mundane social reality. Just as the

119

medieval rulers of Europe tried to legitimize their power by claiming to be the champions on earth of a mythical Holy Roman Empire, which —as many a wit has pointed out—was neither holy, Roman, nor an empire, so the ruling groups of Middle America traced their origins back to a mighty political womb, Tollán, which originally had spawned this host of soldier-kings. Descent from the original Toltec rulers and mystical participation in the original Tollán became the *sine qua non* of political legitimacy, without which royal descent remained spurious and political overlordship illegitimate. When all kinds of conquerors, legitimate kings, and upstart cutthroats claim similar descent, it would be antiquarian folly to hope that such various and contradictory claims can ultimately be made to fit a neat and unified pattern. Some Toltec were undoubtedly real; but others were Toltec through myth-making, as all conceptions of Tollán and Toltec soon passed into the realm of myth. Those who came after regarded these mythical original Toltec as a race of supermen, taller than ordinary men and able to run faster than deca-dent later breeds. They were the master artificers, the first scientists, the first astronomers. Like the Mexica god "From the Land of the Sea Snail," who was god of the moon and lord of all the world's riches, they wore turquoise-colored robes and headgear shaped like sea snails. Tollán it-self was said to be a paradise on earth of blue waters, white willows, white sand, colored cotton, water lilies, and the site of the magic ball court. Tula may well have been the first Tollán, but it is evident that historical reality quickly yielded to political myth-making.

To reduce the confusion of claims to the Toltec mantle to some order, we may distinguish between Pioneer Toltec and Epigonal Toltec. To the Pioneer Toltec we owe the first formation of militarist states in Middle America. When the states built by the Pioneer Toltec disintegrated, their legacy passed into the hand of various epigonal groups of claimants and counterclaimants to the Toltec name.

The first Pioneer Toltec group properly to deserve the Toltec name moved around A.D. 800 from the central highland to Salvador and

120

Nicaragua. Their descendants are the latter-day Pipil, whose name translates literally as "children," though probably, as later among the Colhua Mexica, it carried the symbolic meaning of "nobles." According to their traditions their ancestors left Cholula to escape the tyranny of the Olmeca-Xicalanca. One of the Pipil groups, the Nicarao, settled among the Chorotega people of Lake Nicaragua, where they perpetuated a culture with many central Mexican features. The names of Pipil settlements in San Salvador repeat many Mexican place names of regions farther to the north.

A second group of Pioneer Toltec, headed by a mythical Mixcoatl, appears in the valley of Morelos at the beginning of the tenth century A.D. Perhaps it is this group which is associated with the ruins of Xochicalco. Possibly this Toltec group (or groups) is identical or associated with the Toltec ruling groups which spread into the Mixtec-speaking mountains of the southern highlands. Fray Francisco de Burgoa has preserved a story of this conquest by soldier-kings of a people speaking a different language, a people whom they subjugated to their own rule and law. Codices and traditions symbolize this difference between the upper and the lower classes among the Mixtec-speakers by asserting that the Mixtec were born from the earth, while the new rulers descended from trees at Apoala and Achiutla. Mixtec codices and sculptures show a personage called Eight Deer, a great conqueror, who came to dominate most of the Mixtec-speaking area and much of southern Puebla. He is represented as wearing typical Toltec dress; both he and his ancestors wear the characteristic Toltec nose-plug, while all the other people shown in the codices wear simple nose-rods. The nose-plug was given to him in a sort of investiture by a figure called Four Jaguar or Anáhuatl, supposedly a king of Tula. Jiménez Moreno places Eight Deer's life between 1011 and 1063, and thus some hundred years before the fall of Tula.

A third group of Pioneer Toltec is associated with Tula in Hidalgo, and the so-called Toltec Empire, a large state which seems to have reached as far as northern Veracruz to the east, as far as Querétaro to the west. It may well have included the Mixtec kingdoms mentioned above.

Its ruling group was probably primarily Nahuatl-speaking but included also the representatives of local dynasties and of local populations who spoke Otomí, Huastec, and probably Mazateco-Popoloca. The Mazateco-Popoloca may well have been carriers of the culture of Teotihuacán, at least in its breakdown phase at Atzcapotzalco. The Legend of the Sun contains the political myth symbolizing the seizure of power by the Toltec lords, who worshipped the sun, from the moon-worshipping Otomí.

Scattered evidence gives us some insight also into the internal organization of the Tula state. Authority was divided between a sacred and a secular ruler; each ruler had under him two subordinates. The sacred ruler could not pass his office on to members of his family: he was barred from relations with women and not allowed to produce offspring. Kirchhoff has recently reinterpreted the legends surrounding the fall of Tula to show convincingly that this division of authority was in part responsible for the disintegration of the state. A sacred ruler tried to impose his natural son, Quetzalcoatl, in contravention of legitimate succession. The opposition drove Quetzalcoatl into exile, at the same time splitting the loyalties which had hitherto cemented the structure of the empire. These historical events are probably merely surface phenomena of a more thoroughgoing opposition between the sacred rulers who continued the traditions of Theocratic society and the secular, militarily oriented groups which pulled and pushed in opposite directions. This conflict of interests is clearly evident in the fact that Quetzalcoatl, who asserted the supremacy of the sacred rulership, also stood for peaceable sacrifice of jade, snakes, or butterflies, while the opposition wanted to initiate human sacrifice. With the defeat of Quetzalcoatl, wholesale human sacrifice was introduced, still another indication that the secular militarist tendencies were winning out over the theocratic trend.

122

The valley of Mexico, showing the location of the five Epigonal Toltec capitals. (Map by Patrick F. Gallagher.)

The destruction of the Toltec political system of Tula was followed by a period of political fragmentation and chaos. Warrior bands moved in all directions to seize their share of the imperial inheritance. Some sought new homes in the Huastec-speaking area, or along the trade routes to the south. Others were able to solidify their control over some body of territory and its people and found new kingdoms, smaller replicas of the original Toltec empire. Legitimate or upstart, all called themselves Toltec, to underline the righteousness of their claims to populations and tribute, and paraded genealogies which traced back their descent to the primordial Tollán. Five such Epigonal Toltec states rose in the valley of Mexico: The first, centered upon Atzcapotzalco, controlled the west and northwest of the valley. Atzcapotzalco, the epigonal Teotihuacán settlement on the western shores of the lake, became in 1230 the head town of a political system, ruled by an Otomí-speaking group called Tepanec.

The second successor-state in the valley of Mexico was Xaltocan, on the northern shore of the lake system. Organized in 1250 by Otomí-speakers, it controlled the north of the valley. The third was the Acolhua domain on the eastern shore of Lake Texcoco; it was organized by a Chichimec dynasty upon a Toltec base in 1260.

The fourth city-state, Colhuacán, in the southwest of the valley, had real claim to the honor of the Toltec name. Its ruling line appears to have been directly descended from the kings of Tula, and marriages into this line were sought for the sake of prestige by power-seekers throughout the valley. Thus the lowly Mexica, years later, went to Colhuacán to ask for a legitimate "Toltec" ruler to rule over them, and received Acama-pichtli, descended from the Toltec line through his mother. The very name of Colhuacán means "Place of the Grandparents," that is, of those who have illustrious ancestors. Colhuacán may well have been founded directly by refugees from Tula, around 1207. The fifth successor-state in the valley, Xicco, was—like Colhuacán—a Toltec city bearing some part of the legitimate Toltec aura. Dating from 1161, it controlled for a short period the southwestern part of the valley.

Similar political formations, captained by Epigonal Toltec, arose in other parts of Middle America. One of the best known of these is the state of Chichén Itzá in Yucatán. Toltec influence on this old Maya center built near a holy well may go back to the beginning of the Tula empire; it is clearly predominant by A.D. 1000. The ruling group claimed Toltec descent, but seems to have been a Chontal-speaking group from Tabasco. Close ties with Tula are, however, evident in the architecture. At first, the newcomers merely improved and rebuilt an already existing structure, the so-called Observatory, and also used Maya prototypes in the construction of a temple to the Sky Serpent. Soon, however, they introduced the same features that mark the architecture of Tula and that contrast so strikingly with the Theocratic architecture of the Maya. The older Maya style was functionally related to the worship of vegetation gods through special priestly intermediaries. To enter into communica-

Chichén Itzá, Yucatán, Mexico, with the Castillo or Temple of Kukulcán (Quetzalcoatl) at the right, and the Temple of the Warriors surrounded by colonnades in the foreground. About A.D. 1000. (Courtesy of Compañía Mexicana Aerofoto, S.A.)

tion with these gods, the priests entered small, dark, and confined rooms which symbolized the bowels of the earth—the heart of the land—and emerged from these inner sanctums to communicate the will of the gods to the assembled worshippers. The Toltec, on the other hand, worshipped astral bodies—the sun and the moon, the morning star and the evening star—which demanded public hecatombs of sacrificial victims, and needed large precincts for the rites in which warriors were initiated into the military orders and for their ball games. They thus favored a type of construction which lay open to the sky, exemplified by great colonnades which admitted light and allowed direct contact with the celestial beings. These they introduced into Yucatán, together with their patterns of fortified towns and military symbolisms.

Other Epigonal Toltec groups seized power in the highlands. In the valley of Puebla, the Tolteca-Chichimeca drove the Olmeca-Xicalanca from Cholula in 1292. In highland Guatemala, the Quiché and Cakchiquel, both possessed of traditions which allow their dynasties to claim affiliation with the original Tollán, seized control over the more autochthonous Pokomam and Mam. The Quiché established their capital at Kumarcaah (Utatlán) around 1300; the dissident Cakchiquel separated from them and built their own redoubt at Iximché (Tecpán-Guatemala) in the middle of the fifteenth century.

To compound the confusion created by conflicting loyalties and aspirations, the Chichimec also entered the fray. One major migration brought an Otomí-speaking Chichimec group—the so-called Chichimec

Frieze from the Platform of Skulls (tzompantli) at Chichén Itzá,
Yucatán, Mexico, showing skulls impaled on poles. (Photograph by Joseph
Seckendorf.)

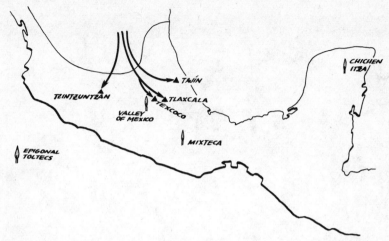

Chichimec invasions of the central highland. (Map by Patrick F. Gallagher.)

of Xolotl—into the eastern part of the valley of Mexico. Here they encountered Toltec remnants whom they subjected to their rule, to found
a new state: the Acolhua domain. Soon, the centripetal imperatives of
statecraft asserted themselves over the centrifugal tendencies of the
Chichimec soldiery, and the new Chichimec dynasty itself became the
primary instrument of acculturation to sedentary patterns. The Chichimec kings began to favor Toltec settlement and to force their unruly
warriors into a peasant existence, driving into exile those who did not
submit. This hybrid state, with its capital at Texcoco, became one of the
great centers of civilization in the valley of Mexico.

Other groups of Chichimec, probably allied with Xolotl and his men,
swept southeastward toward the Gulf. In the course of their expansion
they probably destroyed the old Theocratic center of Tajín, which had
survived the vicissitudes of political upheaval. While Tajín itself was
abandoned around A.D. 1200, the area as a whole remained populated.
Throughout the region, the Chichimec invaders established local dynasties, thus preparing the way for final conquest of the lowlands by the
Acolhua and the Mexica in the second half of the fifteenth century.

Another group of Chichimec, comprising both Nahua and Otomí-
speakers, invaded the northern valley of Puebla and founded Tlaxcala

127

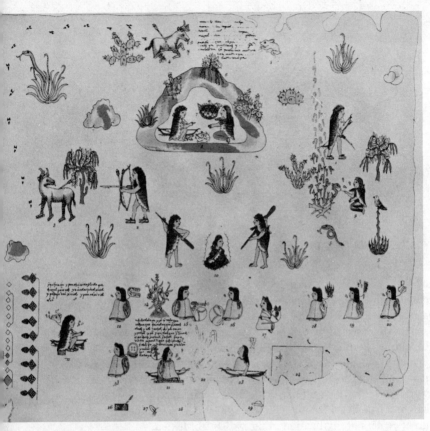

Arrival of the Chichimecs, as depicted in Mapa Quinatzin. Note hunt (left), use of bow and arrow; woman roasting snake (right); man with spear thrower, woman carrying maize (below, center). (Courtesy of American Museum of Natural History.)

in 1348. Here they fused with an older local population and the Toltec refugees who had settled there after the fall of Tula. Tlaxcala quickly developed into a major center of trade between the highland and the lowlands of the Gulf. Probably the fact that the lowland areas were controlled by Chichimec dynasties, related culturally and genealogically to the Tlaxcaltec, eased the acquisition of these trading privileges. The

128

prosperity of Tlaxcala was curtailed only in the mid-fifteenth century, when the Mexica, envious of its wealth, drove a wedge between the highland state and its coastal trade stations.

Similar processes occurred in the west, where farmers and fishermen —this time of Tarascan speech—had settled in the vicinity of Lake Pátzcuaro in Michoacán. In the twelfth century, they came into contact with Tarascan-speaking semi-nomads called Chichimeca-Yanaceo, who occupied the northern fringe of the lake. The leaders of the newcomers fused with the leaders of the established settlers to form a Chichimec dynasty. From its capital at Tzintzuntzan, the dynasty during the fourteenth and fifteenth centuries conquered the area between Balsas and Santiago and beyond. It always emphasized its Chichimec origin, to set itself off from the remainder of the population, whom it depressed to the status of *purépecha* or commoners. The name *purépecha* was later extended to all Tarascans.

When we trace these movements and invasions on the map, it becomes clear that geographically the invasions of the Chichimec were largely confined to the central highland. Splinter groups did reach the Mixtec-speaking area of the southern highland, even as far as Guatulco on the Pacific coast, where the people spoke Nahuat and claimed Chichimec descent at the time of the Conquest; but there they remained unimportant. In the central highlands, however, they played a more important role. True, they soon suffered the cultural fate of so many nomadic or semi-nomadic invaders who set foot among peasant populations: they quickly lost their independence of action and were absorbed into the settled life of countryside and town. But on the political level, they acted as political and military catalysts, speeding the renewed processes toward political integration and state-building. Toltec dynasties with Chichimec allies, or Chichimec dynasties with Toltec allies, labored in competition to return the seat of power to the valley of Mexico, where it had been before the rebellion of the periphery that had spelled the doom of the Theo-cratic world.

129

VII

Soldiers
of the
Sun

The people who brought Militarism to its culmination, and came to
dominate most of Middle America through warfare and commerce were
Chichimec from the outer fringes of the settled Middle American world.
They are known to posterity as Aztec, Tenochca, or Colhua Mexica, their
changing names reflecting their changing fortunes. First they were probably called Aztec, after their mythical home, Aztlán—"Chichimec from
Aztlán," a man from Chalco in the valley of Mexico called them, with
the contempt of the civilized for the barbarian. Later they were called
Tenochca, supposedly after a patriarch Tenoch, who also gave his name
to Tenochtitlán, their lake-bound city. When they accepted the leadership
of an Epigonal Toltec lineage from Colhuacán, they acquired the name
Colhua Mexica, or Colhua of Mexico. It was as Colhua that Columbus
first heard of them in the Antilles, where the Indians answered his inter-
minable questions about lands to the west by repeating, "Colhua,
Colhua!" As empire-builders, they became Mexica, rulers of Mexicayotl,
the Mexica domain.

Few men would have predicted a great future for the Mexica when they were serving as auxiliaries in the armies of Toltec Tula. When Tula collapsed, they entered the valley of Mexico in the wake of other Chicimec invaders, probably at the end of the thirteenth century. Hemmed in on all sides by previous occupants, they finally found refuge on a muddy promontory extending into the lagoon of Texcoco. According to their legends, they were led to the site by their god Hummingbird-on-the-Left, who ordered them to settle where they saw an eagle sitting on a cactus, devouring a snake. There the Mexica would come face to face with their destiny. There they would fight a holy war in support of the sun, against the forces of night and evil. As each night the sun gives battle to the multitude of stars, so the Mexica would capture prisoners of war and sacrifice them; each prisoner would represent one star, fit astral food to sustain the sun in its perilous fight. Painted black and white and wearing a black mask to symbolize the night sky, each victim would mount a holy pyramid, where his captors would tear his heart from his living body so that the sun might eat and rise to fight again. In the lagoon of Texcoco, mythically equated with the Lake of the Moon, near the spring whose waters ran blue and red—symbolic of the glyph "water-fire" (*atl-tlachinolli*) that stands for war—the Mexica were to fulfil their mission as guardians of the sun.

This myth not only recasts reality in symbolic terms to justify warfare and human sacrifice; it also obscures the realities behind the Mexica settlement in the lagoon. The Mexica did not seek refuge in the marshy lake of their own volition; they were driven into the lagoon by their enemies. Nor did their city Tenochtitlán rise pristinely from the waves of the lake without previous antecedents. The Mexica town, built in 1344 or 1345, rose in the shadow of an older city, Tlatelolco, probably in existence since the early Militarist period. Tlatelolco became Tenochtitlán's sister-city, its uneasy ally. Always more interested in commerce than in warfare for its own sake, the Tlatelolca perhaps made use of the Mexica as mercenaries to protect their trade routes; the Mexica in turn claimed, as their own, victories manifestly won by Tlatelolca armies. Undoubtedly Tenochtitlán was long parasitic upon the older city; as soon as they thought themselves strong enough, however, the Mexica turned upon their allies, took Tlatelolco by force, and replaced its king with Mexica officials (1473).

Three stages distinguish the Mexica rise to power after their establishment at Tenochtitlán. During the first stage they took service in the armies of the Epigonal Toltec Tepanecs of Atzcapotzalco, thus sharing as mercenaries in the rapid growth of the Tepanec domain between 1367 and 1418. The year 1427 marks the beginning of the second stage of Mexica expansion. In that year they changed sides and allied themselves with the defeated Acolhua of Texcoco against the Tepanecs. In 1430, Obsidian Snake destroyed the Tepanec capital at Atzcapotzalco. In the wake of this victory, the Mexica of Tenochtitlán, the Acolhua of Texcoco and a liberated part of the Tepanec domain called Tlacopan (modern Tacuba in Mexico City) entered into a "Triple Alliance" which divided both the valley of Mexico and most of Middle America into separate spheres of influence and conquest.

The dominant power during this second stage, however, was not Tenochtitlán, but Texcoco. Under its king, Hungry-Coyote (Netzahual-coyotl), Texcoco had insured its internal food supply through the construction of a great system of dam and canals, opening hitherto marginal lands to cultivation by irrigation. Hungry-Coyote's irrigation engineers also built and maintained the great dike across the lagoon of Texcoco. The dike not only safeguarded Tenochtitlán against floods and drowning but secured chinampa agriculture on the southern margins of the lagoon, barring the entry of salt water from the lake into the fresh water of the lagoon. In contrast to military-aristocratic Tenochtitlán, Texcoco gave both nobles and commoners equal representation on its governing council, granted its merchants a say in the economic administration of the state, and favored the emergence of professional bureaucrats over office tenure by noble warriors. At the same time, it conquered for the Triple Alliance most of the eastern part of the central highland, from

132

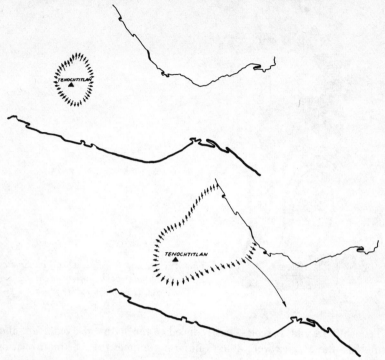

Mexica expansion: to 1440 (above) *to 1481* (below).
(*Maps by Patrick F. Gallagher.*)

the nomad frontier to the Papaloapan, as well as the rich province of Morelos. These tendencies toward military expansion and strong internal consolidation were accompanied by intellectual developments which issued in the enactment of a great legal code, in the growth of a philosophy of monotheism, and in the disavowal of human sacrifice. Texcoco Nahuatl became Classic Nahuatl; at the same time Texcoco cultivated literary Otomí.

Yet none of these tendencies came to fruition, nor did they prevail in the domain of the Triple Alliance. It was blatantly militaristic Tenochtitlán and not Texcoco that left its final imprint upon the culture of Middle America. The year 1500 marks the beginning of the third and final stage of Mexica power, the establishment of Mexica hegemony over the Triple Alliance. Tlacopan, long merely a buffer state between

133

The Mexica king Itzcoatl (Obsidian Snake),
1428–40, founder of the independent
Mexica state. (From Codex Mendoza.)

Tenochtitlán and Texcoco, was reduced to the status of a satellite, and in 1515 the Mexica were able to impose a puppet ruler of their own in Texcoco. Tribute previously gathered separately by the individual members of the Triple Alliance was now concentrated at Tenochtitlán and redistributed from the Mexica treasury to its satellites.

As the external fortunes of the Mexica changed, so did their internal organization. As they cast off the role of mercenaries to the highest bidder and assumed the pretensions of an independent power, they also exchanged the simple social organization of the military band for the complex organization of a conquest state. So thoroughgoing was this change that we find it difficult today to reconstruct their earlier and less stratified social constitution. King Obsidian Snake not only won the war against Atzcapotzalco, thus becoming the initiator of Mexica expansion; he also destroyed the historical records of his tribe and rewrote its history, in the familiar modern manner. Apparently he wished not only to recast in more glorious terms the military and political feats of the Mexica before their rise to power but also to obliterate the memory of their more egalitarian past. As far as we can tell today, the Mexica en-

134

Hummingbird-on-the-Left (Huitzilopochtli), the god of the Mexica state.
(From Codex Borgia.)

tered the valley of Mexico led by two leaders, a war-chief and a priest-chief, who were subject to check by a council which may at some time have comprised the entire weapons-bearing population. On their migrations, they were led by the image of their own god, the terrible young warrior Hummingbird-on-the-Left, just as the migratory bands of Epigonal Toltec had borne with them the image of their god, Smoking Mirror (Tezcatlipoca). Through the medium of priests or priest-chiefs, the image was consulted in all affairs of state.

The tribe itself was divided into twenty subgroups, called Big Houses or *calpulli*. These calpulli have been the subject of an acrimonious scientific debate, a debate which raised questions regarding the basic nature of Mexica society. Some anthropologists have held that the calpulli were none other than kinship groups or clans of the kind that could be found among many other primitive peoples. They drew from this the inference that the Mexica were essentially primitive—on a level, for example, with the Iroquois of upper New York State. Others who interpreted Mexica society as essentially a society divided into social and economic classes thought that the calpulli could not be units of kin at all but merely administrative divisions instituted by a ruling class to accommodate its subject populations. It is more than likely, however, that the question need not be resolved into mutually exclusive alternatives; the Mexica calpulli probably bore features of both class and clan. They were what Paul Kirchhoff has called "conical clans," kinship units which bind their members with common familial ties but which distribute wealth, social standing, and power most unequally among the members of the pseudo-family. Such kin units trace their descent back to an original ancestor, real or fictitious; but, at the same time, they regularly favor his lineal descendants over the junior or "cadet" lines in regulating access to social, economic, or political prerogatives.

It is not unreasonable to suppose that the Mexica possessed similar conical units of fictional kin or that they converted whatever kin groups they had into these more adaptable social instruments. We know that the Mexica did not all share a common ancestor. When they reached the site of Tenochtitlán, their twenty divisions contained not only kin but "allies" as well. Probably they also merged easily with previous settlers, just as they easily accommodated themselves to a ruling dynasty from Colhuacan. Whatever the nature of the calpulli, therefore, its outstanding characteristic was the flexibility with which it adapted itself to the increasing complexity of Mexica society.

Their entrance as mercenaries into the Tepanec armies marked the first stage of Mexica expansion; the acquisition of an Epigonal Toltec lineage from Colhuacan marked the first major stage in the growth of their internal differentiation. Before the new ruler, Acamapichtli, assumed leadership, the Mexica nobility probably consisted largely of the heads of the calpulli, offices which were always filled from members of the same families within the calpulli. After Acamapichtli's accession to the Mexica throne, we witness the development of a hereditary nobility, the "speakers" (sing., *tlatoani*; pl., *tlatoque*) who claimed a descent different from the remainder of the population, a descent hallowed by the mythical aura of the Toltec name. This exclusiveness of descent they reinforced still further by frequent endogamy or marriage within their own blood line, though they also, and at the same time, married commoner wives to strengthen their political ties with their subject population.

Until the fall of Atzcapotzalco, however, this new ruling group and its descendants, the "precious sons" (*tlacopipiltzin* or *tlazopilli*), enjoyed social prerogatives without at the same time possessing a source of economic power that could render them independent of the commoners, organized in their calpulli. The nobles were entitled to receive tribute from the calpulli, but had no access to land as such. The landholding unit was the single calpulli. This situation was reversed at one fell swoop by the defeat of Atzcapotzalco. The successful conclusion of the Tepanec war assured the economic as well as the political power of the Mexica nobility.

The conflict of interests between nobles and commoners emerges clearly from the official records in which the royal historians set forth the motives behind the Atzcapotzalco war. According to this version, the Mexica nobles and commoners held common council on whether to declare war on the Tepanecs. The nobles voted for war, the commoners for peace. Obsidian Snake then rose and said:

If we do not win, we will give ourselves into your hands and you may eat our flesh. Thus may you avenge yourselves upon us; you may eat us, chopped up and fat, in earthen pots. Thus you may disgrace us by eating us.

Then the commoners rose and answered:

Well and good. Now we promise to carry out the following terms, and you yourselves may carry out the sentence. If we succeed in this battle we agree to serve you, to pay you tribute and to be your servants; to build your houses and to serve your fathers and your sons as our lords, in every way. When you go to war, we promise to carry your burdens, your food, and your arms on our backs, serving you on all the roads over which you pass. Finally, we agree to sell ourselves and to subject ourselves to your rule and to put our wealth at your disposal forever.

137

This story—probably apocryphal—expresses the gravity of the changes that beset Mexica society after 1427. The strategic booty of the Tepanec war was land in the conquered provinces—land, and peasants tied to the land. This land was used to underwrite the privileges of a warrior elite independent of popular jurisdiction.

On their new lands, which they secured in permanent inheritance, the nobles also settled their own labor supply drawn from "people who came to them, fleeing from other towns and provinces," the "right hands" (*mayequauh* or *tlalmaitl*). These agricultural laborers did not form part of the calpulli; in exchange for the right to work land and to eat, they forsook the right to mobility. Tied to the land, they were inherited with the land. But apart from this economic bondage, they were free and could own personal property. Their overlords possessed economic but not judicial power over them, as might have been the case in feudal Europe.

The conquest of new land affected the members of the calpulli in still another way. Access to land enabled the rulers to create a nobility of service as well as a nobility of lineage, by rewarding—for the period of a lifetime—commoners who had distinguished themselves in warfare or in trade. The creation of these "knights" (sing., *tecuhtli*; pl. *tecuhtin*) or "Sons of the Eagle" (*quauhpipiltin*) opened avenues of mobility from below; at the same time, it drove a wedge of reward and social recognition between the mass of the population in the calpulli and the aspiring few. As this nobility of service grew increasingly important, however, with the expansion of the Mexica domain, it also entered into conflict with the nobility of lineage over the occupancy of bureaucratic positions. During the last phase of Mexica rule an aristocratic reaction curtailed the privileges of the service nobles in favor of a renewed monopoly of power in the hands of the nobility of descent.

As the Colhua dynasty and its descendants gained rights over tribute, labor, and land, it also came to interest itself in trade. There were essentially two kinds of Mexica trade: local trade, dealing in small quantities

King Nezahualpilli of
Texcoco (1472–1516) in
ceremonial garb, carrying
bouquets of flowers. The
original stems from the
archive of the post-Conquest
Indian historian Fernando
de Alva Ixtlilxochitl
(1568–1648), a descendant
of the royal houses of both
Tenochitlán and Texcoco.
(From Walter Krickeberg,
Altmexikanische Kulturen
[Berlin: Safari Verlag,
1956].)

of low value, and long-distance trade, dealing in products of high value. Local markets served primarily the needs of the common population and the purposes of daily consumption. Some of these markets were exceedingly large: one of the markets of Tenochtitlán—twice as large as the market of Salamanca, said Cortés—served 60,000 buyers and sellers daily. In the provinces, markets were held every five or every twenty days. Selling or buying outside the market was prohibited by law, a rule strengthened by the belief that the god of the market would rise up to smite the sinner. Products which came to market were taxed, and markets had their own courts and judges to settle disputes and punish evildoers. As in Indian markets today, however, traders came not only to buy and sell, but also to worship. Market days were festive occasions and food offerings were brought to the god of the market place.

Long-distance trade, in contrast, dealt in luxury goods, and was in the hands of specialists, called *pochteca* or *oztomeca*. The long-distance traders of Tenochtitlán resided at Tlatelolco. Of an origin different from that of the Mexica, they formed a recognized and semiautonomous unit within Mexica society; organizationally, they may have constituted either a stratified kin group or a guild. They possessed their own emblems, gods, and ceremonies. They administered laws in their own courts under their own judges and were governed by their own officers. Their special customs—ceremonial use of rubber, paper, and tobacco; the offering of blood in worship; the shaving of heads during voyages; artificial cranial deformation; the use of fans; worship of a god, Earth Serpent, and a goddess, Precious Flower—link them either with the Gulf coast or with the older Theocratic cultures of Middle America. They had very likely been traders before the Mexica ever entered the valley. Through long-continued contacts they had built up alliances with merchants from other highland towns and won the privilege of moving peacefully and undisturbed into special commercial sanctuaries, "ports of trade," which lay outside the customary battlegrounds of either Maya or Mexica. Located in the southern Gulf area, these ports of trade were politically independent from all outside interference. Captained by merchant princes or factors whose main interest lay in the steady flow of long-distance commerce, they served primarily to concentrate and to disburse the products of this trade. Exports from Tenochtitlán and the highlands comprised slaves, rich clothing, gold and precious stones, obsidian, herbs, red ochre, cochineal dye, copper bells, and skeins of rabbit fur. From the Gulf lowlands, on the other hand, came the precious symbols of nobility: feathers, especially the feathers of the quetzal bird, turquoise, jade, jaguar skins, feather cloaks, shirts, slaves, and cacao, which served not only as a beverage but also as money.

As the Colhua dynasty cemented its power, it moved to bring under its own administration this trade in the prerogatives of nobility. The conquest of Tlatelolco, the seat of the merchant prices, was probably the first major step in this direction. During the final stage of Mexica power, the king sponsored trade expeditions on his own behalf. Each year, Tenochtitlán received as tribute 2,000,000 cotton cloaks and 300,000 cloaks of century-plant fiber. Part of this tribute was redistributed among the Mexica population; most of it, however, was funneled into trade to buy luxury goods for the king. Economic partner to the merchant effort, the state also protected trade routes and avenged attacks upon its merchants. At the same time, the Mexica traders spied on their customers en route and provided the state with strategic military information. However, while the dynasty made use of the merchant group, it also remained alive to the danger implicit in the existence of a semiautonomous unit within the larger body politic. To curb their aspirations, merchants were barred from the military orders, and during the aristocratic reaction of the final Mexica period, merchants were frequently put to death and their wealth redistributed among the great warriors. The *pochteca* had to make a special effort to appear humble and poor, lest they attract the vegeance of their overlords.

Fortified behind such economic bulwarks, the nobility heavily increased its prerogatives. Special clothing and insignia marked it off

141

from the commoners. The nobles had their own courts, and they alone had the right to polygyny which, in addition to the benefits of extended alliances through marriage, also benefited them economically. Their wives were put to the task of producing great numbers of precious cloaks, valuable commodities in conspicuous consumption and commerce. Ritual and religious training in special schools, the *calmecatl*, became a prerequisite for bureaucratic tenure; only nobles could send their children to these establishments and thus qualify them for the top rungs of the political order.

As the power of the nobility increased, the power of the calpulli necessarily declined. They still retained important economic military and religious functions. The life of the average commoner continued to be lived within the framework of his calpulli. Only the calpulli owned land; the individual had to apply to his calpulli to obtain use rights to his legitimate share. The calpulli paid tribute as a unit. Each calpulli had a war leader, maintained an armory, trained its youth for war in a bachelor house (*telpochcalli*), and served as a unit in warfare. Each calpulli had its own god, its own ceremonies, its own temple. But while the office of calpulli headman remained hereditary within the calpulli, it was shorn of its judicial powers and subjected to supervision by a royal commissar. In long-range perspective, moreover, the economic contribution of the commoner to the total life of the society undoubtedly declined, as the Mexica extended their conquests and gained new sources of land and tribute beyond the confines of their island redoubt. It seems reasonable to assume that, in the course of the second phase of Mexica expansion, the military duties of the calpulli began to overshadow their purely productive functions.

As Mexica society grew more complex, there also developed a servile group (*tlacotli*) whom the Spaniards called slaves. There were three kinds of such slaves: slaves obtained in warfare, contractual slaves, and criminal slaves. Slaves obtained in war were always women and children; male prisoners of war were inevitably sacrificed to the hungry gods.

Moctezuma's palace. Above, The throne room *(center)* and the chambers where the king met the lords of the realm. Below, *Military council room (left), civil council room (right). (Courtesy of American Museum of Natural History.)*

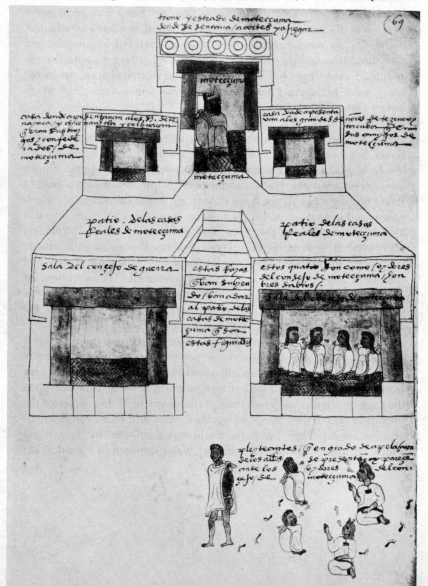

Individuals became slaves by contract if they sold themselves into slavery because they could not pay a personal debt or public tribute; fathers could sell their children in this way. Criminal slaves were usually forced to serve their victim or his family. Thus a man might serve as slave in the family of a man he had murdered or from whom he had stolen. On the other hand, a man could be enslaved because he had committed treason or a similar crime against the larger political community. Slaves were used in the house, in agricultural work, or in the heavy work of carrying burdens, so important in a technology which lacked domesticated animals.

The liens of slavery, however, were quite limited. Slaves could own property. They could maintain families, and their children were never slaves, but freemen. A slave could not be resold without his consent, unless he had committed a crime. Owning property, he could buy his own freedom or allow his relatives to purchase it for him. We even hear of slaves owning other slaves. Such slavery, or rather the temporary servitude which it represented for most, seems to have been a common lot in Mexica society. During the great famines of the mid-fifteenth century, many commoner families sold themselves into slavery to obtain food; others sold themselves to pay for religious ceremonies which they had sponsored and which had left them impoverished. The conditions of Mexica slavery could probably not have been made more stringent without antagonizing the bulk of the population, the masses upon whom the maintenance of Mexica society ultimately depended.

Divided as this society was into social strata and contending interest groups, it nevertheless possessed one powerful cement for social unity in its doomsday ideology. The individual Mexica acquired with his very mother's milk a sense of collective mission in a world balanced upon the edge of destruction. From their predecessors in Middle America the Mexica inherited the concept of worlds created and consumed in recurrent cataclysms. Each successive world was dominated by its own sun which went down in violence: a Sun of Water drowned in a great flood;

144

a Sun of the Jaguar, Night, and Earth came to an end when the sky fell upon the earth; a Sun of Rain or Fire consumed itself when fire fell from the sky; a Sun of Wind collapsed in an earth-sweeping storm. Arrayed against the forces of evil, the Mexica were destined the defend the fifth sun, the Sun-To-End-in-Earthquakes. In the great war to uphold the cosmos, the Mexica saw themselves as fighters on the side of light, sun, valor, courage, sobriety, and sexual control against the forces of night, earth, cowardice, drunkenness, and sexual incontinence. Only continuous warfare and human sacrifice could maintain the sun in its heaven; only continuous military effort could postpone that final day when the present cycle of events would draw to an end, when the world would disintegrate in a cosmic cataclysm.

Human sacrifice has been a recurrent cultural phenomenon: in moments of human crisis, men often can find no greater gift for the gods than one of their own kind. Yet among the cultures permitting human sacrifice the Mexica are unique. No other people on earth has felt it necessary to immolate thousands of victims annually to assure the balance of the heavens. Certainly human sacrifice had an ancient history in Middle America: the Mexica probably inherited the custom from their Toltec predecessors. Again, it is probable that the population of the Mexica domain had grown beyond the capacity of the land to sustain it, an inference supported by the repeated recorded famines of the fifteenth century. Neither population surplus nor custom, however, is in itself sufficient to account for this fanatic obsession with blood and death. No psychoanalytically trained anthropologist or anthropologically trained psychoanalyst has yet attempted an appraisal of Mexica personality. Driven by imaginary and real indignities, cruel against himself and others, doing battle against doom and yet attracted by it, as its victim succumbs to the fascination of a snake, haunted by omens, the Mexica warrior constituted an extreme among possible psychological types, ever engaged in fulfilling his prophecies of destruction by acting upon the assumption of imminent catastrophe.

While Hummingbird-on-the-Left remained the special god of the Mexica, they worshipped other gods too. Thus they took over Smoking Mirror from the Toltec who had preceded them in the conquest of the valley, often identifying him with Hummingbird-on-the-Left. They adopted Tlaloc, He Who Makes the Plants Spring Up, and his household of rain gods, as well as a plethora of local earth and fertility goddesses who controlled the reproduction of plants as well as of men. They rendered homage to Our Lord the Flayed One (Xipe Totec) whose skin symbolized the old mantle of vegetation, with its promise of renewal. And they worshipped the Shining Serpent (Quetzalcoatl). Under Obsidian Snake, the victor of Atzcapotzalco, the Mexica also standardized their pantheon and their ceremonies of worship. It remained a characteristic of their religion, however—as of all Middle American religion—that the multiple deities were never conceived as essentially distinct from one another, each exercising dominion over a separate realm of well-defined functions. Rather, they often interpenetrated one another, sometimes blending their attributes and prerogatives, sometimes united in polar opposition, still at other times indifferent to one another and exercising similar functions side by side. Thus Hummingbird-on-the-Left becomes a Blue Obsidian Mirror, symbolizing the blue sky of day and associated with the south, just as the Flayed Lord can be a Red Obsidian Mirror, or a Fire Serpent when he represents the earth parched by the rays of the sun, or a Plumed Serpent whose feathers symbolize the growing and fecund vegetation. The skin of Our Lord the Flayed One also decorates the body of Filth-Eater (Tlazolteotl), the great earth and fertility goddess whom the Mexica took over from the Huastec-speakers of the Gulf coast, just as the feathers of the Plumed Serpent decorated the face of Tlaloc in his aspect of a fertility god.

These complexities—so exasperating and yet so intriguing to the modern specialist—hardly concerned the Mexica commoner, or the peasant working in his fields under the supervision of a Mexica overseer in Puebla or Morelos. For the commoner peasant or artisan worshipped

146

his local earth goddess—the Lady with the Serpent Skirt (Coatlícue), Serpent-Woman (Cihuacóatl), Our Mother (Tonántzin)—just as today he worships the Virgin of the Remedies or the Virgin of Guadalupe without worrying his head about whether these all represent the same goddess or each is a goddess in her own right. Whether Shining Serpent as White Obsidian Mirror, Hummingbird-on-the-Left as Blue Obsidian Mirror, the Flayed Lord as Red Obsidian Mirror, and Black Obsidian Mirror were different "Obsidian Mirrors" or one quadriune god, was a question not for the average believer but for the sophisticated religious specialist whose intellectual bent and social position raised this problem to one of religious importance. Paul Radin has shown us that all cultures, even the most primitive, contain men whose temperament is essentially religious and who strive to make the universe coherent and intelligible. Priesthoods everywhere have attracted such individuals, and there can be no doubt that the Mexica were confronted with intellectual imperatives, as well as with military and political ones. They had to ask questions regarding the relation of their own gods to the gods of the people they conquered or overran; and one solution was to make the various gods incarnations of each other, so that a Flayed God might be an Obsidian Mirror in certain of his attributes, just as God, the Son of God, and the Holy Ghost could be incarnations of each other in one context and distinguishable concepts in another.

Hand in hand with this process of building a systematic or more systematized pantheon, went a process of esoteric elaboration in which the same symbol could stand for one or more referents, or one referent could be represented by wholly different symbols. One way in which referents and symbols could thus be extended was through the use of a concept of duality which could make things magically the same, and yet magically different. Thus the Plumed Serpent, in his role as the planet Venus, could be both morning star and evening star; or he could be magically split into twins, one of whom—the morning star—lived in the east and bore the color red, while the other—the evening star—was associated with the west and the color white. The night sky and the earth were to some extent opposite, and yet magically the same, while terrestrial phenomena could be linked to astral bodies. Thus an earth goddess, Obsidian Butterfly, could also be the moon; stags or fish could be the stars. It was thus possible to symbolize the struggle of the growing moon who feeds on the stars by showing Obsidian Butterfly feeding on stag hearts.

This esoteric component of Middle American religion undoubtedly received further impetus through the use of religious symbols in divination. In Middle American divination, days, and the fate of men born on those days, are associated with the several directions of the cosmos, with animals, plants, colors, good or evil, and with the gods with their several complicated attributes. Any divinatory system must allow for some choice in interpretation, to allow for the exercise of skill in forecasting. Thus even in a small modern village in Guatemala, Todos Santos Cuchumatán, the 30-odd curers and diviners use at least five different systems of divination, each involving different associations of symbols. This process is an old one in Middle America, and the complexities of the pantheon may well have been reinforced by the requirements of divinatory practice.

Finally, every religion lends itself to interpretation, and differences in interpretation are one of the causes of religious growth and development. As old values fail and new values grip the imagination of people, new thoughts make for new religious formulations. The expressive forms used may remain the same, and yet express a wholly different spirit. As Mexica society consolidated itself, and the tasks of administration and trade became as important as warfare, there also developed a series of alternate cults, as reflexes of the social situation. We have already mentioned the growth of monotheism in Texcoco. It centered upon the cult of Tloque Nahuaque or Ipalnemohuani, the God of the Immediate Present or the God to Whom We All Owe Our Lives. Their counterparts in Tenochtitlán, never as fully developed as in the allied Acolhua domain,

148

were interpretations of the cult of the Shining Serpent which—not unlike Christianity—stressed peaceful and sober behavior, though always within the context of a dominant militarist cosmology.

The coming of the Spaniards in 1519 thus found most of Middle America united under the Mexica aegis. From their island redoubt in the lagoon of Texcoco, their armies ranged far afield, to quell disturbances on the Pacific coast of the southern highland or to secure the main route of trade into the southeastern highlands against Mixtec and Zapotec opposition. Yet their power proved more apparent than real. There is little profit in predicting what might have happened had the Mexica been able to work out their destiny undisturbed. Perhaps they would have consolidated and integrated their vast holdings more efficiently and more competently than they managed to do in their brief span of absolute domination. Yet, in essence, the Mexica remained little more than a band of pirates, sallying forth from their great city to loot and plunder and to submit vast areas to tribute payment, without altering the essential social constitution of their victims.

The Mexica might drag off the gods of the defeated to put them under lock and key at Tenochtitlán, or effect a political marriage between a defeated king and their own ruling line. In and around the valley of Mexico they might on occasion assign land to the use of their own nobles. In most of Middle America, however, they allowed the population to retain both their traditional customs and their traditional rulers, reminding them of their binding duties to Tenochtitlán only by inviting their underlings to witness a display of mass sacrifice in their lacustrine capital. In this loose domination of the periphery from a strong center, they remind one of the Assyrians of the Middle East rather than a Pharaonic Egypt or the Inca of Peru. Just as the Assyrian armies swept annually into the mountains of Kurdistan and Persia or returned time after time to sack the rich cities of the Levant, but then retreated into their strongholds in the Valley between the Rivers, so the Mexica preferred the fast raid to permanent occupation, the incursion of tribute gatherers to per-

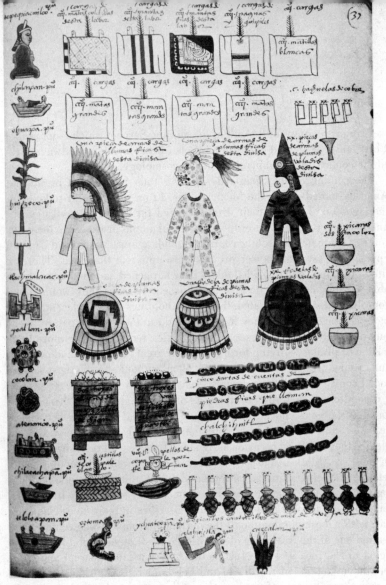

Mexica tribute list for towns in Guerrero, southern highland. (From Codex Mendoza.) The area paid tribute in costly mantles, military uniforms, shields, precious gourds, lime-leaved sage and amaranth, and jade.

manent administration. Thus also they left intact not only the traditional alignments of their subject populations but also hatred of the conquerors, a fact the Spaniards were quick to realize and to exploit.

Nor was the area of Mexica domination ever of one piece. Within the body of the "empire" there remained large areas that either retained their complete independence or felt the weight of Mexica power only intermittently. Thus near the very borders of their valley lay two Chichimec states, wholly independent of the Mexica, Tlaxcala and Metztitlán. The Mexica surrounded Tlaxcala and cut it off from its trade contacts on the coast, but they never subdued it. Nor did the Mexica fare well in their battles with the Tarascan kingdom to the west. Though they attempted several times to penetrate the Tarascan defenses, they were thrown back each time in ignominious defeat. Similarly they retained but a weak grip on their main trade route to Guatemala. While they successfully manned a series of garrisons along the way to the rich cacao lands of Soconusco, the country to either side of the trade route remained in the hands of Mixtec or Zapotec kings, only tenuously subjected to Mexica dictation. Into Maya-speaking Yucatán they never penetrated. There numerous small warring principalities, heirs of Epigonal Toltec dynasties, maintained their fragmented independence until the coming of the Spaniards. In social and political organization, these tiny units closely duplicated the Mexica pattern, with its hereditary ruler committed to human sacrifice and warfare, its monopolistic nobility, its fictitious kinship units linking nobles and commoners, and its slaves.

The rule of the Mexica thus had its inherent limitations. Possessed of a powerful apparatus for conquest, they did not overcome the essentially insular character of Middle American society. They merely terrorized the constituent islands into temporary submission. As they sowed the dragon's teeth of terror, they reaped the whirlwind. As a society and as a culture, they were doomed to disappear in a holocaust of their own creation.

VIII

Conquest
of
Utopia

In 1492, Christopher Columbus, sailing under the flag of Castile, discovered the islands of the Caribbean and planted upon their shores the standard of his sovereigns and the cross of his Savior. From these islands, the newcomers began to probe the Middle American coast. In Easter week, 1519, a young adventurer, Hernán Cortés—lawyer by professional training and military man through baptism of fire on Santo Domingo —landed in the vicinity of San Juan de Ulua in Veracruz. He brought with him an army of 508 soldiers—32 of whom were crossbowmen and carried harquebuses—16 horses, and 14 pieces of artillery, together with a navy of 11 ships and 100 sailors. In July and August of that year, Cortés beached his ships and embarked on the conquest of Tenochtitlán. Two years later, on August 13, 1521, Tenochtitlán fell into Spanish hands. One cycle of history had come to an end and another cycle began.

How is one to explain this sudden irreversible change in the fate of Middle America? The entire enterprise of the Spanish Conquest seems shrouded in a curious air of unreality. Hernán Cortés conquers an empire embracing millions of people. For lack of holy water, a Fray Pedro

152

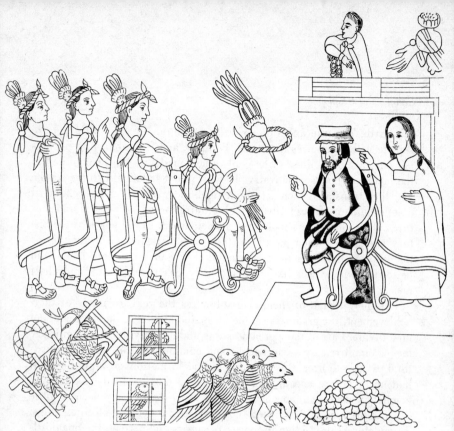

The encounter between Cortés and Moctezuma, as shown in the post-Conquest Lienzo de Tlaxcala. Behind Cortés stands his Indian mistress and adviser Malintzin. (Courtesy of American Museum of Natural History.)

de Gante baptizes hundreds of thousands of Indians with his saliva. A Nuñez Cabeza de Vaca sets out to find the golden cities of Cíbola and the Fountain of Youth, to be shipwrecked, reduced to starvation, nearly eaten by cannibals, only to return to the fray as soon as he is rescued. Actors, acts, and motives seem superhuman: their lust for gold and for salvation, their undivided loyalty to a distant monarch, their courage in the face of a thousand obstacles seem to defy simple psychological explanations. They not only made history; they struck poses against the backdrop of history, conscious of their role as makers and shakers of this earth. The utterances of a Cortés, a Panfilo Narváez, a Garay, are replete with references to Caesar, Pompey, and Hannibal. Cortés plays not only at being himself; he is also the Amadís of Gaul celebrated in the medieval books of chivalry. They were not satisfied with the simple act; they translated each act into a symbolic statement, an evocation of a superhuman purpose. Struck with admiration of their deeds and postures, their chroniclers took them at their word. In the pages of the history books these men parade in the guise of their own evaluation of themselves: half centaurs, pawing the ground with their hoofs and bellowing with voices like cannon, half gods, therefore, and only half men.

But their image of themselves obscures the real greatness of their achievement, for greatness can be measured only on a human scale, not on a divine. Part of their greatness was undoubtedly due to the military tactics employed by a courageous and cunning general. The Spaniards used cavalry to break through the massed formations of an enemy that had never before encountered horses; they thus avoided hand-to-hand combat in which gunpowder and iron arms would have been of little avail in the face of the wicked Indian swords, beset with obsidian chips. To counteract the Indian firepower of spears and arrows, the Spaniards used the crossbow, the instrument that gained them such a decisive victory in the great battle of Pavia against the remnants of French knighthood. When Spanish cavalry, artillery, and infantry proved impotent against Indian canoes manned by archers in the canals and lagoons surrounding Tenochtitlán, Cortés again carried the battle to the enemy, attacking the embattled capital across the water, from the boards of thirteen ships built on the spot.

None of these military successes would have been possible, however, without the Indian allies Cortés won in Middle America. From the first, he enlisted on his side rulers and peoples who had suffered grievously at the hands of their Mexica enemies. In a decisive way, as Ralph Beals has put it, "the conquest of Tenochtitlán was less a conquest than it was

The Spaniards attack the great temple at Tenochtitlán. (From the Lienzo de Tlaxcala. Courtesy of American Museum of Natural History.)

a revolt of dominated peoples." Spanish firepower and cavalry would have been impotent against the Mexica armies without the Tlaxcaltec, Texocans and others who joined the Spanish cause. They furnished the bulk of the infantry and manned the canoes that covered the advance of the brigantines across the lagoon of Tenochtitlán. They provided, transported, and prepared the food supplies needed to sustain an army in the field. They maintained lines of communication between coast and highland, and they policed occupied and pacified areas. They supplied the raw materials and muscular energy for the construction of the ships that decided the siege of the Mexica capital. Spanish military equipment and tactics carried the day, but Indian assistance determined the outcome of the war.

In an ultimate sense, the time was ripe for a redress in the balance of power in Middle America. Even Moctezuma, in his abode at Tenochtitlán, must have felt this, for we can read in his hesitations, in his hearkening to omens of doom, evidence of the doubt and uncertainty

155

which was gnawing at the vitals of Mexica domination. The Spaniards provided the indispensable additional energy required to reverse the dominant political trend. Yet they were not mere agents of the indigenous will, mere leaders of an indigenous revolt. Cortés' genius lay precisely in his ability to play this role, to surround himself with charisma in the eyes of the Indians. Cortés played this role to the hilt, but with calculated duplicity. For the Spaniards had not come to Middle America to restore an indigenous society. They acted from autonomous motives which were not those of their Indian allies. Accepting the command of a people deeply accustomed to obedience through long participation in a hierarchical social order, they began to enact their own purposes, to realize their own ends, which were those of Spanish society and therefore alien and hostile to those of the Indians among whom they had begun to move.

To understand these ends, we must try to understand Spanish society of that time, a task in which we moderns experience a particular difficulty. The reduced and impoverished Spain of today obscures our understanding of the once wealthy and powerful empire upon which the sun never set. All too often, we tend to interpret the past by reconstructing it in the image of the present. Again, too often, we view Spain through the lens of a powerful political mythology, a mythology forged both consciously and unconsciously in Protestant countries to advance the liberating cause of Protestantism and republican institutions against Catholicism and monarchical absolutism. According to this mythology, a singularly partisan deity ranged himself on the side of human freedom and economic progress against "feudal" Spain. While in northern Europe right-thinking and industrious men put their shoulders to the wheel of the Industrial Revolution, the Catholic South remained sunk in medieval sloth. But the rise and decline of a society is not explained by recourse to political demonology; the truth is at once simpler and more complex.

Let us not forget that the Mediterranean and not the European North is the homeland of capitalism and of the Industrial Revolution. Italy,

156

southern France, Spain, and southern Germany witnessed the rise of the first factories, the first banks, the first great fairs. At the time of the discovery of America, the Iberian Peninsula harbored thriving cities, humming with expanding wealth and trade. The sources of this prosperity were manifold: the sale of wool to England or to Flanders; the sale of iron wares to the Levant; the seizure and sale of slaves from the African coast; the quick raid on a Saracen stronghold or a pirate's lair. These were enterprises which demanded the utmost in individual stamina and personal valor; they were also exceedingly profitable. And in response the culture which fed upon an extension of these enterprises elaborated its peculiar image of the manly ideal: the overweening personality possessed of skill and courage. This ideal belonged as much to the medieval past as to the commercial future. It was inherently contradictory and revealed in its contradiction the opposing forces at work within the social system that gave it birth. Its heroes act; but the cultural forms of their acts are not only rich in the symbolic pageantry of the medieval knight-crusader but also supreme examples of the exaltation of Renaissance man pioneering on new frontiers of thought and human behavior. Covertly, more than once, the goal of the act is profit, conceived as personal enhancement through the acquisition of gold and riches.

There were in reality two Spains, or two tendencies at work in the Iberian Peninsula. The first tendency was aristocratic, oriented toward warfare and the gain of riches by warfare. It was exemplified most clearly by the armies of Castile, composed of a warlike nobility and a warlike peasantry. These armies had been forged in the fight against the Moors, first in raid and counterraid, later in the systematic reconquest of the Moorish southland. The nobility, partly organized into religious orders of monastic warriors, saw in warfare a ready source of ego enhancement and looted wealth. Its traditional economic interest lay in the extension of grazing range for its herds of cattle and sheep, coupled with a flourishing export trade in wool to northern Europe. The peasantry, on the other hand, consisted of soldier-cultivators, recruited into the army by promises and guaranties of freedom from servile encumbrances and charters of local self-rule. These peasants desired land, free land, to divide among their sons. In warfare, both nobility and peasantry gained their divergent ends.

The other Spain, the other Spanish trend, was less involved in warfare; it pointed toward capital accumulation through rising industry and trade in the hands of a town-based bourgeoisie. Such entrepreneurs existed in all Peninsular towns; but only in eastern Spain, centered in Catalonia, had they gained sufficient power to check the expansionist desires of the aristocratic soldiery. In this part of Spain, a bloody peasant war had smashed the remnants of a feudal system of the classic European kind. Traditional relationships in which a lord exercised economic, judicial, and social control of a group of serfs had given way to new social ties. A free peasantry populated the countryside; a prosperous bourgeoisie, long oriented toward maritime trade, controlled the towns The country was undergoing incipient industrialization, and the cloth, leather, and iron wares so produced were exchanged in the eastern Mediterranean for the drugs, dyestuffs, and luxury goods of the Orient.

By 1492, these two Spains were headed for collision, a conflict which might well have altered the face of Spain but for the discovery of America. The fall of the last Moorish redoubt put an end to the limitless acquisition of land by conquest and to the easy accumulation of wealth by forceful seizure; 1492 marked the closing of the Spanish frontier. As land became scarce, interests which had run parallel up to that time began to conflict; while the soldier-peasant wanted unencumbered land, the aristocrat wanted open range for sheep and cattle or land for dependent cultivators. With the distribution of the fruits of conquest among the conquerors, moreover, readily available wealth became unavailable. How was new wealth to be produced? To this problem the merchant-entrepreneur of the towns had an answer: capital investment in industry coupled with the reduction of aristocratic power. At this moment, how-

158

ever, the doors to the New World swung wide open to reveal a new frontier: dream cities of gold, endless expanses of land, huge reservoirs of dependent labor. The merchant-entrepreneur receded into obscurity; the knight-adventurer, the visionary of wealth through seizure at sword's point, gained new impetus.

It was this new frontier which settled the fate of Spain. Paradoxically, Spanish industry was to be swamped in a tide of gold from the Indies, which spelled its ultimate ruin; paradoxically, also, the new frontier destroyed the class which might have carried such industrialization to a successful conclusion. For in this New World, all men—peasant, merchant, impoverished noble, noble merchant-prince—could dream of becoming lords of land, Indians, and gold. Men who in Spain might have allied themselves politically and economically with the entrepreneurs and traders of the towns against the aristocrat could in this new venture identify themselves with the ideal of the mounted noble. Men who in Spain might have spurred the growth of the middle classes were here converted into its opponents. The year 1492 might have marked Spain's awakening to a new reality; instead, it marked the coming of a new dream, a new utopia.

Where men of varied pasts and varied interests engage in a common enterprise, belief in a universal utopia renders possible their common action. Utopia asks no questions of reality; it serves to bind men in the service of a dream. Belief in it postpones the day of reckoning on which the spoils will be divided and men will draw their swords to validate their personal utopia against the counterclaims of their comrades-in-arms. Some came to the New World to find gold; others to find order; still others to save souls. Yet in their common dream they asked no questions of one another. For the time being, their dream was validated by their common experience on board ship, by their common sufferings in the face of the enemy, by their common victory.

In the course of their common adventure in utopia they also achieved a set of common usages and understandings which made "the culture of the Conquest" different from their ancestral culture and from the culture still to be in the New World. Their purposes had a transcendental simplicity: gold, subjects, souls. This simplicity patterned their behavior and their thought, some of it conscious, self-imposed. The colonist-to-be in search of his liberty casts off the traditional forms which he has experienced as shackles and encumbrances. The royal official in search of order abhors the tangle of inherited forms of the Old World. The friar leaves behind him a world which is old and corrupt; in utopia he seeks austerity and clarity. The very process of migration produces a simplified stock of cultural forms.

Men drawn from all walks of life, the conquerors were not a complete sample of their ancestral society. They did not bring with them complete knowledge of the gamut of Spanish culture. Some of this age-old heritage they could not reproduce in the New World because they lacked acquaintance with it. Some of it, however, vanished in the crucible of their common experience, in their need to develop a common cultural denominator to facilitate their common task. Spain, but recently unified under one crown, had remained a cultural plural, a mosaic of many parts. Yet the culture of the conquerors was, by contrast, highly homogeneous. This simplification extended to material goods: only one plow, of the many Spanish plows, was transmitted to the New World; only a few techniques of fishing were selected from the plethora of Spanish fishing techniques and transplanted into the new setting. Simplification extended also to symbolic behavior: speech undergoes a leveling, a planing-down of the formalities of Castilian Spanish into a plain and utilitarian idiom. Left behind are the many Spanish folk fiestas in honor of a multitude of beloved local saints; they yield in the New World to the measured and standardized performance of the formal celebrations of way stations in the life of Christ. The culture of the conquest was, as George Foster has pointed out, *sui generis*. In vain one looks in the culture of these men for the rich varied regional heritage of the mother country.

Some of the conquerors wanted gold—gold, the actual tangible substance, not the intangible "promises to pay" of later capitalism. In this they were children of their times, caught in the contradiction between medieval magic and the modern search for profits. All over Europe men longed for gold, encountered gold in dreams, dug for it under trees and in caves, sold their souls to the devil for it, labored over retorts to obtain it from base metals such as•iron or lead. It was a kind of illness, and Cortés stated it that way—half cynically and half realistically—in addressing the first Mexica noble he met: "The Spaniards are troubled with a disease of the heart for which gold is the specific remedy." The illness was greed, but beyond greed the desire for personal liberty, escape of the ego from bondage to other men, "spiritual autarchy," as Eliseo Vivas has said, "which is achieved only when you are able to say to another man, *a mi no me manda nadie*—no one bosses me; I am lord because I have land and gold and Indians, and I need not beg any favors from you or any one else." This is the new self-made man talking, the medieval adventurer on the threshold of capitalism, knight-errant in cultural form but primitive capitalist in disguise. The goal is medieval—never again to bend one's will to that of another—but the instrument is modern: the instrument of wealth.

Utopia thus bears at the outset the mark of a contradiction between past and future, a contradiction never wholly overcome. The contradiction is most startlingly illuminated when the Spanish entrepreneur is compared with his contemporary English rival. "The Englishmen," says Salvador de Madariaga, "though on the surface more self-seeking, were in depth more socially minded; the Spaniards, though in appearance more statesmanlike and creative, more intent on 'ennobling' cities and setting up kingdoms, were more self-centered. The Englishman, with his dividends, socialized his adventures, gain, booty; the Spaniard, with his hospitals, foundations, cathedrals, colleges and marquisates, raised a monument to his own self. . . ." The rise of puritanism in the Anglo-American world, so brilliantly analyzed by Max Weber and Richard

Tawney, destroyed the contradiction between individual goals and cultural means. For in accepting the Protestant ethic of work and capital accumulation as virtue, the entrepreneur made himself an instrument of production, harnessed himself to the process of capital formation. In Anglo-America, the very means thus became the ends; in Ibero-America, means and ends remained at war with one another, contradictory, unresolved.

If some came in search of gold and its promise of personal liberty, others came in search of order. Their deity was the absolute monarch; their religion the new religion of the reason of state. At the end of the fifteenth century the Spanish crown had just emerged victorious in its political battles against its rivals. With the help of the rising middle classes and the peasantry, it had successfully defeated the attempts of the aristocrats who wished to reduce the king once again to the passive position of a mere *primus inter pares*. Yet this political success but threatened to put the king into the hands of the penny-wise merchants who wished to trade support for a veto over his military and bureaucratic expenditures. The long period of the reconquest had also brought with it a spate of *fueros* or local charters which exempted one or the other local or professional body from the application of the general law; many a king had traded local autonomy for support against the Moorish enemy.

In the conquest of the New World, the crown saw its opportunity to escape the limitations of internal Spanish politics. Gold from the Indies would enrich not only the eager adventurer; a fifth of all gold and silver mined in the New World would be the king's, to finance a royal army, navy, and officialdom, to build the bases of absolutist power upon institutions wholly independent of nobility, middle classes, or peasant cultivators. Wealth from the Indies would underwrite a state standing above all classes, above the endless quarrels of contending interest groups. This state would speak with a new voice, with a new will. It would no longer be bound by precedent; it would set aside solutions which had become traditional, overgrown with the "cake of custom" and with compromise.

162

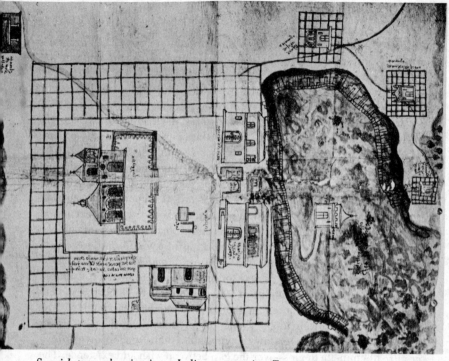

*Spanish town planning in an Indian community: Teutenanco, now
Tenango del Valle, Mexico, about 1580. (From Francisco del Paso y Troncoso,
Papeles de la Nueva España [Madrid: Tip. Sucesores de Rivadeneyra, 1905].
Courtesy of George Kubler.)*

The New World would not have to grow, piecemeal, in the shadows of
ancient complexities: it would be a planned world, projected into reality
by the royal will and its executioners. Thus utopia would become law,
and law utopian. If Spanish towns had been small, cramped within their
rings of fortifications, crowded around small irregular squares, then the
towns of the New World would be large, open, unfortified; built upon
the gridiron plan; centered upon a spacious square dominated by church

163

and city-hall as twin symbols of sacred and secular power; an architectural utopia conceived by Italian architect-dreamers and built in the New World by royal mandate.

Was it true that many Indians lived in scattered hamlets instead of stationary, circumscribed, concentrated settlements? Then let there be a law to force them to live in nucleated towns, each with its own church, each surrounded by its own fields—within a measured radius of 560 yards from the church steeple—so that they could learn to order their lives to the tolling of church bells and to the commands of royal officers. Land and people of utopia had both been conquered by the sword; but it would be the dry scratching of the goose-quill pen upon parchment that would turn utopia into reality. Let each Indian keep twelve chickens and six turkeys and sell them for no more than 4 reales per turkey and $1\frac{1}{2}$ reales per chicken; let each Indian working in a textile mill receive a daily ration of eighteen tortillas or fourteen tamales, plus chili, chickpeas, and beans. No problem was too insignificant to demand solution, and all solutions were solutions of law. Utopia was to be born also with this fatal deficiency implicit in the contradiction of law and reality. Reality is too protean to be wholly covered by law; it soon grows through, around, and over law, leaving but a hollow shell of words, a gesture of etiquette to gloss over the gap between wish and existence. The Latin American world still bears this legacy of law as a gesture to initiate action, to create a new order, and—when the energy of the gesture is spent—to use the law as wish, to wipe out a reality grown beyond law and order, beyond utopia.

Utopia contained many houses. If some men longed for gold, to build upon it their untrammeled liberty, and if others sought Indian subjects to rule and exercise in the spirit of the new order, so there were men who came to save souls. Upon the ruins of pagan shrines and idols in a new continent filled with souls hungry for salvation, yet uncorrupted by the age-old vices of the Old World, they would erect their own utopia: the prelude on earth of the Kingdom of Heaven. To these prophets of sal-

164

vation, the conquest of the New World was the call to a great spiritual task: the defeat of Satan in his own redoubt, the redemption of souls languishing in his power, the annunciation of the faith in the one true God. The shock troops of this new faith were the friars, members of the monastic orders, strongly influenced by the reformist religious currents of the times. In some countries, such movements were soon to feed the flames of the Protestant revolution. If this did not happen in Spain, it was not because Spain lacked inflammable intellectual tinder. The economic and political development of the country had given strong impetus to men who began to question long-accepted opinions and to explore new interpretations of Catholicism. Most of these questioners were influenced by Erasmus of Rotterdam (1466–1536), whose teaching de-emphasized the importance of formal ritual and stressed the promptings to piety of an "inner" voice, and by the utopian and reformist thought of Thomas More (1478–1535) and Luis Vives (1492–1540).

The reason that this new religious current did not explode into open rebellion against accepted religious forms is to be found in the character of the Spanish state and the circumstances which surrounded it rather than in the intellectual heterodoxy of the movement. The Spanish state had no need to break with the papacy: it dictated ecclesiastical appointments in its own territory; it possessed the right to read and suppress papal bulls before making them public; it controlled the office of the Inquisition; it even sponsored autonomy in doctrinal matters through its support of the belief in the immaculate conception of the Virgin Mary, long before this belief became official church dogma at the Council of Trent (1545–63). In other European states the hunger for land and capital was one of the chief underlying motives for religious reformation; after the break with Rome, the estates of the church were divided among the members of the Protestant faction. In Spain, the frontiers had not yet closed. Until 1492 land and wealth were still to be had by fighting the Moors in southern Spain in the name of religion, and that year witnessed the opening of the new frontier in the New World, with its promise of gold and glory for all takers.

Under Cardinal Ximénez de Cisneros, the Erasmists received royal approval. The crown saw in their effort to restore the simplicity and austerity of primitive Christianity—in the face of decay and corruption—a spiritual counterpart to its own efforts to centralize Spain and to endow the new empire with a unified sense of mission. Many of the friars who came to the New World had taken part in this religious renewal. The first twelve friars to set foot in New Spain—the so-called Apostolic Twelve—had all worked to spread the gospel of primitive Christendom in southern Spain. Fray Juan de Zumárraga (1461?–1548), the first archbishop of Mexico, was a follower of Erasmus and familiar with the utopian writings of Sir Thomas More. Vasco de Quiroga (1470–1565), the first bishop of Michoacán, actually established a replica of Sir Thomas More's Utopia among the Indian communities of his bishopric. All these soldiers of the faith favored poverty over wealth, communal property over private property. Carefully they labored to purge Catholicism of the accumulation of ritual, selecting from the profusion of religious ritual only the major ceremonials celebrating the way-stations of Christ's life. This desire for purity and simplicity they also expressed in their great single-naved churches, symbolic of the homogeneity of primitive Christian worship, uncluttered by devotion to smaller altars and lateral naves.

The utopia of gold and liberty crumbled in the tension between exaltation of the self, through valiant deeds, and wealth, the instrument selected for their validation. The utopia of order remained arrested in the legal gesture, attempting to stem the tide of real behavior. The utopia of faith, too, was to founder, hoped-for morality all too often impotent in the face of stubborn secular demand. And yet, conversion proved a success. The romanticists have long delighted in discovering the idols behind altars, the Gods of the Cave transformed into Christs hanging upon the Cross, the earth goddesses disguised as Catholic Virgins, the braziers

166

burning copal gum on the steps of the churches, and other evidences of pre-Conquest heritage in the religious beliefs and practices of modern Indians. There is much that is Indian in the Catholicism of Middle America; but more surprising than the numerous survivals of pre-Conquest ideas and rituals is the organizational success of the Catholic utopia in a country of different religions and languages. Wherever you go in Middle America, you encounter the images of the Catholic saints and the churches built by the conquerors. Christ and the Virgin may have been transmuted by the adoration of men who had worshipped the Sun and the Moon and the Earth and the Lords of the Four Directions; but when an Indian speaks of a human being today, he does not say "a man"; he says "a Christian," a believer.

How is this success to be explained? It is easy to dismember men with cannons; it is more difficult to tame their minds. Certainly military defeat played a part, because it provided a visible demonstration of the impotence and decadence of the Mexica gods. The Children of the Sun had died by the sword as they had lived by the sword. The old gods had failed. When the Spaniards had demanded that the Totonac of Cempoala destroy their idols, the people had recoiled in horror; yet when the conquerors hurled the idols to the ground and broke them to pieces, the idols had remained mute and defenseless. They had not smitten the foreigners; they had failed to show the power that was in them. When the priests released the stones from the Pyramid of Cholula which held back the magic water that was in the mountain so that it would drown the strange men in a flood, the channel remained dry, and their magic deserted them. When the Children of the Sun, the Toltec rulers of Tenochtitlán, called down the wrath of their terrible idol Hummingbird-on-the-Left upon their enemies, Hummingbird-on-the-Left remained silent. The mutilated idols of their gods now rested on the bottom of the lake from which they had set out to conquer the universe for the sun; and the rubble of their temples served as fill for the new city of Mexico which was to arise upon these ruins. The old gods were dead, and powerless.

Not that these old gods had been so greatly loved. We know—or we can guess—that the will of these gods and the burden of human sacrifice rested heavily upon the land. Worship of warrior gods and human sacrifice were religious activities consonant with the military character of Mexica expansion. Inevitably, however, peace and political consolidation brought to the fore alternative religious explanations of a less militaristic character. Quetzalcoatl, the Shining Serpent, served as a symbolic form through which these new interpretations and longings could find expression. His latter-day attributes as a harbinger of peaceful productivity and human wisdom bear surprising similarity to the ideological dictates of Christianity. Indeed, the Spanish friars came to believe that Quetzalcoatl had been none other than the apostle Thomas, come to the New World to convert the Indians. The longing for peace and for an

168

end to bloodshed provided a fertile soil for the diffusion of the Christian message.

Both religions, moreover, believed in a structured and ordered supernatural world, in which more powerful, unseen, and unfathomable divinities stood above local supernatural mediators of lesser scope and power that were yet more immediately tangible. The Middle American peasant, like his Spanish counterpart, focused his religious interest on these lowlier supernatural helpers. He was more interested in the powers that affected his crops, his children, his family, and the people with whom he was in immediate and personal contact, than in the ultimate powers and their manifestations, which absorbed the interest of the religious specialist. Among the gods of a multi-headed pantheon, his daily concern was with the gods of the earth, fertility, rain and water, with illness, with the immediate short-range future, with the malevolence of his neighbors. Where the Spanish peasant worshipped wooden saints, the Middle American peasant worshipped clay idols; both had recourse to the magical practices of folk medicine; both had a strong sense of omens; and both believed in the reality of witches who could be ordinary everyday people during the day and malevolent spirits in animal disguise at night.

The priests, the specialists of both religions, on the other hand, were the heirs of rich and complex intellectual traditions, trained in the esoteric interpretation of religious symbols whether these symbols concerned multiple incarnations of Tezcatlipoca or the implications of the Revelation of St. John the Divine. The concern of the priest was not the concern of the peasant, and yet the same religious structure could embrace both. As long as the priests remained in command, as ultimate mediators between gods and men and ultimate interpreters of this relationship, men could adapt the manifold religious patterns to suit their personal and local concerns. What was true of religious concerns also held true of gods. A god could be one or triune, unique or multiple, and interpretation could stress his oneness at one time, his multiplicity at an-

169

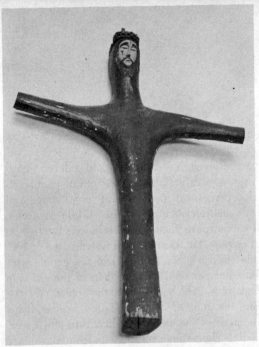

Our Lord of the Tree. This image, to which miraculous powers were ascribed after it was rescued intact from a burning church, is now in the State Museum of Michoacán, Morelia, Mexico. It represents an interesting fusion of pre-Hispanic and post-Hispanic artistic and religious concepts.
(*Copyright 1951 by Pál Kelemen. Reproduced by permission from* Baroque and Rococo in Latin America [*New York: Macmillan Co., 1951*]. *Photograph by Elizabeth Z. Kelemen.*)

other. The Mexica pantheon had embraced many local gods, and the Mexica priesthood had labored to equate these gods with their own inherited deities or with one another. The Catholic Church had a similar tradition of flexibility. Just as the cloak of the Virgin hid many a local Persephone or Isis along the shores of the European Mediterranean, or as an Odin hanging himself from the tree of life became a Christ, so a Hummingbird-on-the-Left became a Spanish St. James riding down upon the heathens; a Tlaloc, a Christian Señor de Sacromonte; a God of the Cave, the Lord of Chalma; and Our Lady Spirit, the Virgin of Guadalupe.

The Catholic Church drove out the priests of the old gods and manned

170

the pivotal points of the religious hierarchy with men ordained in its own cult. It destroyed the old idols and put an end to human sacrifices, burned the sacred picture books and relegated to oblivion much of the calendric and divinatory knowledge of its predecessors; but it also offered the common man a way in which he could cast his traditional attachments into new forms. The Catholic Church, like the solar religion of the Mexica rigid at the heights of command but flexible on the level of the peasant household, built a bridge from the old order to the new. As Frank Tannenbaum has said, "It gave the Indian an opportunity . . . to save his faith in his own gods."

This transition from the old to the new was eased also by an astonishing similarity in ritual and symbol between the old and the new religion. A Nahua or an Otomí would hardly know what to make of a Spanish friar who, hampered by the language barrier, pointed first to the sky to indicate heaven and then to earth to indicate hell, as a first lesson in Catholic catechism. But rituals can be observed and learned by imitation. Both religious traditions had a rite of baptism. In Catholicism, the child was baptized and named, thus including him among the true believers. The Mexica similarly bathed and named the child in a religious rite, and the Maya celebrated with a ceremony the first time the child was carried astride the hip. Both religious traditions had a kind of confession. The Mexica and the inhabitants of the Gulf coast confessed their sexual transgressions to a priest of the earth goddess Filth-Eater; the Zapotec had annual public confessions; and the Maya confessed themselves either to priests or members of their families in case of illness. Both religious traditions possessed a ritual of communion. The Catholics drank wine and swallowed a wafer to symbolize their contact with the divine blood and body of Christ; the Mexica consumed images of the gods made of amaranth and liberally anointed with sacrificial blood. Both people used incense in their churches; both fasted and did penance; both went on pilgrimages to holy places; both kept houses of celibate virgins. Both believed in the existence of a supernatural mother; and

171

both believed in virgin birth. Where Catholics held that Mary conceived immaculately through the power of the Holy Spirit, the Mexica believed that their goddess Coatlícue had given birth to Hummingbird-on-the-Left, impregnated by an obsidian knife which fell from the sky. Both people made use of the cross. A white St. Andrew's Cross, representing the four directions of the universe, often graced the hat and shield of the Shining Serpent, and the Maya made frequent use of the symbol of the foliated cross. The Spaniards represented their sacred stories in passion plays; the Middle Americans represented the annual changes of vegetation and activities in their sacrifices.

The Catholic missionaries well recognized the danger which lay in the maintenance of similar outward forms of ritual upon conversion. Yet they were themselves unable to decide whether these similarities were merely the work of Satan laboring to duplicate in his hellish church the rituals of the church sanctified by God, or whether they might not indeed represent the precipitate of some previous Christian teaching, brought to the New World perhaps by no less a personage than the apostle Thomas. Whatever their doubts, the formal similarities between the two religious traditions permitted an easy transition for the worshipper and gave him continuity precisely in the realm in which continuity was vital: the realm of religious behavior.

Nor did the psychology of Spanish Catholicism differ greatly from the psychology of the Mesoamerican solar cult. The Spanish ideal of the austere knight, defending his honor and the Virgin against Moors or other unbelievers, was not far removed from the Mexica ideal of the jaguar-eagle knight, whose obsidian sword insured victory and sacrificial victims for the hungry deities of war. In both religions cruelty against others in warfare and exalted pride went hand in hand with sacrificial penance—cruelty against the self, performed by a Spanish conqueror in a hairshirt, by a Mexica noble torturing his flesh with the sharp spikes of the century plant.

True to their hierarchical habits, the Spaniards expended their great-

172

est religious effort in converting the nobles, who became their first converts, partly because of the similarity of motivation, partly because of a desire to achieve a secure place in the new Spanish hierarchy through baptism and Christian vows. At Tlaxcala, the first center of the Spanish missionary effort, the local aristocracy strove mightily to reserve for itself a monopoly of all new religious offices, even those of cook, janitor, and gardener in the new monasteries. Their children were the first beneficiaries of Spanish ecclesiastical schooling. They used their power to set the feet of their own tributaries upon the new road to salvation; these tributaries thus came to church, as Fray Mendieta said, "more for the sake of outer appearance, to follow the orders of the *principales* who wanted to deceive them than to find a remedy for their souls." With the nobles firmly dedicated to the worship of the new religion, the commoners could be converted in mass, often with no more than a token understanding of the new divinities they were to worship. Pedro de Gante, exemplary Franciscan and kinsman of Charles V, baptized Indians in Mexico City at a daily rate of 14,000.

To the task of mass conversion, moreover, the church brought an exemplary table of organization. Like the Middle American religion, it drew a line between religious specialists and lay worshippers. In both traditions, the priests were the final spokesmen of the divine realm, in contact with a world to which ordinary men had no access. In both religions, long training was required to make a man worthy of his special role, and in both religions fasts, penances, self-torture, and sexual abstinence were required of priests to maintain their spiritual worth in the sight of the divine powers. Throughout the exercise of their spiritual role on earth, dress, residence, speech, and comportment marked them off from ordinary men. Such parallelism again eased the transition from the worship of the old gods to the worship of the new, maintaining as it did the hierarchy of channels through which supernatural commands were passed down to the lay believer.

To be sure, the Catholic Church was organized internally to take maximum advantage of the opportunities so offered. Its division into holy orders and secular clergy made for great flexibility in a situation where an advance guard was needed to establish new beachheads of the faith, while a rear-guard took over and consolidated the gains. The friars were the advance guard; the abiding missionary work of the sixteenth century which laid the basis for all later religious efforts was probably carried out by no more than one thousand individuals. Established in fortified churches within the core areas of the newly won land, they spread out in "missions of penetration" into areas where Spanish political control was often still in doubt, sometimes ahead of Spanish armies, sometimes in their wake. Always they linked these outposts with their home bases through "liaison missions," to which they could retreat or where they could seek new strength to carry on their task of penetration. The secular clergy, the ordinary priesthood, carried out the work of consolidation.

Inevitably there were quarrels and conflicts of jurisdiction as the work progressed, as well as conflicts of temperament. The holy orders recruited men whose personalities differed markedly from those characteristic of the regular clergy. The friars favored individuals who were more adventurous and utopian in outlook, as well as less amenable to routine and less adapted to the day-to-day life of a going society. The secular clergy showed more conservatism, less of a tendency to sacrifice reality to otherworldly visions and schemes. Thus the larger church benefited by its possession of both kinds of men, both kinds of organization. When the task of conversion was completed, the work of shepherding the flock through its daily tribulations could be turned over to men capable of preserving the gains.

The eventual adjustment of the religious dream to mundane reality was less than utopia, and yet it left an impress on the Indian population such as no other religious or political current has done to this day. Ultimately the message of salvation spelled hope for the Indian, not only hope in the transcendental realm of a supernatural life after death but hope on earth, where utopia was yielding to the pressure of all too

174

secular interests. Men would labor to deny him his humanity, to defend his use as a resource, a tool to be used and discarded at will; but against such claims of politicians, lawyers, and theologians, Pope Paul III would in 1537 assert, in his bull "Sublimis Deus":

The sublime God so loved the human race that He not only created man in such wise that he might participate in the good that other creatures enjoy, but also endowed him with capacity to attain to the inaccessible and invisible Supreme Good and behold it face to face[;] . . . all are capable of receiving the doctrines of the faith. . . . We . . . consider . . . that the Indians are truly men. . . .

To the Indian, the rite of baptism thus proved an assertion of his essential humanity, to be a man with human claims upon other men. Of this right no colonist or royal official could rob him. When the Indian re-emerges from beneath the wreckage of utopia, we find that he has re-built and cemented his new life with bonds drawn from the new religion, at once his opium, his consolation, and his hope of ultimate justice.

IX

New Lords of the Land

The Indian before the Conquest had been a cultivator, a seed-planter. The conquering Spaniard became a mining entrepreneur, a producer of commercial crops, a rancher, a merchant. The strategic economic relationship of the pre-Conquest period united Indian peasant and Indian lord, tribute-producer and tribute-consumer. The goal of the Indian noble was to consume wealth commensurate with his social position. The Spanish colonist, however, labored for different ends. He wanted to convert wealth and labor into salable goods—into gold and silver, hides and wool, wheat and sugar cane. No Spaniard could count himself wealthy as a mere recipient of loads of maize, pieces of jade, or cacao beans. Wealth to him meant wealth invested in Spanish goods, capital multiplying miraculously in the process of exchange. He had not braved the hardships of the Indies merely to come into the inheritance of his Indian predecessor; he wanted to organize and press the human resources under his command, to pay his debts, to enlarge his estate, to take his place among the other men grown rich and powerful in the new utopia.

The motor of this capitalism was mining, carried on first in the footsteps of the Indians, later in deep deposits discovered by Spanish prospectors. The Indians had worked gold and silver before the Conquest, but they had obtained these elements from small placers or shallow pits where the ore-bearing veins ran close to the surface. Spanish exploration for placer mines began very early. Even before the fall of Tenochtitlán, members of Cortés' party had located placers in the headwaters of the Papaloapan and Balsas rivers; shortly after the Conquest, other placers were found on the Caribbean coast of Honduras. Such mining has remained a feature of Middle American life to this day. Cheap, requiring no outlay for mechanical equipment beyond the large wooden bowl or *batea*, it has always been open to the adventurous individual willing to stake his few worldly possessions on the hope of gaining a sudden and overwhelming fortune.

Such small-scale mining, however, was quickly superseded as a major source of capital accumulation. Large and deep deposits of mineral wealth were discovered in 1543, near Compostela, just northwest of modern Guadalajara. In 1546, Zacatecas began to produce silver; in 1548, Guanajuato; in 1549, Taxco, Sultepec, and Temalscaltepec; in 1551, Pachuca; in 1555, Sombrerete and Durango; in 1569, Fresnillo. The year 1557 witnessed the introduction of the patio process in which silver is extracted from ore with the aid of mercury. This process, invented by the Mexican miner Bartolomé de Medina, revolutionized the mining industry. It permitted profitable exploitation of low-grade ores, where the older method of smelting required high-grade ores. So successful was this procedure that it was not replaced until the introduction of the cyanide process in the late nineteenth century. This new exploitation of deep mines was also immensely more expensive than the exploitation of placers. Capital was required to pay for the construction of stamp mills and refineries, for the sinking of shafts and timbering, for the purchase of mules, labor, food, and mercury, for drainage equipment and pumps. Where placer mining remained in the hands of single individuals, laboring to enter the utopia of wealth through a small door,

Mining constituted the motor of New Spanish economy, despite the virtual lack of technological change. This picture shows the interior of the Rayas mine, Guanajuato, Mexico. Carriers averaged burdens of between 225 and 250 pounds on exceedingly steep ascents. (From D. T. Egerton, Egerton's Views of Mexico [London: D. T. Egerton, 1840].)

deep mining produced the capitalist of whom Henrie Hawks, English merchant to New Spain, wrote in 1572 that they were "princes in keeping of their houses, and bountiful in all manner of things." By the end of the sixteenth century, most of the great mining districts of New Spain had been located, and the technology of large-scale capitalist mining was firmly established.

Mining enriched some men; others took to planting and selling agricultural crops. The Indians had raised maize and amaranth for their own consumption and for tribute; but in their new habitat the Spaniards, heirs of different food habits, longed for their native wheat, to turn into their accustomed bread. Using oxen and plow, on land taken over from

178

a pagan temple or from the patrimony of the shattered Mexica state, or uncultivated or purloined—together with the strategic water supply—from some Indian community, new entrepreneurs set out to meet this need for wheat by growing it for the rising cities and the mushrooming mining camps. By the end of the sixteenth century, wheat farms and mills to grind wheat had spread out along the new axis of trade and control linking Mexico City with Veracruz to the east and with Guadalajara to the west, and were fast spreading northward—beyond the confines of pre-Conquest agriculture—to feed the newly opened mines along the arid periphery of Middle America.

In the lowlands, on the other hand, the main crop produced for sale was sugar cane. Cane-farming could be carried on by small-scale operators, using hand-powered or animal-powered mills to grind the cane, but as output rose, sugar-raising—like mining—fast became a large-scale capitalist form of enterprise. The strategic factor in this process was the high cost of a large-scale mill needed to grind the cane. Only a person or a group of persons possessed of considerable wealth could purchase one of these *ingenios* or "engines." In the course of the seventeenth century, the entrepreneurs capable of shouldering such costs proved to be mostly religious bodies, who had accumulated wealth through donations. The output of these large-scale mills, exported in the beginning, also gave rise to the pervading Middle American taste for sweets, immortalized in innumerable shapes and kinds of candy and other confections, and to a new beverage, *aguardiente* or firewater, distilled to a high potency in the novel stills, also imported for the first time by the new lords of the land.

Another product which demanded considerable capital outlay in production was indigo, a blue dye of great natural fastness. Just as deep mining, wheat-farming, and cane-farming, it was taken over entirely by colonist entrepreneurs. Indigo is obtained from the leaves of a shrublike plant (*Indigofera suffruticosa* Mill.), varieties of which are found both in the Old and New World. The pigment is found only in the leaves.

179

Since the amount of pigment per leaf is small, the dye is expensive. The plants are cut, then steeped in water; the sludge formed is allowed to oxidate, then heated, cooled, filtered, and made into paste, cut into bars and finally into the so-called indigo cakes. The first indigo exported came from Guatemala, but it was soon raised elsewhere in the Middle American lowlands, especially in Yucatán. By the fourth quarter of the sixteenth century, more than fifty Spanish-owned indigo "factories" were in operation in the peninsula, each equipped with its mule-driven water pump, its vats and cauldrons. As in the case of sugar production and deep mining, the cost of the mill tended to render indigo production prohibitive to small operators and furthered the emergence of capitalist entrepreneurs in the field. Indigo dye remained a viable commercial product until the advent of aniline dyes in the mid-nineteenth century.

The Spaniards thus reserved to themselves the production, processing, and distribution of all products which required high outlays of capital in processing machinery. They did, however, intrust to the Indians all raising of commercial products which did not require much capital and equipment to produce and process, retaining for themselves the handsome profits of their distribution. Such products were cotton, silk, cacao, and cochineal dye. Cotton production remained largely in Indian hands and was grown along the Pacific and Atlantic coasts of the southern highlands; Spaniards reaped the rewards of its distribution. Cotton-growing was soon supplemented by silk-raising, first upon a mulberry native to Middle America, later upon black mulberries imported from the Old World. The valley of Puebla and the southern highlands benefited especially from this new pursuit; for half a century the Mixtec-speaking highlands became the center of silk production in the New World. Many Indians grew rich in the process, though the major profits went to the Spaniards, who monopolized the spinning and weaving of the new thread. But silk-raising had only a relatively brief period of efflorescence; it was sacrificed to Chinese competition toward the end of the sixteenth century.

Indians laboring on a Spanish estate. (From the post-Hispanic Codex Osuna, written partly in Nahuatl, partly in Spanish.)

Cacao had served the Indians not merely as a beverage but as money, and for some time after the Conquest the cacao bean continued to serve as a ready medium of exchange. Most cacao production remained in Indian hands, with the Spaniards again playing the role of middlemen and distributors. The colonists themselves began to fancy the Indian drink *chocolatl*, prepared from the cacao bean, and soon introduced this new exotic taste into Europe. The Indians also remained the primary producers of cochineal. Cochineal is a source of red dyes produced from insects (*Coccus cacti*) which feed on a cactus (*Cactus nopalea cochinellifera*). About 70,000 dried insects produced one pound of dye. The Indians collected the insects, extracted the dye, and delivered the product to the Spanish entrepreneurs who mediated the trade with Spain. For a long time, New Spain remained the only producer of cochineal. The Spanish government guarded its monopoly jealously; and for the better part of two centuries Europeans remained ignorant of how the dye was produced. Only in the late eighteenth century were the dye-producing insects brought to Spain.

True to their Peninsular tradition, the Spaniards also took up stock-raising: cattle primarily for their hides and tallow, sheep largely for their wool. Leather was then in high demand both in Europe and in New Spain. Leather containers and cables were needed in mines and factories and leather constituted one of the chief requirements of the expanding armies of the day. Wool, on the other hand, was everywhere beginning to replace homespun linen. The Spaniards brought with them two kinds of cattle, the broad and heavy-horned dun type of general European affiliation and the black Iberians, ancestors of the Spanish fighting bull. In sheep they favored the *rasa*, which yields both wool and meat, and the *merino*, which yields fine wool but poor meat, over the hardy *churro*, which yields milk but poor wool. Introduced into an entirely new environment, unaffected by past grazing, the new herds began to multiply at an astonishing rate. Like a flood, they inundated cultivated fields and uncultivated range alike, causing severe dislocations in many settled zones of the central highland, until the crown succeeded in diverting the flood to peripheral areas, the arid north country and the lowlands of the Atlantic and Pacific coastlines. To herd the growing livestock, the Spaniards used their horse, bred to great hardihood from Barb or North African strains crossed with dun and striped indigenous Iberians. Often allowed to roam until needed, these horses formed near-wild herds. Such horses were called *mesteños*, which in the mouths of Anglo-American cowboys was to become "mustang."

Indian nobles and Indian communities quickly adopted the raising of sheep and cattle, but stock-raising as a large-scale enterprise remained in Spanish hands, partly because of laws through which the Spaniards barred Indians from owning horses and retained a monopoly of this

182

New forms of transportation: mule-skinners. (From Carlos Nebel, Viaje pintoresco y arqueológico sobre la parte más interesante de la República Mexicana en los años transcurridos desde 1829 hasta 1834 *[Paris: Imprenta de Pablo Renouard, 1839].)*

means of transportation and warfare for themselves, partly because the Indians were unable to finance expansion into the new grazing lands beyond the old agricultural frontier. Indian stock-raising remained confined to an occasional village herd and to chickens, pigs, mules, and donkeys —the minor domesticated animals introduced by the conquerors. Mediterranean breeds of chickens—Andalusians, Minorcas, Leghorns, and others—came to form an important part of Indian household economy, along with the indigenous turkey. The pigs, driven in droves in the train of advancing Spanish armies to provide them with readily available food, were descendants of razor-backed Spanish breeds. Pork and lard quickly became staple ingredients of Middle American cooking. The donkey, derived from Andalusian breeds, grew smaller and sturdier in adapting to the Middle American environment, and together with the mule became an indispensable source of motor power in mines and mills and on the highroads. Transportation on mule-back gave rise to a whole social group of mule-skinners, or mule-drivers, who traveled from market to market, from city to city, from hostelry to hostelry, linking the country in a great network of back-country trails. Still today, the ancient craft survives in out-of-the-way places such as the Tarascan-speaking uplands of Michoacán or the eastern escarpment, where no other form of transportation provides an adequate alternative.

Together with horses, oxen, mules, and donkeys, came the wheel, long known in the Old World but unknown—or rather not utilized—in the New. The Spaniards brought with them their traditional oxcart, put together with wooden pegs and mounted upon spokeless wheels. That the Indians were acquainted with the basic principle of the wheel is clear from finds of fascinating prehistoric toys, mounted upon rollers, from coastal Veracruz. The principle had never been applied, however, to the construction of wheelbarrows or carts to ease men's burdens, or to the mass production of pottery, or to the transmission of wind and water power. Even today there are many Indian villages where the wheel remains an alien artifact and where men rely on their traditional bodily skills to balance heavy burdens upon their backs with the aid of the tumpline, a leather strap laid across the bowed head.

The newly settled towns of the realm also constituted markets for the products of Spanish craftsmen who brought not only their inherited skills but also their traditional technique of organizing craftsmen into guilds. A guild was an association of specialists who alone possessed the right to exercise a given craft; such guilds also protected members against unfair competition from fellow professionals. Detailed statutes regulated the tools and techniques to be used, the number of workers to be employed, and the salaries to be paid. Advertising was prohibited throughout New Spain. Where the craftsmen themselves did not set up such bodies, the municipality in which they resided organized them on its own initiative, with royal sanction. As in the Old World, the guilds soon competed fiercely with one another for the lesser stakes of prestige and privilege, with the merchant guild (*Consulado*) occupying top rank in status and power.

This new organization of production and distribution soon came into conflict with two opposing forces. The organization of the guild and its regulation of production was geared to an essentially static level of consumption. Strongly monopolistic, it abhorred unregulated competition by outsiders and insiders; in fact, it frowned upon all cumulative capitalist activity. Very soon, therefore, it found itself combating capitalist tendencies, especially in the weaving trades. As Spanish craftsmen settled in the accustomed grooves of life, other Spaniards organized industrial establishments, *obrajes*, for the production of wool and cotton textiles. The basic equipment of these establishments was all of Spanish origin: spinning wheel, reel, cards—the wooden paddles set with iron spikes to clean wool—the horizontal loom with pedals to manipulate the sheds. Some capital was needed also to set up the water-driven machinery (*batán*) for soaking woolens in alkaline solution and for beating them until the fibers were felted together to create a uniform surface. The water powering these fulling mills was more often than not obtained from streams which had previously irrigated Indian fields. To obtain the necessary labor force, the *obrajes* frequently made use of forced labor. Workers were prisoners condemned to work off a sentence or a debt, or simply men held against their will. They included not only Indians but also Negroes from Africa and Oriental slaves imported from the Philippines. The crown attempted to regulate these prison-like establishments and to improve working conditions, but they continued to flourish in the shadow of the law and of guild regulations, building their profits upon the outright exploitation of non-guild labor. Conditions in these prison-like mills did not change until the advent of the first steam-driven machinery in the mid-nineteenth century.

Just as the guilds could not prevent such capitalist competition on the part of their fellow Spaniards, so they also had great difficulty in maintaining their monopoly of skill against the free Indian artisans. All the guilds' codes carried restrictive regulations, prohibiting the access to their professions of Indians or the descendants of Indian-Spanish or Negro-Spanish unions. Yet the Indians proved excellent imitators who learned the skills of the conquerors in an astonishingly short period of

185

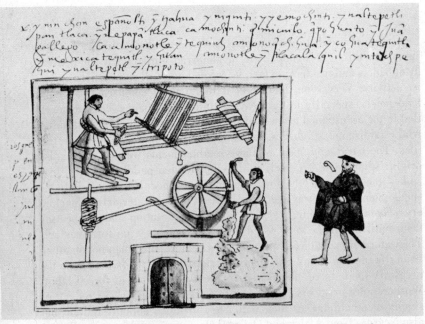

A textile shop or obraje, *third quarter of the sixteenth century. (From the post-Hispanic Codex Osuna, written partly in Nahuatl, partly in Spanish.)*

time. Within the confines of the cities, the guilds could perhaps maintain their restrictive covenants. But in the countryside an Indian craftsman applied his newly won knowledge to the traditional Indian crafts, especially to pottery and the manufacture of textiles.

These Spanish enterprises—mining, agriculture, stock-raising, manufacture—inevitably changed the face of the land and the relation of men to the land they inhabited. Before the Spanish Conquest, Middle America had been landlocked; what shipping there was, was confined to the coast. The Spanish Conquest bridged the oceans and linked New Spain to the Old World through the twin ports of Veracruz on the east coast and Acapulco on the west coast. Veracruz connected New Spain with Cádiz,

186

along the most direct line of Atlantic travel; Acapulco connected the colony with Manila, over a sea route discovered in 1564–65, which was to be used without alteration for three centuries. The connection through Veracruz remained primary; it was the umbilical cord connecting the colony to the mother country.

Under the new order, Middle America was no longer allowed to follow out the logic of its past development. Now part of an empire upon which the sun never set, it was subject to the dictates of an imperial reason of state which transcended local decisions arrived at for local reasons. New Spain, like other parts of the Spanish Empire, was to be a valuable source of raw materials for the homeland, not a primary producer in its own right. Each year a fleet would carry Spanish goods to the Indies and return laden with the produce and precious metals of the colony. Spain would export iron, mercury—essential to mining operations overseas—arms, paper, fine cloth, books, wine, olive oil, and soap and receive in turn silver and gold, sugar and cacao, cochineal and indigo, leather and tallow—the varied products of commercial enterprise overseas.

There was to be no free trade; the crown regarded the link with the Indies as the power cable of its imperial system and shielded it from outside interference by force of arms and minute bureaucratic regulation. Men and goods traveling to and from the Indies could embark only at certain privileged ports. A corps of royal officials, organized in the Casa de Contratación, guarded the Spanish terminus of this imperial lifeline at Cádiz and Seville. A body of privileged merchants with judicial powers over trade, the Consulado, stood watch over the Middle American terminus at Veracruz. The entire commercial rhythm of the colony was geared to the recurrent departures and arrivals of the transatlantic fleet at the east coast port. Goods piled up on the wharves in expectation of the fleet's arrival, and merchants from all over New Spain gathered at the annual fair at Jalapa near Veracruz to receive the staples of their trade for redistribution in the colony. On the goings and comings of these

187

merchants, on their calculations and manipulations, all the commercial enterprises of the colony depended. For it was through their mediation that the colonists acquired the goods which they deemed the proper symbols of their newly won status as lords of the land, and it was through their hands that the commercial products of the land flowed on to their destination in Spain and yielded the purchasing power required to buy the trappings of power and wealth. Similarly, once a year—to the sound of church bells imploring God's favor—the merchants of Mexico City would descend to Acapulco to await the coming of the Manila galleon, to receive from it the riches of China and to load it for the return trip with New Spanish wares.

Just as the economy of New Spain was thus geared to the requirements of the mother country, so it was circumscribed by royal regulation, to fit it as one component part into the larger empire. The crown frowned on the production of goods in the colony which could compete with products of the mother country. The production of olive oil, wine, silken goods, and textiles was therefore forbidden or inhibited. Single colonies might receive exclusive rights to the production of certain other crops; but these rights were frequently reallocated to the detriment of established plantings. Thus in the course of the century, cacao production in New Spain was halted and transferred to Venezuela, to underwrite the economic development of Caracas. This was done in spite of the fact that Middle America was the homeland of cacao and that no cacao had been grown previously along the southern Caribbean littoral. From then on, New Spain had to export silver, flour, sacking, tableware, and copper goods to acquire Venezuelan cacao. At various times, tobacco-growing in New Spain was sacrificed to promote tobacco-growing in Cuba or Louisiana. At intervals New Spanish silver and wheat flour were commandeered to supply the Antilles, where their arrival was celebrated with the joyful ringing of bells and the sound of fifes. New Spain thus took its place in a planned economy in which its economic decisions were subject to revision and censorship by a superior authority thousands of miles away.

Royal command and supervision ordered not only the relations of New Spain to Spain and New Spain to the other Spanish colonies; it also regulated the relation between conquerors and Indians, especially in the economic realm, between the entrepreneurs-to-be and their laborers. To obtain labor for their enterprises, the colonists at first had recourse to two institutions: the institution of slavery and the institution of *encomienda* or trusteeship. The Spaniards were familiar with slavery as an institution; they had but recently sold into slavery the entire population of the Canary Islands. It seemed natural to them, therefore, to brand and sell as slaves Indians captured in war or received in tribute or condemned to expiate some crime, often enough some infraction of an ill-understood new Spanish law. The Middle American Indians had known a kind of limited slavery in which slaves had been permitted to own property, call some of their time their own, and in which the children of slaves were free. They were confronted now with a new, unlimited slavery in which a human being was treated as a mere commodity, to be sold to mines, sugar mills, and farms, and to be used as an expendable resource.

To receive Indians in *encomienda,* on the other hand, meant that the *encomendero* or trustee received rights to tribute payments and unrestricted personal services from a stipulated number of Indians living in stipulated Indian villages. The institution had prototypes in Castile and perhaps in the *iktá* of Islam, as well as in the perquisites of the Indian chiefs before the Conquest. Yet, in the eyes of the colonist, it was not its medieval provenience which lent merit to the institution; it was rather the opportunity it provided for the organization of a capitalist labor force over which he alone would exercise untrammeled sway.

For this reason, both slavery and trusteeship met with royal opposition, for both threatened to raise in the New World the specter of feudalism so recently laid in the Old. The crown, wishing to stand above all men, could not countenance any social arrangement which permitted the re-emergence of power figures who held in their hands combined economic, military, judicial, and social power. In royalist eyes, as Silvio Zavala has said, the nobleman no longer represented a pillar of society, but a source of discord and rebellion. To guard against the rise of combinations of power that could rival the authority of the crown, the king divorced the right to receive Indian tribute from the control of Indian labor. If Indian labor made the wheels turn in this New Spain, then whoever was lord and master of Indians would also be lord and master of the land. With unlimited access to Indian energy, the colonists would soon have no need of Spain or king; hence the crown had to limit this access, supervise it, curtail it. The Indians were thus declared to be direct vassals of the crown, like the colonists themselves. This did not mean that the Indians were to be free to act as they liked, to pursue goals freely chosen with means freely decided upon. It did mean that no private person could lay hands on Indians without prior license from the crown. The Indians were to be royal wards; crown officers would be their tutors upon the road to civilization. These officers would see to it that no Indian remained idle, with satanic thoughts to plague his unoccupied mind. They would work, but they would perform their labor under the watchful eye of royal officers informed of the proper legal prescriptions applying to the particular case.

First, the king abolished all involuntary servitude imposed on individual Indians by individual masters. From 1530 on, Indian slavery was increasingly curtailed; in 1561 the Audiencia of Mexico heard the last cases of slaves to be set free. Only along the northern periphery of New Spain, where Spaniards encountered mobile nomad tribesmen, was slavery maintained as a weapon in the subjugation and pacification of the frontier.

Second, after 1549, the institution of trusteeship no longer included the right to Indian labor. The trustee was to be merely a passive recipient of tribute payments from a given number of Indian villages, but with this tribute—set by royal officials and supervised by the crown— went neither the right to live near his Indians nor to use their labor nor to sit in judgment over them. The trust carried no rights over land. If the crown so desired, it could—and did—allocate land pertaining to one man's Indian villages to another person who applied for a grant of land. Moreover, the grant of tribute was personal and temporary; it applied to the colonist so honored and his son. After the first filial generation, the grant reverted to the king, and the descendants of the original recipient had no claim upon it.

Third, after the middle of the sixteenth century, the crown turned increasingly to a system of compulsory regulated labor, mediated through royal labor exchanges, to fill applications for labor on the part of individuals. In one form or another, this system of regulated labor or *cuatequil* persisted up to the end of the eighteenth century. It bound the employer of Indian labor to pay his workers a standard wage. Labor was to be periodic rather than continuous, allowing workers to return to their native villages after working a stipulated period of time. No more than 4 per cent of the laborers of any community were to be away on outside labor during any given period, nor were they to be taken long distances from their homes. If a trustee wanted Indian labor, he had to hire it from a royal labor exchange at the same price as other men competing for the same precious labor-producing commodity, and no trustee could interfere if a royal officer wished to assign Indians from his tributary villages to the enterprises of another.

The Spanish Conquest was not confined to the Middle America of the cultivators. The conquerors quickly pushed beyond the frontier of agriculture to the north, thus upsetting the balance of core area and periphery which had come to characterize Middle America under Mexica rule. From their capital in the valley of Mexico, the Mexica conquerors had poured eastward, southeastward, and southward. To the west, their expansion had been halted by the redoubtable Tarascans, ensconced in their pine-covered uplands. To the north lay the arid Chichimeca, abandoned to bands of roving food collectors since the collapse of the Toltec power. The Spaniards lost no time in consolidating their grip upon the

191

Mexica possessions. They, too, built their capital in the valley, upon the ruins of the shattered Tenochtitlán. But the main force behind their conquest was the lust for gold and silver, and the main thrust of their expansion took them westward and northward, into the thirsty tableland. The main axis of their push followed the eastern foothills of the western escarpment. Like steppingstones into the great unknown, mining camps and settlements began to reach out toward the north. And where there were mines, there also grew up stock ranches and grain farms: stock ranches to provide the mules and donkeys for the mines, and to produce meat for the miners, hides for sacking and ore-sieves, rawhide for thongs and cables, tallow for candles; grain farms to raise wheat and maize. Mining, stock-raising, and grain-farming all entered the north country together and laid the foundations of Spanish enterprise in the area. By 1590, the great corridor to New Mexico was in Spanish hands.

The new possessions, however, presented a sharp contrast to the Middle America of the civilized seed-planters. The hold of the pre-Conquest urban cultures on this land had always been tenuous. The lack of water in this hot and dry tableland inhibited the growth of a dense population, the rise of cities or towns. At the time of the Conquest only small islands of cultivators survived in the area, surrounded on all sides by hunters and gatherers.

Armed with bows and arrows and stone knives, these nomad warriors were the first obstacle to permanent Spanish colonization. Launching their attacks at first on foot, they were soon riding stolen Spanish horses and raiding their enemies on horseback, often under leaders familiar with Spanish ways from earlier captivity or from childhood training among the missionaries. By the last quarter of the sixteenth century, the horse-riding Indian of the plains had made his appearance, not to be fully subjugated until the last part of the nineteenth century. Like their later North American cousins, these early raiders also scalped and tortured their captives. Traveling in small bands, they ambushed Spanish parties and raided settlements, only to vanish again into the arid steppe before the cumbersome Spanish soldiery could catch up with them.

To deal with such a mobile and scattered enemy, maneuvering against the backdrop of large open spaces, the colonists developed new techniques, many of which anticipated similar methods to be employed two and a half centuries later on the expanding United States frontier. The newly invented covered wagon came increasingly into its own after 1550. The soldiery adopted light leather armor and organized itself into flying detachments for purposes of patrols and escort. The fort or *presidio* made its appearance, alongside the mission. In addition to the use of such new methods in warfare, the Spaniards established colonies of armed Indian peasants from the urban area as strategic outposts in the hostile countryside. Tlaxcaltec colonists were established in several such settlements throughout San Luis Potosı.

The nomads presented not only a military obstacle to colonization. They also affected the nature of the labor supply in the new northern provinces. Food collectors do not lend themselves to easy pacification. When Chichimec prisoners were enslaved and put to work in the mines or on ranches and farms, they sickened and died. Nor was their number sufficient to cover the labor requirements of the new northern enterprises. Negro slaves were introduced in considerable numbers, but their high cost tended to discourage the growth of an African labor force. More important, in the long run, than either Chichimec or Negro slaves were free laborers, both Indian and Spanish, who came to live on the northern frontier of their own will and were willing to work for wages or perquisites rendered in kind. Most of them were Indians from the urban belt to the south who were attempting to escape either the burdens of tribute payment or personal services to the new conquerors, or were trying to escape the tribulations of personal and communal disorganization in the area to the south. Some were poor Spaniards, whose deeds had gone unrecognized in the distribution of rewards after the Conquest and who sought employment and adventure in the north country under the aegis of a more powerful protector. All, however, were individuals who found little to recommend in the settled and stable existence of the southern heartland; they belonged to the typically mobile men attracted by any frontier. The North would organize its communities by drawing together such individuals in associations of common self-interest. In contrast, the South would always rely upon the Indians, old upon the land long before the Conquest. The frontiersmen would lose their separate cultural heritages in the common experience of the frontier. In the South, the Indian would persist, increasingly unwilling to forego the security of living in communities of men of his own cultural kind. In the North, as later on the frontier of the United States, the only good Indian would be a dead Indian.

The costs of exploration, warfare, imported labor, and settlement in areas so far removed from the centers of supply to the south could not be sustained by the average colonist. The northward expansion was the work of great capitalists, grown rich in mining, stock-raising, and commercial agriculture, not of subsistence farmers, patiently staking a claim for themselves and for their families, as on the later western frontier of North America. When mining output and revenues declined at the end of the sixteenth century, the advance was maintained by stock-breeders, looking for new pastures to feed their enormous herds. Stock-breeding, not cultivation, thus provided the "cutting edge" of the northward Spanish advance. Here and there communities of Spanish farmers reached into New Mexico, Arizona, or California to found irrigated oases settlements. But they remained isolated islands in a wide-open stock-breeding countryside, just as before the Conquest settlements of cultivators had constituted islands in a sea of hunters and gatherers.

By the end of the sixteenth century, the ranching frontier extended from Culiacán in the west to Monterrey in the east. As distance increased, however, between the traditional core area of New Spain—with its bases of supply—and the far-distant outposts to the north, the military threat presented by the armed nomads grew correspondingly. At the same time,

194

further advance in strength into the north also encountered environmental barriers. Just as the Great Plains held up United States expansion until the nineteenth century, so they impeded expansion from the south. Not until the advent of a new technology, equipped with iron plowshare, barbed-wire fence, windmill, six-shooter, and repeating rifle, did the conquest of the Plains become a profitable undertaking. And this conquest was undertaken not by the Spaniards from the south but by the United States from the east. Important as the northern periphery thus became to New Spain, its northernmost edges remained shadowy and ill-defined and ultimately prey to annexation by an expanding and rapacious power from the north.

It is one of the ironies of the Spanish Conquest that the enterprise and expansion of the colonists produced not utopia but collapse. Like Tantalus reaching in vain for the fruit that would still his hunger and thirst, the conqueror extended his hand for the fruits of victory, only to find that they turned to ashes at the touch of his fingers.

All the claims to utopia—economic, religious, and political—rested ultimately upon the management and control of but one resource: the indigenous population of the colony. The conquerors wanted Indian labor, the crown Indian subjects, the friars Indian souls. The Conquest was to initiate utopia; instead, it produced a biological catastrophe. Between 1519 and 1650, six-sevenths of the Indian population of Middle America was wiped out; only a seventh remained to turn the wheels of paradise. Like the baroque altars soon to arise in the colony, the splendor and wealth of the new possessions but covered a grinning skull.

Pleaders of special causes ascribed the decimation of the Indian population to Spanish cruelty, but the Spaniards were neither more nor less cruel than other conquerors, past or present. Faced with a large and pliable native population, they perhaps grew accustomed too quickly to the lavish use of Indian services. Yet even the most senseless mismanagement of human resources cannot alone account for such hideous decimation. The chief factor in this disaster appears to have been not conscious maltreatment of the Indian but the introduction of new diseases to which the Indians were not immune. Every population is a feeding ground for micro-organisms that labor to reduce living organic substance to inorganic matter. Most populations sooner or later strike a balance in this battle against biological disintegration; they pay the price of temporary disease and death for the acquisition of more permanent immunities and fight the disease organism to a standstill along new battle lines.

Such a spread of micro-organisms and resultant immunities had gone on within both hemispheres since they were first settled by man. Up to the time of the Spanish Conquest, however, the Pacific and the Atlantic had acted as barriers against their universal extension. The disease organisms of the Old World were not those of the New, nor the immunities of the New World population those of the Old. Disease and death were thus presented with new victims. From the New World, the Spaniards returned to Europe with but one major disease—syphilis—which in its passage through the new hosts developed a virulence unknown in pre-Conquest America. But in the Indian population of the New World, the disease organisms of the Old World encountered a vast undefended pasture ground. The Spaniards introduced smallpox, which struck in virulent epidemics in 1520, 1531, and 1545; typhoid fever, which brought on epidemics in 1545, 1576, 1735, and twenty-nine times thereafter during the period of Spanish rule; measles, which exploded in a great epidemic in 1595; and—imported apparently in the hold of slave ships from Africa—malaria and yellow fever, the twin scourges of the American tropical lowlands. The Indian population possessed no antibodies against these plagues; they spread without obstruction.

Yet we must remember that such epidemics were not peculiar to the New World in this age; they were common everywhere in the Old World. Indeed, the sixteenth century seems to have been a period of open warfare between men and micro-organisms. During this time Europe experienced more disastrous epidemics than in any other century of modern history. Typhus, pox, sweating disease (1529), bubonic plague

196

(1552–64), and influenza (1580–92) sent multitudes to their common graves. The rich art of the baroque decorated not only the insides of churches but also the "plague columns" whose agonized figures writhing in the grip of disease are still a feature of many a European market square. The Spanish conquerors noted that many Indians died; but death by epidemic disease must have been a rather more familiar sight to them than it would be to the modern observer.

Biological disaster was intensified by economic factors. It appears that at the time of the Conquest population in Middle America had begun to outgrow the available food supply. There were several severe famines in the valley of Mexico in the course of the fifteenth century and the prevalence of human sacrifice would seem to indicate that Indian society had begun to produce more people than it could integrate into its everyday life. The introduction of new economic purposes into such a tenuously poised situation easily tilted the balance against human survival. For the Spanish Conquest did not merely add the conquerors to the number of people already living upon the land. As we have seen, it also altered significantly the relationship between man and his environment. Spanish economy, indeed western European economy in general, was inimical to men upon the land. While Indian cultivation made some intensive use of land, the Spaniards used land extensively. While Indian economy massed labor in cultivation, the Spaniards massed animals and tools.

The Indians had possessed no large domesticated animals; the Spaniards let loose upon New Spain a flood of cattle and sheep. Encountering a grazing range rich in its original vegetative cover or fed with the nutriments of cultivated fields, the Spanish herds multiplied rapidly. Following suit, Indian communities and Indian nobles also filled agricultural land with livestock. Only some of this land was land cultivated by the Indian population; a great deal of new range had probably never been under cultivation. But even a small amount of land withdrawn from agriculture had a considerable effect on the distribution of the Indian

197

population. Livestock-keeping implies a notably more extensive use of land than cultivation, which can support many more people per unit of land than pasture range. Nor did livestock-keeping affect only land in actual cultivation. In many cases, it engulfed land which the Indians did not farm during any given year but which constituted the indispensable reserve in their system of field-to-forest rotation. Occupation of this reserve imperiled the continued productivity of the field left in Indian hands and thus also the Indian population which lived off that land. Sheep produced wool, cattle produced hides; both produced meat. These products could be sold for good money; yet the wealth so obtained was won at the expense of hungry mouths. "Sheep eat men," went the saying when livestock-raising replaced farming in seventeenth- and eighteenth-century England. Sheep also ate men in Middle America.

Where the Indians had farmed land with a dibble, the Spaniards introduced a light plow drawn by oxen and capable of making shallow furrows and conserving moisture in the soil. With this new instrument, men were probably able to farm land which they had not farmed before: the plow with a metal tip is a much better tool for loosening deep sod and breaking up the tangle of roots and rhizomes than the hoe. Undoubtedly, therefore, the conquerors took under cultivation land which the Indian had not utilized and thus added to the total stock of land available for food production. But in its net effect, the plow also upset the balance of Indian life upon the land. The plow is efficient only where land is plentiful but labor is scarce. Plow agriculture does not produce as much as hoe cultivation on any given unit of land: in modern Tepoztlán, men achieve twice the yield with hoe cultivation as with plow agriculture. Also, plow agriculture means that oxen must be fed, and some land must be devoted to their care. What the plow accomplishes is a saving in labor; the plow performs the work of the hoe cultivator in a third of the time. But it was not labor that was scarce in pre-Conquest Middle America. On the other hand, every unit of land withdrawn from Indian agriculture meant a halving of the food supply produced on that land, and

198

thus a halving also of the population dependent on that food supply. And when that land was planted to wheat to feed the Spanish conquerors rather than the Indian inhabitants of the land, the growing imbalance between man and land was intensified.

Finally, the Spaniards also laid hands on the scarcest and most strategic resource of Middle American ecology: water. They needed water to irrigate their newly plowed fields, to water their stock, to drive the mills that ground their wheat into flour and the mills that fulled their woolens. Sons of a dry land themselves, they were master builders of aqueducts and wells; but all too often they appropriated the canals of the native population and impounded the streams behind their own dams. In a country in which a large percentage of the population had depended for their food supply on intensive cultivation made possible by irrigation, this wrecked a pattern of life precariously balanced between sufficiency and starvation. In a population ravaged by disease, such loss of land and water must have had a snowballing effect; it condemned a large percentage of the population to obsolescence and decay.

But the Conquest not only destroyed people physically; it also rent asunder the accustomed fabric of their lives and the pattern of motives that animated that life. Pre-Hispanic society and the new society established by the Conquest both rested on the exploitation of man by man; but they differed both in the means of their exploitation and in the ends to which it was directed. Under the Mexica, a peasantry had labored to maintain a ruling class with the surpluses derived from the intensive cultivation of its fields. But these rulers, in turn, were the armed knights of the sun who labored through sacrifice and warfare to maintain the balance of the universe. In the face of divergent interests, such a society possessed both a common transcendental purpose—to keep the sun in its heaven—and a common ritual idiom for the articulation of this purpose. The society produced by the Spanish Conquest, however, lacked both a common purpose and a common idiom in which such a purpose could be made manifest. It not only replaced intensive seed-planting with extensive pursuits; it also sacrificed men to the production of objects intended to serve no end beyond the maximization of profit and glory of the individual conqueror. Moreover, each group of conquerors—ecclesiastic, official, colonist—pursued a separate and divergent utopia.

Laboring in alien field or mine or mill, bewildered by the conflicting demands upon his loyalty, the exploited Indian could perceive no universal meaning in his suffering. It was not exploitation as such that was new; it was rather that men found no sense of participation in the process to which they offered up their lives. Only the religious forms of the conquerors drew Indian loyalty; around these forms the Indians finally rebuilt their impaired morale. Yet Christianity did not bring salvation for all. Like Carlos Moctezuma, the Indian ruler of Texcoco, executed by the Inquisition for his stiff-necked adherence to the old gods, many Indians could not make the transition from a religion which assuaged fear and guilt through repeated human sacrifice to a view of the world in which salvation was to be assured through the single and unique sacrifice of Christ. Such men, orphaned by the old gods yet unsaved by the new, despaired of the world in which they had to live out their lives.

Many Spaniards, especially the friars, labored valiantly to aid and comfort the Indian sick. Yet it is likely that some of their own cultural practices, introduced into this new cultural medium, proved directly lethal rather than beneficial. The Spanish insistence, for example, that the Indians be concentrated in towns where they could receive the direct benefits of royal law and Christian religion accentuated rather than abated the danger of infection. The friars' battle against the Indian sweat bath, the *temazcalli*, also played a part. Indian use of the sweat bath was a religious rite of purification, carried out under the auspices of the earth goddess. The friars, however, associated bathing with the paganism of the ancient Mediterranean and with the Islamic enemy whom they had just extirpated in southern Spain. They condemned the Indian sweat bath out of religious conviction and in so doing removed still another defense against attacks of germ-borne disease and death.

200

Yet the labor of these sick and dying Indians was to have made the wheels go round in the new utopia. Without Indian labor, there could be neither silver nor crops for the market. The mines were especially hard hit, for by 1580 they had run out of rich surface deposits. They had begun to work the less accessible ores which required ever new increments of labor. Yields declined steadily from 1600 on. Not until 1690 did mining output again attain the 1560 level. Food supplies underwent a parallel decline. From 1579 to 1700, the colonists found it difficult to obtain adequate food deliveries to towns and mines, except in an occasional bumper year. Spanish cities had to initiate mandatory deliveries from the surrounding countryside and set up public granaries to stockpile grain for resale at fixed prices during lean years. Silk production suffered and declined, as the labor needed during the peak harvesting periods also declined. By 1600 the industry was moribund. Cacao production witnessed a similar fate, as disease and death took toll of the hands required to harvest and process the bean. The decline in mining in turn affected stock-raising, which had counted upon the mines as one of the chief outlets for its multiple by-products. The country faced an emergency; increasingly it abandoned large-scale commercial enterprises in favor of restricted exchange, coupled with production for subsistence purposes. The bubble of unlimited expansion had burst, together with the utopian dream of wealth unlimited.

About 1600, too, the mother country began to suffer the unforeseen consequences of its overseas expansion. Its industry swamped by the gold and silver of the New World, inflation ran rampant, raising prices for Spanish goods at the very same time that purchasing power in the colonies declined toward the vanishing point. Nor could the mother country absorb the wool, hides, and dyes which the colony was still able to supply. Spain and New Spain, linked together by an umbilical cord from which both were to take rich nourishment, found themselves trapped in common misfortune.

201

X

*Retreat
from
Utopia*

Had Spain sustained the cumulative development of the sixteenth century, Middle America might well have achieved a new and vital synthesis. But the depression of the seventeenth century put an end to utopian dreaming; the bankrupt dream passed into receivership. As in past periods of social and political catabolism, Middle America again retreated into its countryside. The wider galaxies dissolved once more into their component solar systems to allow for reintegration on more parochial levels.

In the course of this retreat there emerged two new patterns for such integration: the *hacienda*, the privately owned landed estate of the colonist, and the tightly knit community of the Indian peasantry, the *república de indios*, as it is often called in the colonial records. Each produced its characteristic cultural design, and each imprinted this design so strongly on its carriers that the outlines of the two patterns are visible in the Middle American fabric to this day. The purposes which animated the two institutions were clearly divergent: one was an instrument of the conquerors, the other an instrument of the conquered. Yet in their divergence they shared a common denominator. Both were institutions of re-treat, both were designed to stem the tide of disorder. And both met the challenge of depression in the same way, for both bought a reduction in the risks of living at the price of progress.

The colonists had come to America in search of gold and—through the possession of gold—of liberty. But falling prices in a depressed mar-ket and the catastrophically declining labor force quickly ended the hopes of limitless wealth and untrammeled self-determination. As reality encroached upon the utopian dream, it again forced men to recognize its terms, terms which made a sack of doubloons in the hand weigh more in the balance than the hidden treasure of Moctezuma, a string of mules worth more than the waters of the Fountain of Eternal Youth. Some of course never acknowledged this confrontation and were lost in search of their personal El Dorados. Others were deprived of access to legitimate tangible claims or cheated of them: only forty years after the Conquest there were four thousand Spaniards in New Spain without visible means of support. But some there were who through guile or personal energy or bureaucratic favor shouldered aside their competitors and laid hold of the means of production required to support them in the fashion to which they wished to become accustomed. These men—recruited from all man-ner of men who had come from the mother country—became the mem-bers of a new colonial elite.

The characteristic cultural form through which they exercised their domination was no longer the trusteeship over Indians but the outright ownership of land in the hacienda, the large privately owned estate. The title to this land they acquired through purchase, by paying good money into an increasingly depleted royal treasury. The trusteeship had in-cluded rights to Indian produce only, and not to land; it had left the trustee passively dependent, at the mercy of royal favor. When a man succeeded in obtaining an outright grant of land, however, he became a director of property he could call his own, property to which he could add, which he might pawn, or which he could sell. To work this new property, the colonists needed labor. This they sought extralegally, by circumventing the royal labor code. The system was deceptive in its simplicity. They invited workers to settle permanently on or near their new estates. The entrepreneur would undertake to pay their tribute to the royal authorities and offer to pay them wages, usually in kind. At the same time, he would grant the worker the right to purchase goods on credit or, as needed, advance him small sums of money. The worker's account would be debited to the extent of the sums involved, in return for a promise to repay the money through labor. Such workers became known as *gañanes, laborios, naborías, tlaquehuales,* or *peones,* the system of labor use *gañanía* or peonage. Upon the twin foundations of landownership and peonage, the colonists thus erected their new economic edifice, the mainstay of their new social order.

Organized for commercial ends, the hacienda proved strangely hybrid in its characteristics. It combined in practice features which seem oddly contradictory in theory. Geared to sell products in a market, it yet aimed at having little to sell. Voracious for land, it deliberately made inefficient use of it. Operating with large numbers of workers, it nevertheless personalized the relation between worker and owner. Created to produce a profit, it consumed a large part of its substance in conspicuous and unproductive displays of wealth. Some writers have called the institution "feudal," because it involved the rule of a dominant landowner over his dependent laborers. But it lacked the legal guaranties of security which compensated the feudal serf for his lack of liberty and self-determination. Others have called it "capitalist," and so it was, but strangely different from the commercial establishments in agriculture with which we are familiar in the modern commercial and industrial world. Half "feudal," half "capitalist," caught between past and future, it exhibited characteristics of both ways of life, as well as their inherent contradiction.

Offspring of an economic depression, the hacienda was set up to feed a limited demand. With its external markets dried up by an economic downturn and by political weakness in the mother country, it relied on markets within the colony. In New Spain, however, only the towns and the mining camps represented secure outlets for agricultural produce; the Indians of the countryside secured their own foodstuffs and fed themselves. And means of transportation were neither rapid nor plentiful enough to allow surpluses from an area with a good harvest to be transferred quickly to an area of food shortage. Markets were limited not only by the food habits of the Indian population and by the distribution of the Spanish settlements but also by the limited capacity of any region to absorb its own products. A glut quickly lowered prices to the point where commercial agriculture met its ruin. Thus the hacienda played safe by always producing below capacity. It never staked all or even most of its land on the vagaries of the market. In times of uncertainty, it could always fall back on its own resources and feed itself. It possessed its own defenses, which it never jeopardized.

Inefficient in its use of land, it was yet greedy for it. It needed and wanted more land, not to raise more crops, but to take land from the Indians in order to force them to leave their holdings and to become dependent on the hacienda for land and work. Once this land was in its possession, the hacienda readily let it out to the inhabitants of the deprived villages for farming and stock-raising, but at the price of a stipulated number of workdays on the cash-crop–producing lands of the hacienda. Such workers, obtained through indirect means of coercion, constituted the bulk of a hacienda's labor force. They were called *peones baldíos,* because they made use of the hacienda's *baldío* or uncultivated land.

To produce the cash crop, a hacienda would farm only a small portion of its total land resources—its best land—but would do so with an unchanging and antiquated sixteenth-century technology, based on the use of the wooden plow and oxen in the fields and on the water-powered wheel in processing. Its cash crop would be a product of many hands, laboring within the *casco* or core of the hacienda, the sum of many indi-

205

vidual efforts each operating at a low level of productivity but considerable in the aggregate through the mere process of addition.

The greater part of this labor was drawn from the non-resident inhabitants of the hacienda's periphery, but the tempo and intensity of the work effort were sustained by a corps of resident laborers, the *peones acasillados*. An *acasillado* had both more rights and more duties than a *baldillo*. Paid in tokens, he could make advance purchases at the store owned and operated by the hacienda, the *tienda de raya*. There he could always obtain maize for himself and his family at lower than market prices. In the highlands, he was entitled to a daily ration of pulque, usually ladled out after a day's work, at the completion of the religious services which peon and owner both attended in the hacienda's chapel. Each man was given a house, and—if he proved faithful and obedient— a plot of land on which he could raise crops for himself. If a man proved properly submissive, moreover, the owner would finance his wedding or a baptism or a religious devotion, or aid him in other times of financial need. To repay these advances, such a worker would then bind himself to work for the owner until the debt was paid, an occurrence not marked by its frequency.

From 1540 on, growing numbers of Indians accepted the liabilities of peonage. Often they welcomed the system as a way of freeing themselves from the increasingly onerous bondage to Indian communities ravaged by death and disease, threatened with loss of land and water, yet all too often required to bear burdens of tribute and labor services assessed on the basis of their past number of inhabitants. Many of the newcomers were attracted also by the novel goods of Spanish manufacture, more accessible through hacienda channels than in the impoverished Indian villages. Extralegal as the system of peonage was, the new worker and his employer soon found themselves partners in a conspiracy to elude royal supervision. Crown officials, aware that they could not stem the tide of peonage, nevertheless strove to limit it by placing a ceiling of five pesos on the sums which could be advanced to any Indian, though they showed no parallel concern for the debt limit of the offspring of mixed Euro-Afro-Indian unions. But soon the new kind of life which developed on the haciendas—favorable to intermarriage and transculturation, providing shared experiences and growing kinship—bound the workers to their common place of residence as much as the accumulating debts bound them to the owner of the hacienda.

Thus the system had advantages for both owner and worker: the owner was guaranteed labor, the worker a measure of novelty, together with security. The system, however, also exacted its social and psychological costs, for—as in all systems of bondage—security was purchased only at the price of liberty. The peon was dependent on the owner, both economically and psychologically. He abrogated his right to decide his own fate; the owner of the hacienda became his guardian and judge, as well as his employer.

Such relations between owner and worker are so different from those to which we are accustomed in modern industrial society that they seem to possess the closeness of personal ties which many tend to miss in present-day life, where superiors and subordinates go their separate, impersonal ways. This has caused some writers to idealize the hacienda, as others have idealized the slaveholding plantation of the ante-bellum South. But there exists a distinction between personal relations, such as those familiar to anthropologists from the study of closely knit small primitive tribes, and personalized relations, in which the relationship bears the guise of a personal relation but serves an impersonal function. Neither hacienda nor slave plantation existed to provide satisfactory relationships between persons. They existed to realize returns on invested capital, to produce profits, functions that take no account of kinship or friendship, of personal needs or desires. The hacienda, like the slave plantation, was a system designed to produce goods by marshaling human beings regardless of their qualities and involvements as persons, an institution of the "technical order," as Robert Redfield has called it, instead of the "moral order." And yet the hacienda personalized many aspects of the relation between owner and worker where modern industrial or commercial organizations substitute the neutral mechanisms of impersonal management through a faceless bureaucracy.

There are relationships which are so basic to all human life that we remain their prisoners as well as their beneficiaries throughout our adult lives. These are the relationships which we experience in growing up in families. When an appropriate situation in adulthood reproduces our infantile condition, we react with emotions learned long ago toward father or mother or siblings, figures often now distant or dead. These emotions provide the fuel for adult institutions which manage to counterfeit the character of the original situation that first produced them. The hacienda achieved this end by elevating the hacienda owner to the role of a stern and irascible father, prepared to guide the steps of his worker-children, ready to unleash his temper and anger upon them when provoked. As long as the worker remained dependent and submissive, he received his just reward: a sum of money, a draft of pulque, a plot for growing corn. When he rebelled against authority, or provoked its anger, he was tied to the whipping post, possessed by every hacienda, and cruelly lashed. Thus the hacienda bound men not only through debts or through force but also through ties of love and hate.

Deprived of their ability to rule their own lives, the workers in turn invested the relation of owner and worker with the elements of personalization. The owner's person became the governor of their lives, their relation with this person the major guaranty of the security and stability on which depended their daily bread and a roof over their heads. Only the owner could materially raise a man's prospects in life, only he could reduce the risks to which the worker was subject. This person, clad in authority and living a life far beyond the reach of his laborers, had to be won over, placated into benevolence, by a show of humility, a pantomime of servitude. The worker not only put his labor time at his owner's disposal; he also offered himself and his family, to secure perhaps yet another advantage in the struggle for support. But each gain of benevolence was achieved only at the expense of competition and conflict with his fellow workers. Where all strove for the same goal, only a few could gain access to the generosity of the master; most remained for life outside the charmed, personalized circle. This competition for imaginary stakes, however, bound the worker with invisible bonds. He set his hopes upon the person of the master. If he succeeded in his ritual pantomime of submission, the master received the credit. If he failed, he blamed himself, or others more successful than he. At the same time, he cut himself off from others in a like condition.

No human institution, not even the most inhuman, can rely wholly on bayonets; it must build also on the motivations of its participants. On the hacienda, personal motives were harnessed to maintain the regime of labor. Given the appropriate social conditions, men make peons of themselves.

Limited in capital, the hacienda presents a further paradox in the display of power and wealth of its owner: wealth invested in the big house, with its high walls, gateways, courtyards, chapel, jail, and outbuildings; wealth invested in rich clothing and silver trappings for horses; wealth displayed in great feasts and public ostentation. This show of grandeur, however, also had its functions, functions appropriate to the context in which the hacienda arose. It underlined the owner's dominance over his workers, it enhanced his self-esteem, it impressed others. In impressing others, it enshrined an economic purpose, today served by departments of public relations or advertising. A *hacendado*'s display was a public demonstration of his credit rating, an assertion that—in the midst of an economy starved for capital—he deserved credit because his enterprise was capable of generating capital and wealth.

Moreover, such display gave him still another psychological hold over his workers, for it encouraged their vicarious identification with his splendor. Children admire and yet fear an overweening father; they also identify with him. His well-being becomes a symbol of the well-being of the entire family. Overpowered and restrained by him, they also wish to

209

see him acknowledged as powerful by others, to make their own submission seem logical and right. Thus, on the hacienda, workers identified with the figure of the owner. His person became symbolic of the enterprise as a whole, his well-being the justification of their collective effort. Dominated by his will, they yet identified with his mastery, his ability to command respect from others. His glory became theirs; it furnished the element of drama in their earth-bound and restricted lives.

The hacienda system was here to stay. The dual nature of the hacienda —its ability to retrench in times of adverse markets, its ability to increase production if demand rose—allowed it to adapt even to conditions which differed from those that gave it birth. When the depression

Hacienda owner and his foreman. (From Carlos Nebel, Viaje pintoresco y arqueológico sobre la parte más interesante da la República Mexicana en los años transcurridos desde 1829 hasta 1834 *[Paris: Imprenta de Pablo Renouard, 1839].)*

of the seventeenth century came to an end in the economic upswing of the eighteenth century, the hacienda, too, participated in the renewed expansion. Peonage, which at the outset had served to bind and hold a labor supply in the face of a diminishing population, became the foundation of an onerous and exploitative system of labor as population again increased. Squads of peons gave rise to peon companies, peon companies to entire armies of peons, all born within the framework of the haciendas and bound to them through debt and past condition of servitude. By the end of the seventeenth century, New Spain was securely in the hands of a class of great landed proprietors, self-made nobles, commanding thousands of dependent laborers, captains of private armies, living in splendid houses, and leading the life of a new aristocracy on horseback, with its display of equestrian skill in competitive games. In sharp contrast with Europe, where a decline of population and an improved technology had freed the feudal serf and turned him into an owner or renter of agricultural property, but much as in Russia during the late eighteenth and nineteenth centuries, the growth of capitalism in New Spain did not produce a greater measure of liberty and freedom for the laborer; instead it sharpened exploitation and increased bondage.

In the retreat from utopia, the strong sought refuge against instability in the control of men and land through the organizational form of the hacienda. But the rest of the countryside, inhabited by the submerged Indian population, witnessed a parallel movement toward consolidation. The Indian, like the Spaniard, sought security, but he had to avail himself of other means.

The Spanish colonist ultimately had access to an apparatus of power managed by others like himself. But the Conquest had deprived the Indian of access to state power. Knowingly, the conquerors had destroyed the connection between the Indian present and the pre-Hispanic past. In dismantling the Mexica state, they had removed also the cortex of the Middle American political organism and severed the nerves which bound communities and regions to the larger economic and political cen-

ters. The Indian state was not rebuilt. Royal decree carefully circumscribed the position of the Indian commoners. They were enjoined from
wearing Spanish dress and forced to don "Indian" costume, a combination of Spanish and Indian articles of clothing. Indian commoners could
not own or use horses and saddles and were prohibited from bearing
arms. They had to pay tribute, but, because they paid tribute, they were
endowed with economic personality and therefore with judicial personality. They could present their cases in special "Indian" courts and were
defined as "free vassals" of the king. They were exempt from military
service and from such taxes as the tithe and the sales tax, imposed on
Spaniards and others. But legal rights were not accompanied by common
political representation. Where Indian officials had once exercised power
on the national and regional level, Spanish officials now held sway. The
Indian political apparatus had been smashed by the Conquest; and the
conquerors were not ill-advised enough to countenance its reconstruction.

With the assumption of power by the Spaniards, the Indian ruling
class lost its functions. Some of the chiefs moved to town, adopted Spanish dress and manners, learned to speak Spanish, and became commercial entrepreneurs employing European technology and working land
with Indian tributaries and Negro slaves. Spanish law abetted this
process by equating them socially with the nobility of Spain and economically with the Spanish *encomenderos*. Since the new law took inade-
quate account of the pre-Hispanic division between nobility of office and
nobility of lineage, granting to all nobles the privileges of hereditary
descent, many Indian nobles even added to the pre-Hispanic perquisites
of their rank and gained title to lands which had previously belonged
either to a community or to a non-hereditary office. Also, the Indian
noble who was treated like a Spanish *encomendero* received rights to
tribute and personal services and, like other *encomenderos*, began to in-
vest in the process of building capital through capitalist enterprise. Frequently, intermarriage with the conquerors still further dissipated their
Indian identity, until they lost touch with the Indian commoners who in

212

the midst of death and upheaval were building a new Indian life in the countryside.

Nobles who remained in the villages, on the other hand, were reduced by loss of wealth and standing to the position of their Indian fellow citizens. Because his person was still suffused with the magic of past power, a former priest or local chieftain here and there assumed a post in a local community, but he soon lost the ability to command tribute or labor-power to which his ancestors had been accustomed. The new Indian communities were communities of the poor, too overburdened to sustain a class that had lost its function.

With the disappearance of the Indian political elite, there also vanished the specialists who had depended on elite demands: the priests, the chroniclers, the scribes, the artisans, the long-distance traders of pre-Hispanic society. Spanish entrepreneurs replaced the *pochteca*; Spanish artisans took the place of Indian feather-workers and jade-carvers; Spanish priests displaced the Indian religious specialists. Soon there was no longer anyone who knew how to make feather cloaks and decorations, how to find and carve jade, how to recall the deeds of gods and ancestors in days gone by. For a brief period the Indians strove valiantly to learn the new arts of the Mediterranean, and men like Bernardino de Sahagún (1499–1590) and the scholars of the short-lived college of Santiago de Tlatelolco (1536–1606) labored to maintain and enrich the intellectual patterns of Indian culture. But the return to ruralism of the seventeenth century put an end to these hopes and endeavors.

Under the new dispensation, the Indian was to be a peasant, the Indian community a community of peasants. Stripped of their elite and urban components, the Indians were relegated to the countryside. Thus the Indians suffered not only exploitation and biological collapse but also deculturation—cultural loss—and in the course of such ill use lost also the feeling of belonging to a social order which made such poor use of its human resources. They became strangers in it, divided from its purposes and agents by an abyss of distrust. The new society could command their labor, but it could not command their loyalty. Nor has this gulf healed in the course of time. The trauma of the Conquest remains an open wound upon the body of Middle American society to this day.

The strategic unit of the new Indian life was to be not the individual but the Indian community. This the crown protected and furthered, as a double check upon the colonists—ever eager to subjugate the Indians to their exclusive control—as well as upon the Indians themselves, whose individual freedom it wished to curb. To this end, it underwrote the legal separateness and identity of each Indian commune.

Each commune was to be a self-contained economic unit, holding a guaranteed 6.5 square miles of agricultural land, land which its members could sell only after special review by the viceroy. In every commune the duly constituted Indian authorities would collect the tribute and levy the labor services for which the members of the commune were to be jointly responsible (not until the eighteenth century was tribute payment individualized). A portion of this tribute would go into the royal coffers, but part of it would be set aside in a "community chest" (*caja de comunidad*) to finance community projects. Communal officials were to administer the law through the instrumentality of their traditional custom, wherever that custom did not conflict with the demands of church and state. The officers of the crown retained the privilege of judging major crimes and legal cases involving more than one community; but the Indian authorities received sufficient power to guarantee peace and order in the new communes. The autonomy which the crown denied to the Indian sector of society as a whole, it willingly granted to the local social unit.

This model for reconstruction did not envisage a return of the pre-Hispanic community. Yet so well did it meet the needs of the Indian peasant that he could take it up and make it his own. Poised precariously on the abyss of disintegration, the commune proved remarkably resilient. It has undergone great changes since the time when it was first consti-tuted in a shattered countryside three centuries ago, but its essential

214

features are still visible in the Indian communities today, especially in the southern and southeastern highlands. Thus it is still possible to speak of this community in the present tense, to regard the present-day Indian community as a direct descendant of the reconstructed community of the seventeenth century.

The core of this kind of community is its political and religious system. In this system, the burden of religious worship is rotated among the households of the community. Each year, a different group of men undertakes to carry out the tasks of religious office; each year a different group of men makes itself responsible for the purchase and ritual disposal of food, liquor, candles, incense, fireworks, and for all other attendant expenditures. A tour of religious duty may leave a man impoverished for several years, yet in the eyes of his fellow citizens he has added greatly to his prestige. This spurs men to renewed labor toward the day when they will be able to underwrite another set of ceremonies; and a man will sponsor several such ceremonials in the course of his life. Each tour of sponsorship will add to the esteem in which he is held by his fellow men, until—old and poor—he reaches the pinnacle of prestige and commands the respect of the entire community. The essential element in repeated sponsorship is therefore time: the older a man is, the greater the likelihood that he has repeatedly acted as religious sponsor. Thus old age itself becomes a source of prestige for Indians: an old man is one who has labored in the interests of the community for many years and whose repeated religious activity has brought him ever closer to the state of grace and secular wisdom.

Since all men have an equal opportunity to enlist in carrying the burdens of the gods, and thus to gain prestige, the religious system allows all households to be ranked along a scale of religious participation, prestige, and age. At one end of the scale, the Indians will place the young household which has but recently come into existence and whose head is just beginning to play his part in keeping the balance between community and universe. At the other end, he will place the households of the very old, whose moral ascendancy over the community is very great, owing to their years of faithful service and ritual expenditure.

Certainly this religious pattern has Spanish prototypes in the Iberian *cofradía* or religious sodality, a voluntary association of men for religious purposes. But it is also pre-Hispanic in origin. "There were some," says the Spanish friar Toribio de Benavente of the days before the Conquest, "who labored two or three years and acquired as much as possible for the purpose of honoring the demon with a feast. On such a feast they not only spent all that they possessed but even went into debt, so that they would have to do service a year and sometimes two years in order to get out of debt." In the reconstructed Indian community of the post-Conquest period, this religious pattern was charged with additional functions. It became the chief mechanism through which people gained prestige, as well as the balance wheel of communal economics. Each year, religious participation wipes out considerable sums of goods and money; each year part of the surplus of the community is consumed in offerings or exploded in fireworks to please the saints. The system takes from those who have, in order to make all men have-nots. By liquidating the surpluses, it makes all men rich in sacred experience but poor in earthly goods. Since it levels differences of wealth, it also inhibits the growth of class distinctions based on wealth. Like the thermostat activated by an increase in heat to shut off the furnace, expenditure in religious worship returns the distribution of wealth to a state of balance, wiping out any accumulation of wealth that might upset the existing equilibrium. In engineering parlance, it acts as a feedback, returning a system that is beginning to oscillate to its original course.

The religious complex also has aesthetic functions. The *fiesta*, with its processions, burning incense, fireworks, crowds, color, is not merely a mechanism of prestige and of economic justice. It is also "a work of art," the creation of a magic moment in mythological time, in which men and women transcend the realities of everyday life in their entry and procession through the magical space of the vaulted, incense-filled

216

Quiché-Maya
from
Santo Tomás
Chichi-
castenango,
Guatemala.
(Photograph by
Joseph
Seckendorf.)

church, let their souls soar on the temporary trajectory of a rocket, or wash away the pains of life in holy-day drunkenness. For the Indians, time is not linear, as it is for the citizens of the industrialized North Atlantic world, where each moment points toward a future of new effort, new experience, and new goals. The Indian scheme of life moves in an endless round, in which everyday labor issues into the magic moment of religious ritual, only to have the ritual dissolve again into the everyday labor that began the cycle. The Indian community has now forgotten its pre-Hispanic past; its past and its future have merged in a timeless rhythm of alternating mundane and holy days.

The social, economic, aesthetic, and ritual mechanisms of the religious complex do not stand alone. They are part and parcel of a larger system which makes political and religious behavior mutually interdependent. For participation in the religious system qualifies a man also for political office. In Indian eyes, a man who has won prestige for himself by bearing the burden of the community in its relations with the gods is expected and—more than expected—required to assume political office. Thus men who have laid down their burdens as religious sponsors will be asked next to serve as community officials. Qualified for office by past religious participation, they are the ones who transact the business of the community: allocating land, settling boundary disputes, investigating thefts, confirming marriages, disarming disturbers of the peace, dealing with the emissaries of outside power. A man cannot seek political office for its own sake, nor can he bend political power to his individual end. Power is bestowed by the community, and reallocated at intervals to a new group of officeholders. It is the office that governs men, not its occupant. In this democracy of the poor, there is no way to monopolize power. It is divorced from persons and distributed, through election, among all in turn.

The Indian cannot control men; he only wishes to come to terms with them. This process of mutual adjustment has become a group concern. The group counts more than the individual; it limits individual auton-

Procession in Santa María Jesus, near Antigua, Guatemala.
(Photograph by Joseph Seckendorf.)

omy and initiative. It is suspicious of conflict, tireless in the advocacy of
"adjustment." People raised in cultures that thrive on the conflicts of
individual with individual would find it difficult to fit into such a community; yet the community can be understood in terms of its context, a
larger social order in which men continually fight for power and are ever
willing to pay for its fruits the price of their own corruption. In this
setting, the Indian community shows great consistency in refusing to
play a game that will always seek its first victims among its members.
For navigation in troubled water its politico-religious system is a steer-
ing mechanism of great resilience.

As the Indian community leveled differences of class, so it obliterated other internal divisions intervening between its jurisdiction and the households that composed it. The diligent ethnologist may still find, among the Otomí-speakers on the fringes of the valley of Mexico, hamlets based on common descent in the male line and enforced marriage outside the community; or patrilineal kinship units sharing a common name, a common saint, and a measure of social solidarity among the Tzeltal-Tzotzil–speakers of Chiapas, though there too they have lost their former exogamy and the common residence which they possessed in the past. But these examples remain the fascinating exceptions to the general rule that, among Middle American Indians as a whole, common territoriality in one community and common participation in communal life have long since robbed such units of any separatist jurisdiction they may at one time have exercised. This holds also for the divisions called *barrios* or sections, which some have traced back to the pre-Hispanic *calpulli* and which in many cases go back to joint settlement in one community—voluntary or enforced—of groups of different origins, in both pre-Hispanic and post-Hispanic times. In most cases these units have simply been transformed into religious sodalities, each concerned with the support of its special saint and socially amorphous in any context other than the religious, although mutual name-calling, backbiting, or slander of one another's reputation may serve to drain off some of the minor irritations of daily life.

It is the household, then, that makes the basic decisions within both the politico-religious and the economic field, the household being usually composed of husband, wife, and children. Such unions are customarily formed through monogamous marriages; polygyny, the marriage of one male to more than one female, occurs but rarely. An unmarried man or woman is not regarded as an adult member of the community and cannot take up his responsibilities in communal life. A person who has lost a marriage partner through divorce or death must remarry before the community will again ratify the social standing he enjoyed before the breakup or end of his marriage. Nor is it marriage alone that bestows

220

Interior courtyard of an Indian house. Santo Tomás Chichicastenango, Guatemala. (Photograph by Joseph Seckendorf.)

full rights of citizenship. A couple must have children to validate their claim to complete adult status; a sterile marriage quickly falls prey to conflict and divorce. Marriage therefore, and a marriage blessed with children, is the common goal of the Indian men and women.

Economically, a marriage is a union of two technological specialists: a male specialist skilled in field labor and house-building, a female specialist skilled in tending the kitchen garden, caring for the small livestock, making pots and clothing, raising children, preparing the daily meal. The functions of the division of labor and of reproduction take precedence in people's minds over marriage as an outlet for sexual impulses. Marriages are often arranged by the parents of the prospective

221

Indian mother and child from Santiago Atitlán, Guatemala. (Courtesy of Pan American Union.)

couple, through the services of a go-between. The Indian man seeks a woman to bear his children and to keep up his home: there is little romantic love. Ideally, people conform to strict standards of marital fidelity. In practice, however, there is considerable latitude for sexual adventure outside marriage, and philandering does not usually endanger the bonds of the union. Nor do Indians engage in sexual conquest as a validation of their masculinity; sexual conquest does not add luster to the reputation of the individual. Exploitation of one sex by the other encounters little sympathy, just as political or economic exploitation of one man by another is not countenanced within the boundaries of the community.

Throughout their marriage, the partners retain a rough equality, though, ideally, wives are held subordinate to husbands. Women own the movable goods which they bring with them into the marriage. If a woman owns land, her husband may farm it for her, but the proceeds from the sale of produce raised on such a field is her own, as are the proceeds from the sales of her handicraft products. If she owns livestock, she retains her rights of ownership. In case of divorce, the family herd is divided equally between the divorcing partners. When one of the partners dies, his property is divided equally among the children; the surviving partner retains his share. Women do not occupy political or religious office, but they help their husbands in making the relevant decisions and in carrying out the attendant obligations. Within the home, the woman has a great deal to say, in strongly marked contrast to her non-Indian sister.

Just as the questions of participation in religio-political life are raised and settled within the household, so the day-to-day economic decisions are also made on the household level. It is the household that plants its fields to crops, that sells its maize or chili, that buys the needed kerosene or pottery. It is the men and women of these unit households who handle the money derived from these sales and act as individual economic agents. This apparent contradiction between the behavior of the

223

Indian as a member of his community on the religio-political plane and his behavior as an economic agent has so impressed some observers that they have lost sight of the communal involvements of the Indian and treated him in terms of capitalist economic theory. Indeed, Sol Tax has spoken of the Indians as "penny capitalists," presumably in contrast to more affluent "nickel" or "dime" or "millionaire" capitalists, thus drawing attention at once to his comparative poverty and characterizing his participation in the wider economy as an individual agent, and a capitalist to boot. Certainly the Indian is poor, and no Middle American Indian community ever existed on a desert island; it always formed part and parcel of a larger society. Its economic agents, the members of its households, are subject to a wider economy and to its laws. For instance, the value of the money they use and the prices of the commodities they buy and sell are often influenced, if not directly determined, by national conditions. The recent inflation, to name but one case, has affected Indians and non-Indians alike.

But the Indian is not merely quantitatively different in his economic involvements from other members of society. He differs qualitatively from the poor non-Indian Mexican or Guatemalan because he is culturally different from them. Superficially, he may resemble the individual economic agent of classical economics, unrestrictedly exchanging goods in a capitalist market. But he is not a capitalist, nor free of restrictions. His economic goal is not capital accumulation but subsistence and participation in the religio-political system of his community. He handles money; but he does not use money to build capital. It is for him merely one way of reckoning equivalences, of appraising the value of goods in exchange. The Indian works first so that he may eat. When he feels that he has accomplished this goal, he labors to build a surplus so that he can sponsor a ceremony and gain prestige in the eyes of his fellow Indians. In the course of his sponsorship, he redistributes or destroys his surplus by providing displays of fireworks or dressing the saint's image in a new cloak. Clearly, the quality of his involvement in the national economy

Church and market in Santo Tomás Chichicastenango, Guatemala. Note the worshippers burning copal-gum incense on the church steps before entering. (Photograph by Joseph Seckendorf.)

differs from that of the commercial farmer, industrial worker, or entrepreneur.

Moreover, this pattern of consumption operates within cultural limitations laid down and maintained by his community. When we see the solitary Indian bent over his patch of maize, we seem to see a lone economic agent engaged in isolated production. But this man is enmeshed in a

225

complicated web of traditional rights to land maintained by his community. Spanish rule granted each community sovereign jurisdiction over a well-defined amount of land. With the passage of time, general communal rights over land have become attenuated, usually in favor of a mixed system of ownership, where the richer bottom lands along the valley floors are now owned by individual members of the community, while the community retains communal rights over hilly land and forests. Yet the community still retains jurisdictional rights over land everywhere, rights which remove land from the category of free commodities. The most important of these rights states that members of the community may not sell land to outsiders. This is usually reinforced by a stringent rule of endogamy, which prohibits members of the community from marrying outsiders and thus endangering the man-land balance. Frequently this taboo is strengthened by other sanctions: the right allowing existing members of the community to glean or the right to graze their livestock on any land within the community after the harvest. Such rights frequently imply sanctions in their turn. A man cannot put a fence around his piece of land or grow crops that mature at variance with the crops of his neighbors. Both land and crops are thus subject to negative limitations, even though the actual process of production is intrusted to the several separate households.

Such limitations also apply to the craft products made in a given community. We may see a woman shaping a pot or a man weaving a hat, and taking pot or hat to market. Again, we apparently see an individual agent engaged in autonomous economic activity. We must however realize that the producer is not "free" to choose the object he wishes to produce and market. What looks like individual craft specialization is but an aspect of a pattern of specialization by communities. There is a general tendency for each community to engage in one or several crafts that are not shared by other communities in its vicinity. Thus, in the Tarascan-speaking area, for instance, Cocucho makes pottery, Tanaco weaves with century-plant fibers, Paracho manufactures wooden objects and

226

cotton cloth, Nahuatzen weaves woolens, Uruapan paints gourds, and Santa Clara del Cobre produces items of beaten copper.

The Indian market is a place where the members of the different communities meet to exchange their products. Such a market brings together a very large and varied supply of articles, larger and more varied than could be sold by any permanent storekeeper in the market town, and does so at prices low enough to match the low income of the Indians. Thus, while the individual producer enters a market that is highly heterogeneous in the variety of goods offered, his particular individual contribution is homogeneous with that of other members of his community. In

Indian merchants, on their way to market, embarking at Panajachel for Santiago Atitlán, Lake Atitlán, Guatemala. (Photograph by Joseph Seckendorf.)

the characteristic Indian marketing pattern, where the sellers of similar types of objects are arranged together in carefully drawn-up rows, what looks to the casual observer like a mere grouping of individuals is actually a grouping of communities.

We must conclude, therefore, that the Indian's economic involvements are different from those of other participants in the national economy. The individual Indian household is indeed *in* the economy, but not *of* it. For added to the household's general purposes of self-maintenance are the community's purposes aiming at maintaining the Indian social group intact in its possession of land and membership, despite the corrosive influences that continually surround it. A peasantry needs land, and the Indian community defends its land against outsiders through the twin weapons of endogamy and the prohibition of sale to non-members. A peasantry faces the risks of class differentiation. As soon as one man accumulates wealth and is allowed to keep and reinvest it, he threatens, in the straitened circumstances of Indian life, to take from others the instruments of their own livelihood. More seriously, wealth breeds power, and power—unless adequately checked—corrupts, stacking the political cards in favor of some men to the detriment of others. Thus the Indian community strives to abolish wealth and to redistribute power. It even frowns on any display of wealth, any individual assertion of independence that may upset the balance of egalitarian poverty. Its social ideal is the social conformist, not the innovator, the controlled individual, not the seeker after untrammeled power. It places its faith in an equality of risk-taking.

It is doubtful whether the Indian community could have achieved these ends by itself alone. Certainly, without the world beyond its confines, it could not have solved its population problem. Each new generation born to it threatens to upset again and again the balance between mouths to feed and land available to feed them. It can solve this problem only by continually exporting population. To stay in the running, it must continually sacrifice some of its sons and daughters to the outside world,

Indian selling medicinal herbs and other remedies in the market at Uruapan, Michoacán, Mexico. (Courtesy of American Geographical Society. Photograph by Jim McClure.)

thus ever feeding the forces which it attempts to resist. Increasing its own security by exporting people, it at the same time endangers the security of the larger society. Neither Indian peasant nor colonist entrepreneur, the emigrants fall into no ordered category, occupy no defined place in the social order. They become the Ishmaels of Middle America, its marginal men. Cast out into the shadows, with no stake in the existing order, they are forced to seek their own vindication, their place in the sun. If this is impossible within the social framework, then it must needs be against it. Thus the Indian community perpetually creates a body of potential antagonists, ready to invade it and benefit by its destruction.

Without the outside world, moreover, the Indian can never close the ever opening gap between his production and his needs. Robbed of land and water by the Conquest and subsequent encroachment, the Indian community can rarely be self-sufficient. It must not only export people; it must also export craft produce and labor. Each Indian who goes off to work seasonally in other men's fields strengthens his community; each hat, fire fan, or reed mat sold beyond the limits of the community adds to its capacity to resist encroachment. Each Indian who, in the past, enlisted on a hacienda as a *peón baldillo* thus benefited his community. Paradoxically, he also benefited the hacienda that used his labor. Assured of seasonal laborers who would do its bidding at the critical periods in the process of production, the haciendas welcomed the presence of Indian communities on their fringes. For such a community constituted a convenient reservoir of laborers where men maintained their labor power until needed, at no additional cost to the entrepreneur. Suddenly we find, therefore, that the institution of the conquerors and the institution of the conquered were linked phenomena. Each was a self-limiting system, powered by antagonism to the other; and yet their coexistence produced a perpetual if hostile symbiosis, in which one was wedded to the other in a series of interlocking functions.

If colonists and Indians achieved symbiosis, they did not achieve synthesis. While the great landowners secured virtual political and economic autonomy behind the walls of their great estates, they remained ideologically tied to Spain and, through Spain, to Europe. If the Conquest deculturated the conquered, it also affected the conquerors. First it narrowed the range of patterns carried by the newcomers, only to render them doubly provincial in the enforced readaptation to the ruralism of the seventeenth century. If the Conquest ended, once and for all, the isolation of America from the cultural development of the Old World, the ensuing decline of Spain left the new colonies on the margins of the new and larger world into which they had so suddenly been introduced. Here they suffered the fate of any marginal area isolated from its center of cultural productivity.

At the same time, the Conquest cut the lines of communication with the pre-Hispanic past: the conquerors could not take over the culture of the conquered. But neither could they develop a cultural configuration of their own. Communication with Europe remained formalistic and empty. The intellectual and artistic currency of the Old World was sought more for the sake of provincial display than for the sake of a new vital synthesis. Thus, for example, what is astonishing about the colonial architecture of New Spain is not the degree of indigenous influence in its construction but the virtual absence of it. Churches and palaces were built along European lines, even though greater wealth might render them more ornate or though an occasional decorative symbol might betray the hand of an Indian craftsman as yet untutored in the canons of Occidental art. Similarly, New Spain borrowed from Europe the models of sophisticated thought, first the intellectual formulas of the Counter-Reformation, later those of an Enlightenment tempered with Thomism, still later—in rapid succession—the phraseology of Jacobinism, English Liberalism, Comtean Positivism, only to see the European catchwords produce a sterile harvest in the Middle American soil. Thus the society of the post-Conquest period suffered not only from the deepening cleavage between Indian and non-Indian. It also clogged the wellsprings of autonomous cultural creativity. Product of the meeting of two

231

cultural traditions, it should have been the richer for their encounter. But design and circumstance both reduced the capacity of each component to quicken and stimulate the other into new cultural growth, and to be quickened in turn by stimuli from outside. Instead of organic synthesis, the meeting of Indian and Spaniard resulted in a social unity that remained culturally mechanical.

XI

The Power-Seekers

Hacienda and Indian community divided the countryside between them, but, like all monopolies, they created the forces for their own undoing. For, claiming exclusive power over men and land, they left no room for a social group neither Indian nor colonist which grew rapidly after the mid-seventeenth century. This new grouping drew its recruits from the sons of Indians who had left the encysting communities because they could no longer make a living there or because they preferred a freer life outside; from the descendants of African slaves, those manumitted by their owners or runaways hiding in the shadows of the law; from the offspring of mixed Indo-Afro-European unions, often illegitimate, who found a home neither in the Indian communities nor in the precincts of the Spaniards. With the passage of time, all these were joined also by descendants of poor conquerors, men who had come off second best in the distribution of riches; by men who had staked their all and lost it in one turn of fortune's wheel; and by men who found the cards stacked against them in their search for an adequate and respectable livelihood.

233

There were many of these. To gain wealth, to improve his chances in life, to secure a newly won position against competitors, a man needed connections. Only royal good will could grant the merchant his license to trade, the royal official his delegated power. Only the royal signature gave the landowner title to his land or the right to keep his estate undivided upon inheritance. Only through political connections and connivance could the mighty build their armies of peons or extend their sway over lands claimed by others. In the strongly centralized government of New Spain, only a few doors led into the sanctuary of power in Mexico City; only the wealthiest and the most powerful could gain entrance, through ties of marriage or offers of profitable collusion. Inevitably, therefore, the colonists came to be divided into the well-connected, for whom all things were easy, and the unconnected, who found their paths barred by invisible hands, their holdings and wealth eroded by lack of political guaranties. Where the well-connected flourished, the unconnected had to content themselves with humbler returns on their capital. Increasingly, they found themselves edged out, pushed into provincial areas too mountainous or too far from city markets or lacking in potential labor to support large holdings. Steadily and implacably, they came to feel the narrowness of their circumstances. As holdings grew smaller, fathers found it ever more difficult to provide their daughters with proper dowries, their sons with farms adequate to maintain them. Their inability to entail their estates, to keep their wealth inviolate, forced many of the sons into the poorly paid priesthood or into petty officialdom.

Other ruling elites, in other places and at other times, have shared their power gradually and carefully with the disadvantaged. But this the colonial elite either would not or could not do. Such a step would have demanded that the favored merchant yield his prerogatives to his own best customers; that the privileged landowner relinquish the political guaranties of his stability in favor of his competitors; and that the royal official—mediating between colonist and Indian—abdicate his power to the colonist party. Rather than resign their positions, the elite families bound themselves ever more tightly to Spain, seeking in the mother country both their marriage partners and their political replacements. For the unconnected, the pattern of life descended from dignified poverty to bare existence, without title to property, without guaranties in court.

Deprived of a place in the sun, relegated to the byways and back alleys of society, all these varieties of men encountered one another in common destitution along the trail, in mining camps, in hostelries, in city taverns. Recognizing their common fate, they produced common offspring, resulting in an ever increasing number of mixed physical types. These the colonial authorities called "colored" people or *castas*, following the traditional Iberian usage of "caste" for color. Later it became fashionable to call them *mestizos* or mixed-bloods, or—harking back to the days of the Roman Empire when Spain had been Romanized—*ladinos*, a term which meant somebody Latinized and therefore wise to the ways of the world.

At first, the members of this group were relatively few. In 1650—when the Indian population of New Spain had declined to its lowest point—the mestizo element consisted of only 130,000 persons, as compared with some 1,270,000 Indians and 120,000 people socially defined as white. By the end of the eighteenth century the Indian population of New Spain had quadrupled, to a total of about 5,200,000, but the *castas* had increased more than seventeen times, to a total of 2,270,000. From the end of the eighteenth century to the present, the Indian population of what was once New Spain has remained surprisingly stable. But during the same period, partly through steady recruitment from the Indian communities, partly through natural increase, the mestizo population of Mexico and Guatemala has increased more than a hundredfold. In numbers the Indian has held his own; but it is clearly the mestizo who represents the future of Middle America.

The terms *casta* and *mestizo* are both opprobrious, but it would be a

235

mistake to read into them the twentieth-century prejudice against race mixture which informs similar terms in the North Atlantic world. The negative sentiment that adheres to them is social prejudice, not racial prejudice. Social prejudice, the dislike of the in-group for the out-group, the prejudice of the initiated for the encroaching stranger, is attested by the remnants of cannibalistic meals eaten half a million years ago in the Chinese cave of Chouk'outien. But racial prejudice is no older than the experience of Negro slavery in the New World and the rise of industrialism in Europe. The first European contacts with members of other races were formulated in religious and not in racial terms: all men were capable of salvation, all men were children of Adam and therefore brothers. This argument held even in seventeenth-century Virginia, where authorities still drew the legal line between "heathen" and "Christian," and not between "white" and "black," and where Negro slaves baptized in Africa were freed, equipped with dowries, and married to desirable mates. Only the rising economic importance of Negro slavery in America and the development of industrial wage labor in Europe produced the racist attempt to convert people into things by denying them a common humanity and by degrading them through various kinds of pseudo-science to the status of the burden-bearing animal.

This form of prejudice did not take root in Latin America until the nineteenth century, and then only briefly in restricted areas of the Caribbean, when the institution of Negro slavery was nearing its end. But in Middle America, the prejudice against *castas*, as indeed the prejudice against Indians, remained social prejudice. If the offspring of a mixed union gained wealth and standing, he could obtain from the pertinent authorities a legal paper that declared him to be "white" (*que se tenga por blanco*). Thus the white group quickly became a social, not a racial, group, just as an Indian was any person, whatever his parents, acknowledged to be a member of an Indian community. In like fashion, *castas* or mestizos were neither "white" nor "Indian," but embodiments of all those interstitial human elements whose social position made it impossible for them to join the other two groupings. What the colonial society feared was not the creation of mixed offspring but the growth of a large mass of unattached, disinherited, rootless people in its centers and along its margins. In their fear of the mestizo, men feared for the future of their social order.

Also, because men usually hate, dislike, or fear those of whom they avail themselves in the pursuit of socially concealed ends, feeling toward the mestizos came to be tinged with the mixed emotions of hidden complicity. This was perhaps most obvious in the sexual sphere, where men frequently claimed no responsibility for the mixed offspring they had fathered, leaving them to be raised by their usually destitute mothers. But resentment was generated also in other contacts of social life. There was little correspondence between law and reality in the utopian order of New Spain. The crown wished to deny the colonist his own supply of labor; the colonist obtained it illegally by attaching peons to his person and his land. Royal prescript supported the trade monopoly over goods flowing in and out of the colony; but along the edges of the law moved smugglers, cattle-rustlers, bandits, the buyers and sellers of clandestine produce. To blind the eyes of the law, there arose a multitude of scribes, lawyers, go-betweens, influence peddlers, and under-cover agents, the *coyotes* of modern Middle America, a term that once merely designated one of the physical types produced by mixed unions. In such a society, even the transactions of everyday life could smack of illegality; yet such illegality was the stuff of which this social order was made. Illicit transactions demanded their agents; the army of the disinherited, deprived of alternative sources of employment, provided these agents. Thus a tide of illegality and disorder seemed ever ready to swallow up the precariously defended islands of legality and privilege. At the same time, just as the Masai of East Africa blame their smiths for forcing them to make war by making their weapons, the

237

citizens of New Spain blamed the mestizo for those of their own activities that daily subverted an order of society they were formally committed to uphold.

Disinherited by society, the mestizo was also disinherited culturally. Deprived of a stable place in the social order, he could make only limited use of the heterogeneous cultural heritage left him by his varied ancestors. The Negro, bound in servitude to mill or mine, could not recreate Africa in Middle America; only here and there, in isolated pockets on the Pacific coast of the southern highlands or along the Gulf, did "Negro" or Afro-mestizo groups weave some African culture elements into their on-going life. Similarly, the Indian had little to contribute to the new ways of city, stock ranch, mine, or factory, beyond his inventory of household arts, his techniques for curing illness, his folk beliefs about the supernatural. The heritage of Spain had already undergone the simplification of transatlantic migration and Conquest; much of it the mestizo had to jettison still further, because it was not consonant with the erratic rhythm of his new life. His chances of survival lay neither in accumulating cultural furniture nor in cleaving to cultural norms, but in an ability to change, to adapt, to improvise. The ever shifting nature of his social condition forced him to move with guile and speed through the hidden passageways of society, not to commit himself to any one position or to any one spot. Always he would be called upon to seem both more or less than what he was, to be both more or less than what he seemed.

Thus the mestizo would come to be the very antithesis of the Indian. Where the Indian was rooted in a community, he would be rootless. Where the Indian clung stubbornly to the norms of his group, he would learn to change his behavior as other men assume or doff a mask. Where the Indian remained closed in upon himself, impervious to arguments raised beyond the confines of his local universe, he would have to make himself at home in the market place of goods, ideas, and people. The

238

Indian could turn a face to the outside world that yielded no knowledge and accepted no premise of the larger society; but the mestizo would have to operate with its premises and logic, so as to be counted among "men of reason" (*gente de razón*), as non-Indians are called in Middle America. Where the Indian valued access to land, land to work by the sweat of his brow, the mestizo would value manipulation of people and situations. Above all, he would value power, the instrument that would make people listen where society granted him no voice and obey where the law yielded him no authority. Where the Indian saw power as an attribute of office and redistributed it with care lest it attach itself to persons, the mestizo would value power as an attribute of the self, as personal energy that could subjugate and subject people.

For the mestizo, power is not an attribute of groups. The group exists to back the individual; the individual does not exist for the group. The individual wish, the individual gesture, are paramount, subject only to a man's grip upon his fellow men. The measure of success is the readiness of others to serve him, to underwrite with their services his conspicuous consumption of time and goods. The outcome of defeat is bondage or death. There is no middle ground: if a man does not wish to be victor, he must needs be loser. Ultimately, all means are legitimate in this battle for personal control of people and things, even violence and death.

This struggle for power was more than a means: as a validation of self and of one's station in society, it became an end in itself. To the mestizo, the capacity to exercise power is ultimately sexual in character: a man succeeds because he is truly male (*macho*), possessed of sexual potency. While the Indian strives neither to control nor to exploit other men and women, the mestizo reaches for power over women as over men. As the urge for personal vindication through power is continuous and limitless, so the mestizo possesses "a limitless sexual deficit" which feeds merely upon past conquests. While the Indian man and the Indian woman achieve a measure of balance in their relationship, the mestizo

239

male requires absolute ascendance over women. Thus even familial and personal relationships become battlegrounds of emotion, subject to defeat and to victory.

As men expect hostility and aggression from others, so they rise to defend themselves with hostility and aggression. They advance upon each other, ever circumspect, ever ready to defend themselves, ever willing to take advantage of the chink in their opponent's armor. Personal encounters thus become daily dramas in which the participants transcend the limits of the workaday world through gestures of potency or submission. The ultimate gesture, however, is not the stance of the victor; it is the defiant posture of the victim who can turn defeat and death into triumph by a calm and derisive acceptance of his fate.

There are cultures which preach the acceptance of things as they are; others, seeing the reality of daily life as cold and unpleasant, exalt the wish, the longing, the play of fantasy. The Indian is reality-adjusted and reality-bound. Hard work and its fruits are his primary values; he knows that wishing does not make it so. The mestizo, in contrast, enjoys the play of fantasy. Standing on the edge of society, he has also come to stand on the edge of reality. Uncertain of backing from his fellows, he is thrown back on his own resources; propertyless and alienated, he often feels estranged from society. Wishing to escape reality, he has learned to "drown the pain of living" in alcohol or gambling, creating for himself an unreal world with unreal stakes. Despising life, he has learned to substitute the dream for unfriendly reality. He may rise suddenly on a crest of fantasy into a dream world of personal dominance, only to fall back into a trough of self-denigration, filled with feelings of misfortune and insufficiency. Rarely in tune with things as they are, he is in the words of José Iturriaga, "either above or below them." Yet, suspicious of reality, he is also suspicious of dreams. Dreams do not come true, and in a sudden reversal of moods he may pull himself back to the demands of life with a cynical joke. Thus he does not commit himself easily either to dream or to actuality. The dream may give him wings, unleash the energy for which he strives, but in the pursuit of energy the dream is but a means, the original catalyst. Dreaming, men retain a vast gift for improvisation, an ability to shift both ends and means that enables them to score a personal triumph where critics could predict only the failure of a cause.

To transcend reality, to suggest possibilities and plans that in real life remain unrealized and unrealizable, the mestizo often submerges himself in verbal fantasy that decorates truth with falsehood, falsehood with truth. Yet as he distrusts the dream, he also distrusts the promise of words. He finds their play pleasurable but does not become their captive. His slogans of the moment may be liberal or socialist or fascist or capitalist. But he is not a system-builder; the use of such phrases does not make him a liberal, a socialist, a fascist, or a capitalist. Quick to change ends and means, he is also quick to change the tokens of communication. Moreover, he is often unwilling to commit himself to an unpredictable future; to this end he can use language as a strategy in which explicit meanings disguise implicit messages, and a man can speak with two contradictory tongues, to the confusion of the uninitiated. Often, language is not so much a means of communication, of "putting all your cards on the table," as the North American would have it, as it is a means of avoiding entanglement. Nothing will excite moving-picture audiences in Middle America to greater glee than the antics of their glorious clown Cantínflas (Mario Moreno), who in an eternal round of wish fulfilment steps nimbly around the traps of life with fancy footwork and hilarious doubletalk, traveling lightly through the social corridors. Owning nothing, he can lose nothing; standing neither to gain nor to lose, he lives without responsibilities or commitments.

Denied his patrimony by society, the mestizo was yet destined to be its heir and receiver. Superficially, this rise to power resembles the experience of the European middle classes and their emancipation in a series of "bourgeois" revolutions. But the mestizo mass was not a middle class, or a class at all—if class be defined in terms of differential access to the means of production. The European middle classes occupied a clear-cut position between the rich and powerful and the poor and power-less. Owning property and having traditional claims to the intermediate positions in civil and religious hierarchies, they also possessed a stake in constituted society and—based on that stake—a well-knit system of common behavior and understanding, a common subculture. The mes-tizos, on the other hand, comprised both men who worked with their hands and men who worked with their wits. They shared not a common stake in society but the lack of such a stake; they shared a common condition of social alienation. Relegated to the edges of society, living in permanent insecurity, their reactions were akin not to the firmly anchored, substantial European middle classes but to the groups which Karl Marx called the "Lazarus-layers of the working class" and to the rootless, underemployed, unemployable intelligentsia-in-rags of post-1929 Europe who furnished the *condottiere* of the European Right and Left. In their common estrangement from society, the petty official, the political fixer, the hard-pressed rancher, the hungry priest, found a common denominator with the Indian bereft of the protection of his community, the artisan burning his midnight oil in poverty and religious devotion, the petty trader or cattle-rustler, the half-employed pauper of the streets, the ragamuffin of the Thieves' Market. Such men constituted neither a middle class nor a proletariat; they belonged to a social shadow-world.

Nor was industrial or commercial development in Middle America ever steady and sustained enough to recruit more than a handful from the mestizo mass into what might be a middle class or a proletariat until the advent of the twentieth century. The Industrial Revolution of North Atlantic Europe, advancing steadily both in space and time, generated middle classes and proletariats that could build, coral-like, upon the achievements of their predecessors. The problems of political order were resolved early in the course of industrial growth to insure the victory of the bourgeoisie over feudal lords and to reduce the political struggle

242

to the niceties of parliamentary behavior. In contrast, Middle America —as indeed much of the colonial world—moved economically not in a straight line but in fits and starts, in a succession of upswings and downswings.

The sixteenth century had witnessed the establishment of the colonial utopia and the consequent flow of specie and rapidly growing transatlantic trade. The seventeenth century relapsed into rural isolation and restricted markets: the hacienda became the bulwark of colonial life in the countryside, the Indian community its ruralized Indian counterpart. The eighteenth century again witnessed an upswing in mining, trade, production for export; but independence from Spain drove Middle America back into reliance on the countryside. Thus Middle America entered the nineteenth century without a middle class and without a proletariat. The basic issue of power remained similarly unresolved. Economic power and power won by force of arms remained wedded to each other. The power-seekers had to employ both together; each kind of power fed and reinforced the other.

Yet, paradoxically, the very weakness of the mestizos, their very alienation from society, spelled subterranean strength. As society abdicated to them its informal and unacknowledged business, they became brokers and carriers of the multiple transactions that caused the blood to flow through the veins of the social organism. Beneath the formal veneer of Spanish colonial government and economic organization, their fingers wove the network of social relations and communication through which alone men could bridge the gaps between formal institutions. At the same time, such informal relations drew men together and strengthened their sense of a common fate. Subterranean as they were, they depended on face-to-face relations. They owed nothing to governmental prescript; their organization depended entirely on the vicissitudes of personal power. As men fought their personal battles of loyalty and disloyalty, they unwittingly wove the new patterns of dominance and submission that would serve to organize men into common action within

243

larger groups. Thus in the unacknowledged niches of the powerless, a new social pattern developed, a mestizo pattern, a common etiquette of signaling and receiving. Beneath the integument of Spanish power, the Middle American patterns of nationality were born.

As the mestizos filled with their own web of relationships the social void left by the Spanish overlords, they also projected into the society that harbored them a common emotional force, the passion of nationalism. Nationalism becomes a passion because it allows men to transcend the limits of the separate self and to merge that self with a social body, the nation, to which they impute a magical collective strength. As members of a nation, men need no longer feel isolated and alone; and as they gain in strength through numbers, the collectivity becomes the bearer of their secret wishes. In attacking a common national enemy, they can attack also—on the symbolic level—the inimical forces that threaten their personal well-being. To the Middle American mestizo, this symbolic enemy was inevitably first the Spaniard who had denied him his rightful inheritance; but after Independence it would be the *gringo* from north of the border, whose wealth and self-confident brashness would remain a standing irritant to Middle American pride even after the United States soldiery had withdrawn from the Halls of Montezuma.

A nation, says Ortega y Gasset, is an invitation extended by some men to others to join them in a common undertaking. To make themselves heard in such a venture and to insure continuity of purpose, men must be able to communicate. To become a nation, groups of men must learn to transact social business with one another. They need an etiquette to rule this newly discovered mutuality, a shared grammar of manners and morals and of shared emotional inflections to govern their exchanges in a common market place of goods and ideas, to channel their conflicts in a common political arena. In the hidden passageways of society, as he tightened the informal network of economic, military, and political relations, the mestizo learned just such a new etiquette of communication. Yet the gates to the citadel of power and wealth stood shut. As long as the structure of privilege persisted, his newly found idiom could remain no more than a subterranean jargon. Hacienda and Indian community discoursed endlessly over their closed circuits upon the subject of their separate identities. Trade was in the hands of the great merchants, land and men in the hands of the landowners or the protected Indian communities, craft production in the hands of guild masters, ecclesiastical power in the hands of Spanish-born priests, political power in the hands of Peninsular officials and their friends. To create the future, the mestizo had to war upon privilege, to open the sluice gates of circulation through which goods, land, labor, and power could all flow out as negotiable commodities upon an open market, to impose one grammar of manners and morals—his cultural grammar—as a national means of communication. Only as closed society gave way to open society, closed communication to open communication, could the mestizo win his place in the sun.

To become masters in the Middle American house, the mestizos had first to be apprentices. For a long time they could play no independent political or economic role. Some served their journeymen years in the armies of the large landowners who broke the grip of the Spanish bureaucracy on Middle America, not to create a new and open society, but to tighten more securely their own hold over the supply of available labor. But independence from Spain ushered in no new dawn of liberty. It merely swept away royal protection of the Indians and put an end to labor exchanges, special Indian courts, legal limits to Indian debts, laws governing the duration and kind of work open to Indians. After independence the hacienda emerged with redoubled strength. A decline of mining at the end of the eighteenth century, the disorders of war and rebellion, the sudden removal of Middle America from the economic bloc of the Spanish Empire, all favored, once again, a return to the ramparts of power in the countryside.

Everywhere, too, independence was followed by attempts to divide the Indian communal holdings among the members of the community.

245

or to allocate them to outsiders. The language used to justify this break-up of long-established tenures was the language of economic liberalism, the ostensible aim to create a Middle American yeomanry, a sturdy class of independent property-holders, in the image of the English and French revolutions. In this invasion of the Indian communities mestizos and landowners made common cause. But when the dust of battle had cleared, the haciendas had gained all; the mestizos who had ridden in their service had gained little or nothing. The haciendas had added both land and peons, while in areas too distant or too poor to prove rewarding to the outsider, the Indians had simply withdrawn further into their communal shells, turning the dream of the sturdy Middle American yeoman into merely another political and economic chimera.

Paradoxically, however, this solidification of power on the local level opened a third gate to mestizo participation in politics and civil warfare. It created a power vacuum on the national level. A hacienda could dominate a community, a valley, even a region; but the hacienda system did not give rise to a united national planter class, conscious of its interests. The removal of the Spanish viceroy and his staff left vacant the seats of power; no committee of powerful landowners took his place. Inevitably, this lack of power on the national level drew men into a round of endless conquests for real or imaginary spoils. Sometimes the contestants fought their own battles; at other times they were the witting or unwitting agents of foreign powers taking advantage of the power vacuum to further their own interests. Yet, in the very pursuit of chaos the mestizo emerged from his shadow-world on the edges of society into the full light of day. The prevalent political and economic disorder was his school of public administration and his military academy. In the struggle for the instruments of the state, he learned how to project personal power into public power. If the retreat into the countryside solidified the power of the landowners, it also made the mestizo a force to be reckoned with, for it propelled him—weapons in hand—upon a national stage.

In the second half of the nineteenth century, this time under the stimulus of foreign capital investment, the economic balance began to shift once more away from agriculture. In Mexico, investment speeded the growth of mining, textile production, railroad construction, petroleum exploitation; in Guatemala, it flowed into the commercial cultivation of bananas and coffee. Wherever it penetrated, it quickened the economic pulse and speeded up the circulation of people and goods. Wherever it diffused, it created new hopes for the future. This was true especially of Mexico, and especially of northern and central Mexico as compared with southern Mexico and Guatemala. By 1895 Mexico had an industrial proletariat of 365,000, a rural middle class of 213,000, an urban middle class of 776,000. In comparison with the 7,853,000 living in peon families on haciendas, these represent only a fraction of the population; but their very presence indicates the direction of social and economic growth.

Yet between the possibilities offered by this growth and their realization stood a formidable array of vested interests. These included not only the traditional tenants of power in the rural area but also foreign financiers, fearful for the fate of their investments, and—toward the end of the century—a mestizo cabal which had emerged victorious in the successive political and military eliminations and which lived by selling protection both against the increasingly restless peons and against disorders which might curtail the flow of foreign capital. Poised between past and future, these power-holders maintained an uneasy equilibrium between hostile forces by eliminating, through bribery and violence, all possible rivals from below.

Only a revolution could break through this network of interests and clear the way to an open society; and in the course of this revolution the mestizo would graduate from political apprenticeship to political mastery. The revolution came in Mexico in 1910, belatedly and abortively in 1945 in Guatemala. In these revolutions the mestizo leadership abandoned its alliance with the traditional power-holders and allied itself instead with the submerged elements of the old order, the peons of the haciendas and the Indians of the Indian communities. The economic cement of this alliance was land reform, the division of land among the propertyless; the ideological cement was Indianism, the search for roots in the Indian past.

In the course of land reform, in Mexico, successive revolutionary governments distributed—between 1910 and 1945—close to 76 million acres, including the holdings of foreigners who owned a fifth of all the cultivable land in the Republic. All this land was allocated either to independent smallholders or to communities called *ejidos*, in which the community, not the individual, retained ultimate proprietary rights. Guatemala, in the course of its belated revolution, distributed close to a million acres, including half the holdings of the United States–owned United Fruit Company. Here land remained in the hands of the government; recipients of land grants were to pay a small annual rent to validate their rights of usufruct. In both countries, legal reform accompanied the reform in land tenure, and newly promulgated laws struck at the relationship between landowner and peon. In both countries, too, agricultural workers and peasants formed organizations capable of defending their interests against the vanquished landlord class by force of arms or through recourse to the courts. In Guatemala, counterrevolution reversed these steps in 1954; but in Mexico they became the law of the land.

The ideological counterpart of this social mobilization was the burgeoning and spread of Indianism. This intellectual movement had begun in the nineteenth century as a rather self-conscious attempt on the part of a few individuals to draw moral inspiration for the new order from the legacy of the Indian past. With the coming of the revolution, their symbols and attitudes achieved a new and wider popularity. Indian themes sounded again in the music of a Carlos Chávez, populated the murals of the Mexican Neo-Realists, guided the brush of a Roberto Ossaye in Guatemala, the hand of an architect designing the new uni-

The University City in Mexico City. (Courtesy of Pan American Sanitary Bureau.)

versity in Mexico City. Heroes of the Indian past became national archetypes; the bloodthirsty Mexica tyrants were transfigured into champions of the new united nation. Collective scorn and pity were heaped upon a Malinche, the Indian concubine of Cortés, for the betrayal into Spanish hands of her fellow Indians. In the murals of a Siqueiros, Cuauhtémoc, the last Mexica king, tortured and put to death by Cortés, achieved a new transfiguration, rising from the dead to affirm a new and glorious future, while—in Diego Rivera's hands—his Spanish protagonist emerged as a hydrocephalic, syphilitic idiot. Transmuted into myth, the indigenous past became a golden age, the colonial period a time of trial and darkness, the mestizo present a return to the abundance and innocence of the country's golden youth. The foreigners had been expelled; now Cuauhtémoc would again be master in his own mansions.

But land reform, like Indianism, was only a halfway house to the achievement of the new society. The new order began there; yet it could not stop there. Land reform may be a prelude to solutions; but by itself alone it is incapable of solving any problem on more than a temporary basis. If a country possesses sufficient land for all now living, division of land may postpone a renewal of agrarian conflict for a generation; but population growth alone will soon reopen the question of land to the landless. If a country, like Middle America, lacks sufficient land for all, the very act of distribution will refuel the voices of discord. In Mexico, the average recipient received 10.4 acres of crop land, little of this irrigated. Such a gift would not supply the needs of a growing family for very long.

The ultimate effects of land reform, as of the Indianist movement, were therefore not those foreseen by its early advocates. Land reform solved no economic problem; nor did the archive of the Indianist contain a road map to guide the society on its future path. But land reform had transcendental political effects. It not only broke the monopoly of power of the landholding elite and freed the peons; it created new sources of power in the countryside. For in the very act of distributing land to the landless, the agents of the land reform became the new power-holders in the rural area. In the deed of land the revolutionary government paid its rural citizens an earnest of its intentions; but in the act of bestowal the new government simultaneously laid the foundations of a new political machine to replace the one overturned by the revolution. In the creation of this new political weapon the revolutionary government not only guaranteed its present stability; it also created a set of checks against the vicissitudes of the future.

For the future could no longer be built upon the past. To fulfil the goals of his revolution the mestizo had to go beyond land reform and beyond Indianism to an active transformation of society in his own image. The economic instruments of this transformation are industrialization and the mechanization of agriculture. The political instruments

This small town in southern Mexico could be duplicated in many parts of Middle and South America. Such towns are now being linked by roads and motor transport to a larger nationwide transportation and communication grid. The house on the left contains the office of the local bus line. (Photograph by Joseph Seckendorf.)

of this transformation are the political machines that maintain the peace of the countryside. And the ideological instrument of this transformation is nationalism, together with its concomitant desire not to return to the cultural patterns of the Indian but to put an end to his separate cultural existence. Yet industrialization, political consolidation, and nationalism have a logic of their own. They exact a price, and as that price increases, those who pay it begin to question what goods and services all this blood, sweat, and tears will finally buy. Thus, if the revolution granted the mestizo the levers of power, it also made the maintenance of this power dependent upon his ability to deliver on his promises. Those who unleash the storm must know how to ride it, or become its victims.

The "underdeveloped" countries of the world have a choice of two major patterns of industrialization. The first pattern was adopted by the Soviet Union and by China. It grants priority to the construction of heavy industry; it carries out what Nikolai Bukharin called "war-feudal exploitation of the peasantry" to generate the capital needed for this purpose; and it throttles consumer needs to a minimum. The other pattern is that of the modern capitalist world. For both external and internal political and economic reasons Mexico has followed the second pattern. It involves a combination of various types of economic effort. Some capital is built up through sales of products to the heavily industrialized countries of the world; thus Mexico sells to the outside world a number of raw materials, and snares quantities of mobile dollars through its growing tourist trade and industry. At the same time, there is a growing light industry directed toward an internal market. This industry has its roots in the textile industry of the late nineteenth century; but in contrast to its predecessor it is beginning to supply—often on the instalment plan —goods which until recently were the hallmark of North American mass production: radios, gas stoves, sewing machines, watches, costume jewelry, knives and forks, television sets, aluminum pots, overalls, shoes— the cheap, quickly obsolescent, easily replaceable commodities of the "American way of life." These goods do not go into a foreign market;

252

Mexico on the road toward industrialization: a steel mill in northern Mexico. (Courtesy of Compañía Metalúrgica Peñoles.)

they are marketed in Mexico to an ever growing number of Mexican wage-earners.

This change in the pattern of consumption is a direct function of industrialization. In the narrow sense, it provides a means of fulfilling some of the promises of the revolution. Industrialization everywhere has involved people in the dilemma of "steel versus butter," between consumption now and consumption postponed in favor of continued reinvestment. In the countries of the Soviet bloc industrialization has been subsidized by restricted consumption and discrimination against the agricultural producer; in Mexico, it has been supported by the low real income of the Mexican wage-earner. While the Mexican economy as a whole has witnessed a phenomenal rate of growth, real wages have increased but slightly since 1910. The small increase in wages has not gone into a better diet or into better housing. It has gone into the acquisition of the cheap and expendable items of North American culture. Not everyone can participate in their consumption; but their "demonstration effect" makes "pie in the sky" seem increasingly available in the here and now, thus masking the hidden exploitation of the industrial labor force.

The spread of the new culture pattern also symbolizes the advent, here and now, of the open society of the future. That society, like the society of the United States north of the border, will be based on the premises that mobility is open to everyone; that position in society is measured not by descent but by income and by the goods income can buy; that all elites are temporary and that the tastes and goods of the elite should be distributed among the general population as quickly and as widely as possible; and that unlimited production and ever changing consumption are values in their own right. Hence Middle America borrows in the United States not only some of its capital for economic development but also canons of taste and the goods to satisfy these tastes. As nineteenth-century France offered the world the symbols of consumption that marked off the cultivated and educated man from the boorish and illiterate, so in the twentieth century the United States provides the world with the symbolic small-change of participation in the open society. The result is a cultural hybrid which the Mexicans deride publicly as *pocho* culture, although they are unable to resist its attraction and its advance.

But the spread of *pocho* culture does more than this. Along with a politics based on land reform, it is a powerful solvent of Indian resistance to incorporation. The diffusion of its cheap and expendable goods effectively undermines the scheme of means and ends through which the Indian has hitherto defended his autonomy. Limited wants, covered in limited ways, are yielding to growing wants and to the spread of alternative means to their satisfaction. Each year brings, in this community or that, the breakdown of the ritual system of enforced expenditures which has hitherto checked individual accumulation of wealth. At the

254

same time, each year witnesses—here and there—the abandonment of the traditional unity of secular and sacred offices, up to now the chief defense of the community against the accumulation and misuse of power by one of its members. Each year, in some community, men grown old in the service of their fellow men and of the supernatural yield to young men untried in communal administration but willing to align themselves with the new mobile men in the larger society beyond.

Yet the spread of this pattern raises as many problems as it answers. Many communities have indeed yielded to its temptations, but at the time of telling there still remain everywhere reservoirs of resistance, communities as yet unwilling or unable to open the gates to the flow of new cultural alternatives. Will all these communities eventually be integrated into the mainstream of national life? This would represent a signal triumph for the mestizo cause; yet it would imply, too, the disintegration of that local unity on which Middle America has so often relied for its defense in past times of crisis. But what if the process of integration should encounter limits, as it has so often encountered limits in the past? Perhaps there are still communities so distant from the centers of national life, so poor in resources, that they could not multiply their wants even if they had the will to do so. Perhaps there are still communities so lacking in assets possible to mobilize that any effort to make them part of the nation would outweigh the advantages thus gained. Shall we then witness the unwished-for and unenvisioned emergence of "native reserves," in which the remaining Indians will cling, hillbilly-like, to an ever more barren, ever more impoverished hinterland?

Nor is the spread of *pocho* culture an unmixed boon even for those willing and able to purchase its trappings. Perhaps Middle America can achieve integration and liberation from the dead hand of the past only by borrowing the cultural patterns of its powerful northern neighbor. Yet such borrowing involves a deeper paradox, the paradox of a social unity gained at the price of cultural indebtedness to another society. Would Middle America be willing to pay for such a solution with lowered self-esteem and valuation of its society, and would it then substitute for its hostility against itself the rituals of a nationalism exacerbated rather than attenuated by the growing similarity in the cultural field, in order to preserve its social identity? Or will Middle America eventually find its own voice? Is the great flowering of Mexican painting and architecture evidence of such a new and fruitful synthesis, or will it, too, wither away as Indianism declines in the face of the new utilitarian concerns of the new occupants of power?

Thus men still remain torn between yesterday and tomorrow; and Middle America remains in travail. There can therefore be no finis to this book, nor any prophecy. The rooster has cried a coming dawn, but in the gray daybreak the shadows still lie in dark pools about doorway and alley. Somewhere, an Indian elder bows to the four directions and invokes the rain-givers, the earth-shakers in their mountainous domain. The mouth of the volcano still yawns; the future is not yet. It lies in the walk of that man, shielding his face against the cold; in the gestures of that woman, fanning the embers of her fire and drawing her shawl more closely about her sleeping child; in that lonely figure, setting a signal along a railroad track. There is still time until the sun rises, but men scan the sky; for their lives are mortgaged to tomorrow.

Bibliographical
Notes

I have consciously preserved the reader from contact with the dusty, if necessary, world of scientific footnotes. These notes at the end of the volume therefore serve a double purpose. I want to provide references for those who wish to explore on their own some of the material treated in this book. I also want to show my professional colleagues the color and shape of the markings on my cards. To those whom I have so encouraged I wish most happy hunting and a pleasant encounter upon the trail.

To expedite matters, I have employed the following abbreviations for journals and publications cited more than once in the body of the bibliography:

AA	American Anthropologist
AAA	American Anthropological Association
AAA-M	American Anthropological Association, Memoir
AATQ	American Antiquity
AgH	Agricultural History
AI	América Indígena (Mexico, D.F.)
AMNH-AP	American Museum of Natural History, Anthropological Papers
APS-P	American Philosophical Society, Proceedings
APS-T	American Philosophical Society, Transactions
ASR	American Sociological Review
BAE-B	Bureau of American Ethnology, Bulletin
BBAA	Boletín Bibliográfico de Antropología Americana (Mexico, D.F.)
CA	Cuadernos Americanos (Mexico, D.F.)

CIW-NMAAE	Carnegie Institution of Washington, Notes on Middle American Archaeology and Ethnology
CIW-P	Carnegie Institution of Washington, Publications
CS	Ciencias Sociales (Washington, D.C.), Pan American Union
EAMG	*Estudios antropológicos publicados en homenaje al doctor Manuel Gamio* (Mexico: Dirección de Publicaciones, 1956)
EMA	El México Antiguo (Mexico, D.F.)
GR	Geographical Review
HAC	*Homenaje al doctor Alfonso Caso* (Mexico: Imprenta Nuevo Mundo, 1951)
HAHR	Hispanic American Historical Review
HB	Human Biology
HC	Sol Tax (ed.), *Heritage of Conquest* (Glencoe, Ill.: Free Press, 1952)
HM	Historia Mexicana (Mexico, D.F.)
HT y V	Ignacio Bernal and Eusebio Dávalos Hurtado (eds.), *Huastecos, Totonacos y sus vecinos* (Mexico: Sociedad Mexicana de Antropología, 1953)
IA	Ibero-Americana
ICA	International Congress of Americanists
ICA:XXVI	*XXVI. Congreso Internacional de Americanistas, 1935* (2 vols.; Madrid: S. Aguirre, 1948)
ICA:AA	*Acculturation in the Americas: Proceedings and Selected Papers of the XXIXth International Congress of Americanists*, ed. Sol Tax (Chicago: University of Chicago Press, 1952)
ICA:CAA	*The Civilizations of Ancient America: Selected Papers of the XXIXth International Congress of Americanists*, ed. Sol Tax (Chicago: University of Chicago Press, 1952)
ICA:XXXI	*Anais do XXXI Congreso Internacional de Americanistas* (2 vols., São Paulo: Editorial Anhembi, 1955)
IEA-A	Instituto de Etnografía Americana, Universidad de Cuyo, Anales (now Anales de Arqueología y Etnología [Mendoza, Argentina])
IETM	Institut d'Ethnologie, Université de Paris à la Sorbonne, Travaux et Mémoires
IIN-B	Instituto Indigenista Nacional, Boletín (Guatemala City)

IJAL	International Journal of American Linguistics
INAH	Instituto Nacional de Antropología e Historia (Mexico, D.F.)
INAH-A	Instituto Nacional de Antropología e Historia, Anales (Mexico, D.F.)
INAH-M	Instituto Nacional de Antropología e Historia, Memorias (Mexico, D.F.)
INI-M	Instituto Nacional Indigenista, Memorias (Mexico, D.F.)
IPGH-P	Instituto Panamericano de Geografía e Historia, Publicaciones (Tacubaya, Mexico, D.F.)
JNH	Journal of Negro History
JSAP	Journal de la Société des Américanistes
JWAS	Journal of the Washington Academy of Sciences
KAS-P	Kroeber Anthropological Society, Papers
MARI-P	Middle American Research Institute of Tulane University, Publications
MN	Clarence L. Hay *et al., The Maya and Their Neighbors* (New York: Appleton-Century, 1940)
MO	*Mayas y Olmecas* (Tuxtla Gutiérrez: Sociedad Mexicana de Antropología, 1942)
MOC	Miguel Othón de Mendizábal, *Obras completas* (6 vols.; Mexico: Talleres Gráficos de la Nación, 1946–47)
PM-P	Peabody Museum (Harvard University), Archaeological and Ethnological Papers
PSP	Gordon R. Willey (ed.), *Prehistoric Settlement Patterns in the New World* ("Viking Fund Publications in Anthropology," Vol. XXIII [1956])
RMEA	Revista Mexicana de Estudios Antropológicos (Mexico, D.F.)
SAA-M	Society of American Archaeology, Memoirs
SEN-D	Secretaría de la Economía Nacional, México, Documentos para la historia económica de México (Mexico, D.F.)
SES	Social and Economic Studies (Kingston, Jamaica)
SI-AR	Smithsonian Institution, Annual Reports
SI-ISA	Smithsonian Institution, Institute of Social Anthropology, Publications
SWJA	Southwestern Journal of Anthropology
TE	Trimestre Económico (Mexico, D.F.)
UTILAS	University of Texas, Institute of Latin American Studies (Austin)

CHAPTER I

Much of this chapter is based on a study by Angel Palerm and myself on "Ecological Potential and Cultural Development in Mesoamerica," in *Studies in Human Ecology* (Washington, D.C.: Pan American Union, 1957), pp. 1–37. Oliver G. Ricketson, Jr., wrote "An Outline of Basic Physical Factors Affecting Middle America," in MN, pp. 10–31.

Standard geographies dealing with Mexico are Jorge Tamayo, *Geografía general de México* (2 vols.; Mexico: Talleres Gráficos de la Nación, 1949), and Jorge A. Vivó, *Geografía de México* (Mexico: Fondo de Cultura Económica, 1949). I have learned a great deal from Nathan L. Whetten's summary chapter 1 in his *Rural Mexico* (Chicago: University of Chicago Press, 1948) and from Leo Waibel's paper, "Die wirtschaftsgeographische Gliederung Mexikos," *Geographische Zeitschrift*, XXXV (1929), 416–39.

Unfortunately we do not yet have an up-to-date geography of Guatemala in English. The best studies extant are still the works of Karl Sapper, such as "Grundzüge der physikalischen Geographie von Guatemala," *Petermanns Mitteilungen*, CXIII (1894), 1–59, and "Über Gebirgsbau und Boden des Nördlichen Mittelamerika," in the same series, CXXVII (1899), 1–119, as well as Franz Termer's "Zur Geographie der Republik Guatemala," *Mitteilungen der geographischen Gesellschaft in Hamburg*, XLIV (1936), 89–275, and XLVII (1941), 7–262. I have greatly benefited from reading E. Higbee, "The Agricultural Regions of Guatemala," GR, XXXVII (1947), 177–201, which includes an excellent map.

Most useful have been studies of regional cultural geography such as Felix W. McBryde, *Cultural and Historical Geography of Southwestern Guatemala* (SI-ISA, IV [1945]); William T. Sanders, "The Anthropogeography of Central Veracruz," in HT y V, pp. 27–78; Franz Termer, *Die Halbinsel Yucatán* (Gotha: Veb Geographische Kartographische Anstalt, 1954); Robert C. West, *Cultural Geography of the Modern Tarascan Area* (SI-ISA, VII [1948]).

The myth of repeated cyclical destructions appears, among other sources, in the Indian pictorial manuscript *Anales de Cuauhtitlán*, also called *Codex Chimalpopoca*, translated from Nahuatl into Spanish by Primo Feliciano Velásquez, *Anales de Cuauhtitlán y leyenda de los Soles* (Mexico, D.F.: Universidad Autónoma de México, 1945).

Carl O. Sauer has written on the persisting division between northern and southern Mexico in "The Personality of Mexico," GR, XXXI (1941), 353–64.

Joseph Raymond has surveyed references to "Water in Mexican Place-Names," *The Americas*, IX (1952), 201–5.

Karl A. Wittfogel has explored the implications of irrigation for social control in many writings. The most recent and most comprehensive of his studies is *Oriental Despotism* (New Haven: Yale University Press, 1957). The bearing of his theories on Middle America is discussed in Julian Steward (ed.), *Irrigation Civilizations: A Comparative Study* (Washington, D.C.: Pan American Union, 1955), pp. 58–78.

The study of settlement patterns is a growing concern among archeologists and ethnologists interested in Middle America. Gonzalo Aguirre Beltrán has spoken of the "solar" pattern of Middle American settlement in his "Teoría de los centros coordinadores," CS, VI (1955), 66–67. William T. Sanders has drawn the distinction between "community settlement pattern" and "zonal settlement pattern," or between the spatial distribution of a group in a given locality and the symbiotic interrelationships between groups in different localities in "The Central Mexican Symbiotic Region," in PSP, pp. 115–27. Ángel Palerm has contrasted "planned" and "unplanned" prehistoric civic centers in "La secuencia de la evolución cultural de Mesoamérica (del Arcaico a fines del Clásico)," BBAA, XVII (1954), Part 1, 205–33. Sol Tax developed the useful distinction between nucleated communities and "vacant towns" in "The *Municipios* of the Midwestern Highlands of Guatemala," AA, XXXIX (1937), 423–44, a distinction refined by Gordon R. Willey in his "Problems concerning Prehistoric Settlement Patterns in the Maya Lowlands," in PSP, pp. 107–14. Willey sees a difference between "vacant town" arrangements in which the population is scattered evenly about the town in isolated homesteads and a situation in which they are scattered about a center in small, tightly clustered hamlets. Suzanne W. Miles has grouped together these various kinds of dispersed settlement as variants of one type, in "An Urban Type: Extended Boundary Towns," SWJA, XIV (1958), 339–51. In PSP, moreover, Stephan F. de Borhegyi points to the persistence into modern times of prehistoric types of settlement: "Settlement Patterns in the Guatemalan Highlands: Past and Present," pp. 101–6, a point also raised in a slightly different fashion in Dan Stanislawski's *The Anatomy of Eleven Towns in Michoacán* (UTILAS, X [1950]).

The concept of key area has its origin among the geopoliticians. See, for instance, Friedrich Ratzel, *Politische Geographie* (Munich: R. Ouldenbourg, 1923), pp. 136–37. Its utility for social analysis was first demonstrated in Ch'ao-ting Chi, *Key Economic Areas in Chinese History* (London: Allen & Unwin, 1936). Since then it has been used by Karl A. Wittfogel and Owen Lattimore among students of Chinese history, Julian Steward among American anthropologists, Karl Deutsch among sociologists. In my discussion of the relation between key area and periphery in Middle America I have followed out some leads of Betty Starr's in "Levels of Communal Relations," *American Journal of Sociology*, LX (1954), 125–35.

Bibliographical Notes

CHAPTER II

In my discussion of Amerind origins I have largely followed Joseph B. Birdsell, "The Problem of the Early Peopling of the Americas as Viewed from Asia," in William S. Laughlin (ed.), *Papers on the Physical Anthropology of the American Indian* (New York: Wenner-Gren Foundation for Anthropological Research, 1951), pp. 1–68. Ales Hrdlička's views are conveniently summarized in "Origins and Antiquity of the American Indian," written in 1923 and reprinted in Earl W. Count (ed.), *This Is Race* (New York: Henry Schuman, 1950), pp. 328–38. Environmental adaptation in the New World are treated by Marshall T. Newman, "The Application of Ecological Rules to the Racial Anthropology of the Aboriginal New World," AA, LV (1953), 311–27. A. E. Mourant, *The Distribution of the Human Blood Groups* (Oxford: Blackwell, 1954) is the best source on the subject. On natural selection and the human blood groups, see John Buettner-Janusch, "Natural Selection in Man: The ABO(H) Blood Group System," AA, LXI (1959), 437–56.

Juan Comas has summarized all metrical data for Middle America up to 1943 in *La antropología física en México y Centro América* (IPGH-P, No. 68 [1943]). Jorge A. Vivó has applied José Imbelloni's racial classification to Middle America in *Razas y lenguas indígenas de México* (IPGH-P, No. 52 [1941]). For Imbelloni's classification, see "The Peopling of America," in the volume edited by Earl W. Count, pp. 665–78.

Comas has scrutinized "Olmec" physical remains in "Osteométrica Olmeca: informe preliminar sobre los restos hallados en Cerro de las Mesas, Estado de Veracruz, México," IEA-A, VI (1945), 169–208. Eusebio Dávalos Hurtado and J. M. Ortíz de Zárate interpret the Olmec features as pathologies in "La plástica indígena y la patología," in HT y V, pp. 95–104. See also Sigvald Linné, "Humpbacks in Ancient America," *Ethnos*, VIII (1943), 161–86, on the supernatural significance of the hunchback.

Mourant's book on blood groups also contains the latest data on Spain (p. 59). The metrical features of the Spanish population are surveyed in Carleton S. Coon, *The Races of Europe* (New York: Macmillan Co., 1939), pp. 489–98. George M. Foster has written on the provenience of Spanish migrants in "The Significance to Anthropological Studies of the Places of Origin of Spanish Emigrants to the New World," in ICA: AA, pp. 292–98.

The history of the Negro in Spanish America has received less attention than it deserves. A general summary is provided by James F. King, "Negro History in Continental Spanish America," JNH, XXIX (1944), 7–23. Gonzalo Aguirre

Beltrán has written the standard work on the Negro in Mexico in his "*La población negra de México, 1519–1810* (Mexico, D.F.: Ediciones Fuente Cultural, 1946). See also his "Tribal Origins of the Negro in Mexico," JNH, XXXI (1946), 269–352, and his "The Slave Trade in Mexico," HAHR, XXIV (1944), 412–31. On the Negro component among the Otomí see Eugène Schreider, "Étude de quelques signes de métissage dans une population amérindienne," *Bulletins et Mémoires de la Société d'Anthropologie de Paris*, Ser. 10, VI (1955), 223–34. On Tehuantepec, see Carlos Macías, "Los Tehuantepecanos actuales," *Boletín del Museo Nacional*, II (1912), 18–19.

Post-Conquest immigration of Chinese, Malays, Filipinos, and others from the Asiatic side of the Pacific Ocean via the trade route from Manila to Acapulco deserves a special study, together with the possible influence of such groups on art forms, food habits, dress, etc. An interesting paper dealing with "Chinese in Mexico City in 1635," by H. H. Dubs and R. S. Smith appeared in the *Far Eastern Quarterly*, I (1942), 387–89.

Estimates of pre-Hispanic population range all the way from Alfred L. Kroeber's minimal number of 3,000,000 for the region of higher culture in Mexico and Central America in his *Cultural and Natural Areas of Native North America* (Berkeley and Los Angeles: University of California Press, 1947), pp. 159–60, to a figure of 25,000,000 supported by Andrés Molina Enríquez in *La Revolución Agraria de México* (5 vols.; Mexico, D.F.: Talleres Gráficos del Museo Nacional de Arqueología, Historia, y Etnografía, 1933–37), I, 70. My bias favors studies which attempt to arrive at independent estimates of population figures through the study of extant documents rather than through inferences from other kinds of evidence. Only when we can get agreement among several different lines of investigation, each proceeding on autonomous grounds, are we likely to get an approximation of the truth. Dino Camavitto arrived at an estimate of 9,000,000 on the basis of documents in Iberian and Italian libraries: *La decadenza delle popolazioni messicane al tempo della Conquista* (Rome: Comitato Italiano per lo studio dei problemi della popolazione, 1935). Miguel Othón de Mendizábal set the figure at 9,170,400 in his essay "La demografía Mexicana," MOC, III, 335. The most detailed and well-documented, and to me the most persuasive, estimate is by Sherburne F. Cook and Lesley Byrd Simpson, *The Population of Central Mexico in the Sixteenth Century* (IA, No. 31 [1948]), who arrive at a figure of 11,000,000 for central Mexico alone. These figures tend to favor Karl Sapper's earlier guess that the population of Middle America as a whole was somewhere

around 12,000,000–15,000,000 in "Beiträge zur Frage der Volkzahl und Volks-dichte der vorkolombischen Indianerbevölkerung," ICA: XXVI, I, 456–78.
   Sherburne F. Cook has examined the Spanish census of 1793 in "The Popula-tion of Mexico in 1793," HB, XIV (1942), 499–515. The study of modern mestizo populations in Middle America is still in its infancy. Metrical studies which have been useful to me are: Marcus S. Goldstein, "Observations on Mexican Crania," *American Journal of Physical Anthropology*, N.S., I (1943), 83–93, and his *Demographic and Bodily Changes in Descendants of Mexican Immigrants, with Comparable Data on Parents and Children in Mexico* (UTILAS, 1943); Johanna Faulhaber, *La antropología física de Veracruz* (2 vols.; Jalapa: Gobierno de Veracruz, 1950–56); Gabriel W. Lasker, "Ethnic Identification in an Indian Mestizo Community, II: Racial Characteristics," *Phylon*, XIV (1953), 187–90; Morris Steggerda, *Maya Indians of Yucatán* (CIW-P, No. 531 [1941]); George D. Williams, *Maya-Spanish Crosses in Yucatán* (PM-P, Vol. XIII [1931]).

CHAPTER III

   Language classification has a long history in Middle America. Outstanding among earlier schemes is the largely intuitive but most productive scheme offered by Edward Sapir, "Central and North American Languages," *Encyclopaedia Bri-tannica* (1929 ed.), V, 138–41. The most recent published synthesis is by J. Alden Mason, "The Native Languages of Middle America," MN, pp. 52–87. A verbal summary of achievements in this field was presented by Norman A. McQuown, J. Alden Mason, and Morris Swadesh at the Fifty-fourth Annual Meeting of the AAA on November 17, 1955. This is to be published in a forthcoming monograph by the Social Science Office of the Pan American Union, Washington, D.C. Nor-man A. McQuown has presented a useful inventory of Indian languages in his paper on "Indigenous Languages of Native America," AA, LVII (1955), 501–70.
   Frederick Johnson drew a language map to accompany J. Alden Mason's syn-thesis: "The Linguistic Map of Mexico and Central America," MN, pp. 88–114. Another map of great value is the second revised copy of "Lenguas indígenas de México," by Miguel Othón de Mendizábal and Wigberto Jiménez Moreno, pub-lished in 1939 by IPGH and the Instituto Politécnico Nacional, Mexico.
   The technique of glottochronology was first discussed by Morris Swadesh in "Lexico-Statistic Dating of Prehistoric Ethnic Contacts," APS-P, XCVI (1952), 452–62, and again in "Towards Greater Accuracy in Lexicostatistic Dating," IJAL, XXI (1955), 121–37. Most linguists have accepted Swadesh's basic find-ings, though with qualifications dictated by scientific caution.

My reconstruction of language history in Middle America rests on the language sequences in the Gulf region worked out by Wigberto Jiménez Moreno and on the reconstructions of Morris Swadesh. Jiménez Moreno has presented his reconstructions in "El enigma de los Olmecas," CA, V (1942), 113–45. Swadesh, in addition to the papers already listed, discusses problems of general classification and reconstruction in "Perspectives and Problems of American Comparative Linguistics," *Word*, X (1954), 306–32, and "Towards a Satisfactory Genetic Classification of Amerindian Languages," ICA: XXXI, II, 1001–12. See also Morris Swadesh, George I. Quimby, Henry B. Collins, Emil W. Haury, Gordon Ekholm, and Fred Eggan: "Symposium on Time Depths of American Linguistic Groupings," AA, LVI (1954), 361–77.

The relationship of Chibchan and Uto-Aztecan is discussed by Swadesh in the paper in *Word* mentioned above. The unity of Otomian was established by Stanley Newman and Robert J. Weitlaner in "Central Otomian," IJAL, XVI (1950), 1–19, 73–81. The tie between Mixtec and Otomian is broached by Lawrence Ecker, "Relationship of Mixtec to the Otomian Languages," EMA, IV (1937), 209, and treated by the *Altmeister* of Mexican linguistics, Robert J. Weitlaner, in "Los Pueblos no Nahuas de la historia Tolteca y el grupo lingüístico Macro Otomangue," RMEA, V (1941), 249–69. The unity of Macro-Mayan was proposed on intuitional grounds by Norman McQuown, "Una posible síntesis lingüística Macro-Mayance," MO, pp. 37–38. This is accepted by Swadesh but disputed by William L. Wonderly, "Sobre la propuesta filiación lingüística de la familia Totonaca con las familias Zoqueana y Mayense," HT y V, pp. 105–13.

On Otomí, see Newman and Weitlaner, above, and Jacques Soustelle, *La famille Otomi-Pame du Mexique central* (IETM, Vol. XXVI [1937]). The differentiation of Mixtecan was discussed by Swadesh at the Fifty-sixth Annual Meeting of the AAA on December 27, 1957, on the basis of a recent thesis presented at the Escuela Nacional de Antropología e Historia, Mexico, by Evangelina Arana Osnaya. María Teresa Fernández de Miranda has dealt with Popoloca in *Glotocronología de la familia Popoloca* (Museo Nacional de Antropología, Serie científica 4 [Mexico, D.F., 1956]). For Nahua, see Benjamin L. Whorf, "The Comparative Linguistics of Uto-Aztecan," AA, XXXVII (1935), 600–608, and "The Origin of Aztec *tl*," AA, XXXIX (1937), 265–74. Morris Swadesh has discussed Nahua prehistory and glottochronology in "Algunas fechas glotocronológicas importantes para la prehistoria Nahua," RMEA, XIV (1954–55), 173–92. On Huastec, see Morris Swadesh, "The Language of the Archaeologic Huastecs," CIW-NMAAE, IV (1953), 223–27. On Maya, Norman McQuown, "The Classification of the Maya Languages," IJAL, XXII (1956), 191–95; Abraham M. Halpern, "A Theory of Maya *ts*-sounds," CIW-NMAAE, XIII (1942), 51–62. On Zoquean, William L. Wonderly, "Some Zoquean Phonemic and Morphophonemic Correspondences," IJAL, XV (1949), 1–11.

Not all specialists will agree with me on the location of the area in which Zapotec achieved characterization. Historical sources mention that the Zapotecs came into their present habitat from the north. Archeological evidence demonstrates that Tehuacán in the state of Puebla once constituted a frontier region between the carriers of Teotihuacán culture and the carriers of the culture of Monte Albán. Zapotec, Maya, and Nahua share a loan word for dog, *pekku*, and must therefore once have been in close contact. This is only feasible if we project the former settlement of the Zapotec-speakers northeastward from their present location. Finally, most persuasive of all, Swadesh, on linguistic grounds, places the former home of the Zapotec-speakers north of the Villa Alta mountains and northeast of the Juárez region in "The Phonemic Structure of Proto-Zapotec," IJAL, XIII (1947), 220–30. See also John Paddock, "Some Observations," *Mesoamerican Notes*, IV (1955), 80–92.

The present-day distribution of speakers of native languages in Mexico and Guatemala is mapped and discussed in: Manuel Germán Parra, *Densidad de la población de habla indígena en la República Mexicana* (INI-M, Vol. I, No. 1 [1950]); Antonio Goubaud Carrera, "Distribución de las lenguas indígenas en Guatemala," IIN-B, I, Nos. 2–3 (1946), 63–76, and "La población de habla indígena en Guatemala," IIN-B, I, No. 4 (1946), 17–21. My estimates of populations still speaking various Indian languages are based on various censuses. They include both monolinguals and bilinguals, as well as an estimated 15 per cent of the total population under 5 years of age usually not listed in Mexican censuses.

A most useful instrument for the study of American Spanish is Madeline W. Nichols, *A Bibliographical Guide to Materials on American Spanish* (Cambridge, Mass.: Harvard University Press, 1941). Pedro Henríquez Ureña (ed.), *El español en Méjico, los Estados Unidos y la América Central* (Buenos Aires: Instituto de Filología, Universidad de Buenos Aires, 1938), is a standard work dealing with our area. I have benefited greatly from the works of Amado Alonso, *Castellano, español, idioma nacional: Historia espiritual de tres nombres* (Buenos Aires: Instituto de Filología, Universidad de Buenos Aires, 1938) and *Estudios lingüísticos: Temas hispanoamericanos* (Biblioteca Románica Hispánica, Vol. II [Madrid: Editorial Gredos, 1953]), and from the provocative paper of Richard M. Morse, "Language as a Key to Latin American Historiography," *The Americas*, XI (1955), 517–38.

Nahuatl influence on Mexican Spanish is shown in José Ignacio Dávila Garibi, *Del Nahuatl al Español* (IPGH-P, Vol. XL [1939]). Cecilio A. Robelo compiled a dictionary of Nahuatl words in Mexican usage, *Diccionario de Aztequismos* (Mexico, D.F.: Ediciones Fuente Cultural, 1941). Alfredo Barrera Vásquez discusses the influence of Maya on Yucatec Spanish in "El idioma español en Yucatán," *Enciclopedia Yucatense* (Mexico, D.F.: Gobierno de Yucatán, 1946), VI, 341–75. Anthropologists will be interested in an early study of Spanish influence on an Indian language by Franz Boas, "Spanish Elements in Modern Nahuatl," *Todd Memorial Volume, Philological Studies* (New York: Columbia University, 1930), I, 85–89. An elegant modern study of the influence of Spanish on a native language is William L. Wonderly, "Phonemic Acculturation in Zoque," IJAL, XII (1946), 92–95. The rate at which native languages are disappearing is discussed by Emilio Alanís Patiño in "La población indígena de México," in MOC, I, 29–98.

CHAPTERS IV–VII

These four chapters all deal with Middle American prehistory. I have been greatly helped in their preparation by several recent attempts at synthesis. These are: Pedro Armillas, "A Sequence of Cultural Development in Mesoamerica," in Wendell C. Bennett (ed.), *A Reappraisal of Peruvian Archaeology* (SAA-M, Vol. IV [1948]), pp. 105–11, and his "Tecnología, formaciones socio-económicas y religión en Mesoamérica," ICA: CAA, pp. 19–30; Ignacio Bernal, *Mesoamérica* (IPGH-P, No. 152 [1953]); Alfonso Caso, "New World Culture History: Middle America," in Alfred L. Kroeber (ed.), *Anthropology Today* (Chicago: University of Chicago Press, 1953), pp. 226–37; Ángel Palerm, "La secuencia de la evolución cultural de Mesoamérica," BBAA, XVIII, Part 1 (1954), 205–33; Gordon R. Willey and Philip Phillips, *Method and Theory in American Archaeology* (Chicago: University of Chicago Press, 1958), esp. Part II.

George C. Vaillant's *Aztecs of Mexico* (Garden City, N.Y.: Doubleday, Doran & Co., 1944; also Harmondsworth: Penguin Books, 1950) remains the most widely read source on Middle American archeology, though now heavily out of date, a fact which is not remedied by C. A. Burland's postscript to the Penguin edition. For specific criticisms see John Paddock, "Notas sobre el texto de Vaillant 'Los Aztecas de México,'" *Antología MCC* (Mexico, D.F.: Mexico City College Press, 1956), pp. 187–210. The best book on the ancient cultures of Mexico and highland Guatemala is undoubtedly Walter Krickeberg, *Altmexikanische Kulturen* (Berlin: Safari-Verlag, 1956). Sylvanus G. Morley's *The Ancient Maya* has been brought up to date and revised by George W. Brainerd (3d ed.; Stanford, Calif.:

Stanford University Press, 1956). J. Eric Thompson's *The Rise and Fall of Maya Civilization* (Norman: University of Oklahoma Press, 1954) deals, like Morley, with the Maya of the lowlands.

CHAPTER IV

The gathering cultures of Middle America have been hypothetically grouped with a whole series of so-called desert cultures, said to extend from Oregon to the valley of Mexico by Jesse D. Jennings *et al.*, "The American Southwest," in Robert Wauchope (ed.), *Seminars in American Archaeology* (SAA-M, Vol. XI [1955]), pp. 59–127, esp. p. 69. The recent find of a skull associated with grinding tools in the valley of Mexico, perhaps representative of a seed-grinding group living between 8000 and 6000 B.C. is reported in Helmut de Terra, "A Successor to Tepexpan Man in the Valley of Mexico," *Science*, CXXIX (1959), 563–64.

I have benefited greatly in my understanding of early hunting and gathering cultures from H. M. Wormington's *Ancient Man in North America* (Denver: Denver Museum of Natural History, 1957). A useful critical study of early finds in our area is Luis Aveleyra Arroyo de Anda's *Prehistoria de México* (Mexico, D.F.: Ediciones Mexicanas, 1950). William R. Coe II has written an equally trenchant critique of "Early Man in the Maya Area," AATQ, XX (1955), 271–73. Tepexpan Man was the subject of a special monograph by Helmut de Terra, Javier Romero, and T. Dale Stewart, *Tepexpan Man* ("Viking Fund Publications in Anthropology," Vol. XI [1949]). More recent finds of men, mammoth, and spear points are discussed by Luis Aveleyra de Anda and Manuel Maldonado-Koerdell in "Association of Artifacts with Mammoth in the Valley of Mexico," AATQ, XVIII (1953), 332–40. Robert F. Heizer and Sherburne F. Cook write on "New Evidence of Antiquity of Tepexpan and Other Human Remains from the Valley of Mexico," in SWJA, XV (1959), 36–42.

The monograph on *Tepexpan Man* by De Terra *et al.* also offers a useful first encounter with the problems of correlating geological, faunal, and human data. José L. Lorenzo offers a later summary in "Notas sobre arqueología y cambios climáticos en la Cuenca de México," in *La Cuenca de México* (INAH, Dirección de Prehistoria, Publication No. 2 [1956]), pp. 29–51. The specialized contributions of pollen analysis are treated in Paul B. Sears, "Pollen Profiles and Culture Horizons in the Basin of Mexico," in ICA: CAA, pp. 57–62, and by Edward S. Deevey, Jr., "Pollen Analysis and Mexican Archaeology," AATQ, X (1944), 134–49. Robert Wauchope deals with "Implications of Radiocarbon Dates from Middle and South America," MARI-P, XVIII (1954), 19–40.

The concept of the "neolithic revolution" is discussed by V. Gordon Childe in

What Happened in History (New York: Penguin Books, 1946), chap. 3. Much of what I know about the course of plant and animal domestication in the New World, I have learned from Carl O. Sauer, *Agricultural Origins and Dispersals* (New York: American Geographical Society, 1952). Edgar T. Anderson's paper on "Man as a Maker of New Plants and Plant Communities," in William L. Thomas, Jr. (ed.), *Man's Role in Changing the Face of the Earth* (Chicago: University of Chicago Press, 1956), pp. 753–77, has proved most instructive, as has his book *Plants, Man, and Life* (Boston: Little, Brown & Co., 1952). Robert L. Dressler's "The Pre-Columbian Cultivated Plants of Mexico," *Botanical Museum Leaflets, Harvard University*, XVI (1953), 115–72, has been most useful to me. A fine summary of the history of maize is offered in P. C. Mangelsdorf, "Ancestor of Corn," *Science*, CXXVIII (1958), 1313–20. Jonathan D. Sauer has given us a monograph on "The Grain Amaranths," *Annals of the Missouri Botanical Gardens*, XXXVII (1950), 561–632. Richard MacNeish has discussed his findings of early cultivation in Tamaulipas in "Ancient Maize and Mexico," *Archaeology*, VIII (1955), 108–15, and in Thomas W. Whitaker, Hugh C. Cutler, and Richard S. MacNeish, "Cucurbit Materials from Three Caves in Tamaulipas," AATQ, XXII (1957), 352–58.

George C. Vaillant was the first to define the village cultures of the valley of Mexico. They are described in his *Aztecs of Mexico;* a summary of his various technical papers on the subject is *Early Culture in the Valley of Mexico: Results of the Stratigraphical Project of the American Museum of Natural History in the Valley of Mexico, 1928–1933* (AMNH-AP, Vol. XXV [1935], Part 3). Román Piña Chan, *Las culturas preclásicas de la Cuenca de México* (Mexico, D.F.: Fondo de Cultura Económica, 1955) offers a general view of the subject from the vantage point of more recent evidence. Edwin M. Shook has discussed the "Present Status of Research on the Pre-Classic Horizons of Guatemala, in ICA: CAA, pp. 93–100.

Gonzalo Aguirre Beltrán discusses the Middle American diet in "Cultura y nutrición," EAMG, pp. 227–49, including an excellent general bibliography of the subject. Miguel Othón de Mendizábal has documented the role of salt in Middle American culture in his "Influencia de la sal en la distribución geográfica de los grupos indígenas de México," MOC, II, 181–340. Harlan W. Gilmore, "Cultural Diffusion via Salt," AA, XLVII (1955), 1011–15, regards salt use as a form of addiction. Oswaldo Gonçalves de Lima deals with the cultivation of the century plant and the preparation of pulque in his *El maguey y el pulque en los Códices Mexicanos* (Mexico, D.F.: Fondo de Cultura Económica, 1956). On pulque at Teotihuacán, see Krickeberg, *Altmexikanische Kulturen*, p. 391.

CHAPTER V

Deficient terminology continues to plague us in the study of prehistory as in other fields. I have selected the term "Theocratic" as a lesser of several evils. Had I been more courageous, I should not have hesitated to invent a series of neutral terms for the various stages of Middle American development; but this seems a task for the professional archeologists united *in collegio* rather than for the isolated individual. I do not like terms like "Florescent" and "Classic," not only because they are stylistic terms, but also because they involve us in value-judgments about relative cultural richness or poverty of the preceding and following stages. I have also decided to lump with my Theocratic the Late Pre-Classic or Proto-Classic, usually assigned to the preceding stage, because it shows all the features said to be diagnostic of the full Classic. The courage of my convictions here receives reinforcement from Michael D. Coe's paper on "Pre-Classic Cultures in Mesoamerica: A Comparative Survey," KAS-P, No. 17 (1957), pp. 7–37. My Theocratic thus begins around 1000 B.C.

A recent discussion of the Theocratic as a whole is offered by Donald W. Lathrap, "The Classic Stage in Mesoamerica," KAS-P, No. 17 (1957), pp. 38–74. Pedro Armillas has discussed the pan-Mesoamerican influences of Teotihuacán in his "Teotihuacán, Tula, y los Toltecas," *Runa*, III (1950), 37–70, a paper which also offers insights into the Militarist period.

I see in the Olmec phenomenon one of the roots of the Theocratic. Its stylistic unity was first defined by Miguel Covarrubias, "Orígen y desarrollo del estilo artístico 'Olmeca,' " in MO, pp. 46–49. Its antiquity at the type site is attested by Philip Drucker, Robert F. Heizer, and Robert J. Squier, "Radiocarbon Dates from La Venta, Tabasco," *Science*, CXXVI (1957), 72–73. The interpretation of the Olmec style from a cultural point of view has analogies with the problem posed by the Chavín style in Peru; on this topic see Gordon R. Willey's "The Chavín Problem: A Review and Critique," SWJA, VII (1951), 103–44. For the association of the jaguar with Tlaloc see Pedro Armillas, "Los dioses de Teotihuacán," IEA-A, VI (1945), 35–62; for the ties with the Maya rain gods as well as for a discussion of jade see J. Eric Thompson, "Aquatic Symbols Common to Various Centers of the Classic Period in Mesoamerica," ICA: CAA, pp. 31–36.

A growing literature debates the social implications of cultivation in prehistoric and present-day Middle America. Ángel Palerm deals with "The Agricultural Bases of Urban Civilization in Mesoamerica," in Julian Steward (ed.), *Irrigation Civilizations: A Comparative Study* (Washington, D.C.: Pan American Union,

1955), pp. 28–42. On chinampas see Elisabeth Schilling, *Die 'schwimmenden Gärten' von Xochimilco* (*"Schriften des Geographischen Instituts der Universität Kiel,"* Vol. IX [1939]), and Robert C. West and Pedro Armillas "Las chinampas de México," CA, L (1950), 165–82. The more important papers on the subject of irrigation include: Pedro Armillas, "Notas sobre sistemas de cultivo en Mesoamérica: Cultivos de riego y de humedad en la Cuenca del Río de las Balsas," INAH-A, III (1949), 85–113; René F. Millon, "Irrigation Systems in the Valley of Teotihuacán," AATQ, XXIII (1957), 160–66; Ángel Palerm, "La distribución del regadío en el area central de Mesoamérica," CS, V (1954), 2–15, 64–74, with an excellent map of identified irrigation sites; Eric R. Wolf and Ángel Palerm, "Irrigation in the Old Acolhua Domain," SWJA, XI (1955), 265–81. The prophecy of the Maya priest on the availability of food through irrigation on the other side of the mountains appears in Alfredo Barrera Vásquez and Silvia Rendón, *El libro de los Libros de Chilam Balam* (Mexico, D.F.: Fondo de Cultura Económica, 1948), p. 105.

The connection of priests with cultivation is evident in the murals of Teotihuacán (Teopancaxco, Tepantitla). On the mural of the four priests at Jonacatepec, see Román Piña Chan, *Chacaltzingo, Morelos* (INAH, Dirección de Monumentos Pre-Hispánicos, 1955), p. 69. Connection of the priesthood with agriculture among the Maya is indicated by the post-Conquest Codex Pérez (see Morley and Brainerd, *The Ancient Maya*, p. 132), by the figure of a jaguar priest planting corn with a planting stick in the Codex Tre-Cortesianus (*ibid.*, p 134) and by figures scattering grain depicted on Maya stelae in Tatiana Proskouriakoff, *A Study of Classic Maya Sculpture* (CIW-P, No. 593 [1950]), p. 5.

Theocratic monuments and paintings show various personages carrying weapons, though hardly ever engaged in military action. Early Theocratic monuments which may depict a battle of some sort are stelae 1 and 2 from La Venta; see Miguel Covarrubias, *Indian Art of Mexico and Central America* (New York: Alfred A. Knopf, 1957), pp. 67, 68. The murals of Bonampak show warfare, though J. Eric Thompson interprets them as representations of a minor raid; see K. Ruppert, J. Eric Thompson, Tatiana Proskouriakoff, *Bonampak, Chiapas, Mexico* (CIW-P, No. 602 [1955]). Robert Rands furnishes "Some Evidence of Warfare in Classic Maya Art" (Ann Arbor: University of Michigan Microfilm Publication No. 4233, 1952). Ángel Palerm reviews the problem in the light of later evidence in "Notas sobre las construcciones militares y la guerra en Mesoamérica," CS, VII (1956), 189–202.

William T. Sanders suggests the possibility of markets at Teotihuacán in his paper on "The Central Mexican Symbiotic Region" in PSP, p. 124. The existence of markets in the Maya Theocratic is inferential. Miguel Acosta Saignés has suggested a Theocratic origin for the trading guild in his *Los Pochteca* (Mexico, D.F.: Acta Anthropologica, Vol. I [1945], No. 1). The association of the Amanteca or feather-workers with Teotihuacán follows a suggestion of W. Jiménez Moreno.

The best general treatment of the pantheon of Teotihuacán is Pedro Armillas' paper on "Los dioses de Teotihuacán." The murals of Tepantitla depicting the house of Tlaloc have been interpreted by Alfonso Caso, "El paraíso terrenal en Teotihuacán," CA, VI (1942), 127–36. The movement toward the standardization of figurines in the northern part of Middle America and their disappearance in the south is treated in general perspective by Stephan F. de Borhegyi, "The Development of Folk and Complex Cultures in the Southern Maya Area," AATQ, XXI (1956), 343–56, but especially incisively by John L. Sorenson, "A Chronological Ordering of the Mesoamerican Pre-Classic," MARI-P, XVIII (1955), 41–70, esp. 53–58. Walter Krickeberg has offered his interpretation of the cosmic symbolisms implied in the construction of Middle American temples and temple precincts in "Bauform und Weltbild im alten Mexiko," *Paideuma*, IV (1950), 295–333.

Matthew W. Stirling demonstrated the relationship of the Olmec calendar to the Maya calendar in his reading of a date on stela C, found at La Venta: see his "An Initial Series from Tres Zapotes, Vera Cruz, Mexico" ("National Geographic Society Technical Papers, Mexican Archaeological Series," Vol. I, No. 1 [Washington, D.C., 1940]). All such early calendric monuments have been discussed recently by Michael D. Coe, "Cycle 7 Monuments in Middle America: A Reconsideration," AA, LIX (1957), 597–611. Alfonso Caso has furnished evidence for the presence of the calendar in Monte Albán in his "Calendario y escritura de las antiguas culturas de Monte Albán" in MOC, I, 113–45, as well as for Teotihuacán in "Tenían los teotihuacanos conocimiento del tonalpohualli?" EMA, IV (1937) 131–43.

In my understanding of Middle American art I have benefited greatly by reading Salvador Toscano, *Arte precolombiano de México y de la América Central* (Mexico, D.F.: Instituto de Investigaciones Esteticas, Universidad Nacional Autónoma de México, 1944), Paul Westheim's essay *Arte antiguo de México* (Mexico, D.F.: Fondo de Cultura Económica, 1950), and Miguel Covarrubias, *Indian Art of Mexico and Central America*. Eulalia Guzmán has written an interesting essay about the general characteristics of pre-Hispanic Middle American art, "Carácteres fundamentales del arte," in *México Prehispánico* (Mexico, D.F.: Editorial Emma Hurtado, 1946), pp. 545–51. Tatiana Proskouriakoff's *A Study of Classic Maya*

Sculpture and *Urnas de Oaxaca* by Alfonso Caso and Ignacio Bernal (INAH-M, Vol. II [1952]) deserve special mention.

Descriptions and maps of most Theocratic sites may be found in Ignacio Marquina, *Arquitectura Prehispánica* (INAH-M, Vol. I [1951], as well as in the general works by Krickeberg, *Altmexikanische Kulturen,* and Morley and Brainerd, *The Ancient Maya,* and in Vaillant's *Aztecs of Mexico.* The papers dealing with Middle America in PSP explore various aspects of Theocratic sites. A recent monograph on Cholula by Eduardo Noguera, *La cerámica arqueológica de Cholula* (Mexico, D.F.: Editorial Guaranía, 1954) covers much more than just ceramics. On the Olmeca-Xicalanca, see Pedro Armillas, "Los Olmeca-Xicalanca y los sitios arqueológicos del suroeste de Tlaxcala," RMEA, VIII (1946), 137–45; for their identification with the Mixtec, Wigberto Jiménez Moreno, "El enigma de los Olmecas," CA, V (1942), 113–45. On the recent findings at Dzibilchaltún, see E. Wyllys Andrews, "Dzibilchaltún: Lost City of the Mayas," *National Geographic Magazine,* CXV (1959), 90–109.

CHAPTER VI

The Militarist stage is discussed in general terms by Jane Holden, "The Post-Classic Stage in Mesoamerica," KAS-P, No. 17 (1957), pp. 75–108. Agustín Villagra Caleti describes the murals of Atetelco in "Las pinturas de Atetelco en Teotihuacán," CA, LV (1951), 153–62. The departure of the priests from Copán is discussed by John M. Longyear III, "A Historical Interpretation of Copán Archaeology," in ICA: CAA, 86–92.

Vaillant assigned to deforestation and consequent erosion a large role in the fall of Teotihuacán: see his *Aztecs of Mexico* (Penguin ed.), p. 79. Sherburne F. Cook sees a further causative relationship between increasing population pressure and soil exhaustion in "The Interrelation of Population, Food Supply, and Building in Pre-Conquest Central Mexico," AATQ, XIII (1947), 45–52, as well as his *The Historical Demography and Ecology of the Teotlalpan* (IA, No. 33 [1949]) and *Soil Erosion and Population in Central Mexico* (IA, No. 34 [1949]). The same point is made for the lowland Maya by C. Wythe Cooke, "Why the Mayan Cities of the Petén District, Guatemala, Were Abandoned," JWAS, XXI (1931), 283–87, and, more recently, by Betty J. Meggers, "Environmental Limitation on the Development of Culture," AA, LVI (1954), 801–24, esp. 817–21. This last paper raised a lively controversy: see, for instance, William R. Coe, "Environmental Limitation on Mayan Culture: A Re-examination," AA, LIX (1957), 328–35, and Milton Altschuler, "On the Environmental Limitations of Mayan Cultural Development," SWJA, XIV (1958), 189–98. O. F. Cook in his "Milpa Agriculture, a

273

Primitive Tropical System" (SI-AR 1919 [1921]) cites invasions by grass as a
further cause for social collapse, an explanation also favored by Morley. Limitations of environment and technology may well have exerted a general effect, but
they cannot explain specific circumstances. On the stability of Teotihuacán settlements, see José L. Lorenzo in *La Cuenca de México*, p. 45. The persistence of
Cholula throughout Theocratic and Militaristic times is demonstrated by Noguera
in his book on Cholula pottery. According to Thompson, *The Rise and Fall of
Maya Civilization* (p. 86), Maya sites are not located near grasslands. Longyear
notes no environmental reason for the sudden abandonment of Copán; in fact, the
region as a whole was still populated at the time the Spaniards arrived in the area.
The ceremonial center was abandoned; not so, however, the extremely fertile
valley surrounding it.

Thompson is the chief advocate of the thesis which would explain the fall of
the Maya centers as a result of a series of "peasant revolts": see, for example,
his *Rise and Fall,* p. 87. Religious dissensions may have played some part, though
it is no longer possible to explain the burial of the so-called Temple of Quetzalcoatl
at Teotihuacán under another structure on the basis of historical data which apply
to Tula, some half a millennium later, as Mendizábal attempted to do in MOC, II,
345–53. Ángel Palerm and I have discussed the problems raised by the imbalance
between city and hinterland in our paper on "Ecological Potential and Cultural
Development in Mesoamerica," pp. 32–33.

On jade in the grave of a Maya peasant see Gordon R. Willey, "The Structure
of Ancient Maya Society: Evidence from the Southern Lowlands," AA, LVIII
(1956), 777–82.

On fortifications in Middle America see Pedro Armillas, "Fortalezas Mexicanas," CA, XLI (1948), 143–63 and his "Mesoamerican Fortifications," *Antiquity,* No. 96 (1951), pp. 77–86, as well as Alberto Ruz Lhuillier, "Chichén-Itzá
y Palenque, ciudades fortificadas," HAC, pp. 331–42. The shift from undefended
to defensible hilltop sites is beautifully documented by A. Ledyard Smith in
Archaeological Reconnaissance in Central Guatemala (CIW-P, No. 608 [1955]).
Ángel Palerm's paper on fortifications and warfare has already been cited.

On the trade state of Acalán see France V. Scholes and Ralph L. Roys, *The
Maya Chontal Indians of Acalan-Tixchel* (CIW-P, No. 560 [1948]). On the
"pottery barrier," Robert E. Smith, *Ceramic Sequence at Uaxactun, Guatemala*
(MARI-P, No. 20, Vol. I [1955]), p. 8.

For the identification of the legendary Xibalba with the Petén and its conquest
by the brothers Hunahpu and Xbalemque see Adrián Recinos, Delia Goetz, and
Sylvanus G. Morley, *Popol Vuh* (London: Hodge & Co., 1951), p. 114, n. 6.

Xochicalco is described and discussed by William T. Sanders in PSP. Tula was dealt with specifically in a special issue of RMEA, V (1941) ; especially significant are the papers by Wigberto Jiménez Moreno, Jorge R. Acosta, and Alfonso Caso. Palerm and I have debated the role of Tula in our paper on ecology and cultural potential, pp. 3–4, 32. La Quemada is discussed by Armillas in his studies of fortifications, as well as by J. Charles Kelley in "Settlement Patterns in North-Central Mexico," PSP, pp. 128–39. Toltec finds have appeared in Penitas, Nayarit, an area which may have been much more important in the development of the northern frontier than has hitherto been realized: see news item in AATQ, XXII (1956), 222. Paul Kirchhoff, Ralph Beals, and Carl O. Sauer have discussed the shifting agricultural frontier in northern Mexico in a special issue of AA, LVI (1954), 529–56, devoted wholly to the Southwest of the United States.

Tollán may mean literally "Place of Reeds," but in its wider sense it signifies simply "city." In the Mapa Quinatzin the glyph for Tollán stands for Teotihuacán, in the sense of City of Teotihuacán. In the Codex Sierra, Tenochtitlán–Mexico City is designated as Tollán. In the *Relación de Cholula* by Cristobal de Chávez, Cholula is called Tollán Cholollan. Sahagún refers to Tula, Hidalgo, as Tollán Xicocotitlán, after the mountain still called Jicuco near modern Tula. *Tolteca* or Toltec thus means "city-dweller." The political concept of Tollán as a metropolis with hinterland appears in symbolic representations of the metropolis as the head and heart of an organism, the towns of the hinterland as arms and feet: see *Historia Tolteca-Chichimeca*, where the hands and feet of the Great Tollán are said to consist of 20 towns, and Alfredo Barrera Vásquez and Silvia Rendón, *El libro de los Libros de Chilam Balam* (Mexico, D.F.: Fondo de Cultura Económica, 1948), pp. 108–9 and n. 48. Maya documents often carry maps that show heads, arms, and heart. My continuing doubts about the one-to-one correspondence of the Great Tollán with Tula, Hidalgo, is based on a reading of David H. Kelley's unpublished manuscript *A History of Pre-Spanish Mesoamerica*. Krickeberg, *Altmexikanische Kulturen* (pp. 284–85) well describes the magical character of the Toltec in the minds of later populations. Paul Kirchhoff's "Quetzalcóatl, Huemac y el fin de Tula," CA, LXXXIV (1955), 163–96, illuminates the collapse not only of the Tula political system but of its social and political organization.

On the Epigonal Toltec states in the valley of Mexico, see Wigberto Jiménez Moreno, "Síntesis de la historia precolonial del Valle de México," RMEA, XIV (1954–55), 219–36, as well as his "Historia antigua de México" (Mexico, D.F.: Escuela Nacional de Antropología e Historia, 1953, mimeograph). The history of Mexican intrusions into Yucatán is treated in Thompson, *The Rise and Fall of Maya Civilization*, pp. 97–130. Robert Wauchope has focused his attention on the

Guatemalan highlands in "An Approach to the Maya Correlation Problem through Guatemala Highland Archaeology and Native Annals," AATQ, XIII (1947), 59–66.

The term *Chichimeca* derives from *chichitl* ("dog") and *mecatl* ("tie") and has been interpreted to mean "lineage of the dog." This may be connected with the North American Indian folk tales which trace the origins of the Indians to men-dogs begotten on a human female by a dog, or with a hypothetical affiliation with the dog-headed god Xolotl, who accompanies the sun on its appointed round. The Chichimec-Toltec state of Texcoco has received treatment in Ángel Palerm and Eric R. Wolf, "El desarrollo del área clave del Imperio Texcocano," RMEA, XIV (1954–55), 337–49. Charles Gibson summarizes available historical material on Tlaxcala in his *Tlaxcala in the Sixteenth Century* ("Yale Historical Publications, Miscellany," Vol. LVI [New Haven, 1952]). The historical background of the Tarascan dynasty is conveniently summarized by Donald D. Brand in *Quiroga: A Mexican Municipio* (SI-ISA, Vol. XI [1951]), pp. 9–10. Chichimec inroads toward the Gulf coast are discussed in Isabel Kelly and Ángel Palerm, *The Tajín Totonac* (SI-ISA, Vol. XIII [1952]), pp. 16–20. The Chichimec splinter at Puerto Angel on the Pacific coast is mentioned in Barbara Dahlgren de Jordan, *Le Mixteca* (Mexico, D.F.: Imprenta Universitaria, 1954), p. 64.

Throughout this chapter i have implied a distinction between the earth and vegetation serpent of the Theocratic period and the sky or shining serpent of the Militaristic. Both serpents are usually classified under the common rubric of Quetzalcoatl. The Militarist Quetzalcoatl, however, may differ from the Quetzalcoatl identified with Tlaloc by Pedro Armillas, "La serpiente emplumada," CA, XXXI (1947), 161–79. We may in effect be dealing with two concepts similar in form but different in function.

CHAPTER VII

So much has been written on the Mexica or Aztec that I will cite here only the literature that has been most helpful in preparing this chapter.

Robert H. Barlow discussed the name "Aztec" in his "Some Remarks on the Term 'Aztec Empire,'" *The Americas*, I (1945), 344–49. It was Domingo de San Antón Muñón Chimalpahin Cuauhtlehuanitzin who called the Aztecs "savages from Aztlán": see his *Annales. 6me et 7me Relations*, translated by Rémi Siméon (Bibliothèque Linguistique Américaine, Vol. XII [Paris, 1899]), pp. 55–56. Alfonso Caso has interpreted the symbolisms of day, eagle, nocturnal snake, cactus, and holy lagoon in *El Teocalli de la Guerra Sagrada* (Mexico, D.F.: Talleres

Gráficos de la Nación, 1927). On Huitzilopochtli see Ignacio Bernal, "Huitzilo-pochtli Vivo," CA, XCVI (1957), 127–52.

My account of the social and political changes in Mexica society is based—with minor modifications—on Friedrich Katz, *Die Sozialökonomischen Verhältnisse bei den Azteken im 15. und 16. Jahrhundert* ("Etnographisch-Archaeologische Forschungen," Vol. III, Part 2[Berlin: Veb Deutscher Verlag der Wissenschaften, 1956]). Robert H. Barlow dealt with *The Extent of the Empire of the Culhua Mexica* (IA, No. 28 [1949]). He also discussed "Tlatelolco como tributario de la Triple Alianza," *Memorias de la Academia Mexicana de la Historia,* IV (1945), 200–15. Isabel Kelly and Ángel Palerm have an excellent appendix on the Mexica conquests in their *Tajín Totonac* (SI-ISA, Vol. XIII [1952]), pp. 264–317.

On the *calpulli* see specifically Arturo Monzón, *El Calpulli en la organización social de los Tenochca* (Mexico, D.F.: Instituto de Historia, Universidad Nacional Autónoma de México, 1949). On stratified kin groups, in general, see Paul Kirchhoff's seminal, long-unpublished paper "The Principles of Clanship in Hu-man Society," *Davidson Journal of Anthropology,* I (1955), 1–10, and Morton H. Fried, "The Classification of Corporate Unilineal Descent Groups," *Journal of the Royal Anthropological Institute,* LXXXVII (1957), 1–29. On lineages among the lowland Maya, Ralph L. Roys, *The Indian Background of Colonial Yucatán* (CIW-P, No. 548 [1943]), p. 34; among the highland Maya, Pedro Carrasco, "Kinship and Territorial Groups in Pre-Spanish Guatemala" (Paper delivered at the Fifty-seventh Annual Meeting of the AAA in Washington, D.C., November 20, 1958).

The significance of Itzcoatl for Mexica history was first recognized explicitly by Paul Radin, *Sources and Authenticity of the History of the Ancient Mexicans.* ("University of California Publications in American Archaeology and Ethnol-ogy," Vol. XVII [1920]).

Miguel Acosta Saignés has written on Mexica merchants in his *Los pochteca,* as well as on the Mexica priesthood in "Los teopixque," RMEA, VIII (1946), 147–205. Anne Chapman has written a most insightful study of the Mexica and Maya trade in "Port of Trade Enclaves in Aztec and Maya Civilizations," in Karl Polanyi *et al.* (eds.), *Trade and Market in the Early Empires* (Glencoe, Ill.: Free Press and Falcon Wing's Press, 1957), pp. 114–53. A very well documented doc-toral thesis deals with the economic role of cacao in Middle America: René F. Millon, "When Money Grew on Trees" (Ph.D. diss., Columbia University, 1955). Carlos Bosch García is the author of a book on Mexica slavery, *La esclavitud pre-hispánica entre los Aztecas* (Mexico, D.F.: El Colegio de México, 1944). Mexica religion and world view are treated in Alfonso Caso, *The People of the Sun* (Norman: University of Oklahoma Press, 1958) and in Miguel León Portilla, *La filosofía Nahuatl* (Mexico, D.F.: Instituto Indigenista Interamericano, 1956). Human sacrifice is discussed from the demographic point of view in Sherburne F. Cook, "Human Sacrifice and Warfare as Factors in the Demography of Pre-Colonial Mexico," HB, XVIII (1946), 81–102. On divination and religious symbolism among the Mexica see Krickeberg, *Altmexikanische Kulturen*, pp. 263–64. For an excellent presentation of a modern case, Maud Oakes, *The Two Crosses of Todos Santos* ("Bollingen Series," Vol. XXVII [New York: Pantheon Books, 1951]).

In seeing the Mexica as the Assyrians of Middle America I have followed a suggestion by Ángel Palerm.

For good ethnohistorical studies of pre-Hispanic groups not treated here in detail see Ralph L. Roys's book on the *Indian Background of Colonial Yucatán;* Pedro Carrasco, *Los Otomíes* (Mexico, D.F.: Instituto de Historia, Universidad Nacional Autónoma de México, 1950) ; Barbara Dahlgren de Jordan, *La Mixteca* (Mexico, D.F.: Imprenta Universitaria, 1954) ; Suzanne W. Miles, *The Sixteenth-Century Pokom-Maya*, APS-T, XLVII (1957).

CHAPTER VIII

The Renaissance dreams and postures of the conquerors receive excellent treatment in Ida Rodríguez Prampolini, *Amadises de América: la hazaña de Indias como empresa caballeresca* (Mexico, D.F.: Junta Mexicana de Investigaciones Históricas, 1948). Irving A. Leonard has contributed to this theme in *Books of the Brave* (Cambridge, Mass.: Harvard University Press, 1949), especially in chapters 2–4, and in "Conquerors and Amazons in Mexico," HAHR, XXIV (1944), 561–79.

Much remains to be written about the military tactics and instruments of the Conquest. Mario Alberto Salas has contributed a study of weapons in *Las armas de la Conquista* (Buenos Aires: Emecé, 1950). Robert M. Denhardt writes on "The Equine Strategy of Cortés," HAHR, XVIII (1937), 550–55. C. Harvey Gardiner has unearthed unsuspected dimensions of the Conquest in his excellent *Naval Power in the Conquest of Mexico* (Austin: University of Texas Press, 1956). Ralph Beals comments on the Conquest as a revolt of subject peoples in HC, p. 227.

The background of the Conquest is ably discussed by Charles Verlinden in *Précédents médiévaux de la colonie en Amérique* (IPGH-P, No. 177 [1954]) and by Charles J. Bishko, "The Iberian Background of Latin American History: Recent Progress and Continuing Problems," HAHR, XXXVI (1956), 50–80. My distrust of Weber's correlation of Protestantism and capitalism stems from reading

Lujo Brentano, *Der wirtschaftende Mensch in der Geschichte* (Leipzig: Meiner, 1923); Werner Sombart's *Der moderne Kapitalismus* (4th ed., 2 vols.; Munich-Leipzig: Duncker & Humblot, 1921); and André E. Sayous, "La genèse du système capitaliste: la pratique des affaires et leur mentalité dans l'Espagne du XVIe siècle," *Annales d'Histoire Économique et Sociale,* VIII (1936), 334–54. It has since been reinforced by what I have learned about the course of Spanish history from Ángel Palerm's "El industrialismo y la decadencia," *Presencia,* Nos. 5–6 (1949), pp. 38–80. Somewhat parallel papers are Rodrigo García Treviño, "Los elementos y la síntesis de la Colonia: apuntes para un ensayo," *Universidad Obrera: Revista de cultura moderna,* XVI (1937), 1–29, and Carmelo Viñas y Mey, "De la Edad media a la Moderna: El Cantabrio y el Estrecho de Gibraltar en la historia política española," *Hispania,* I (1940–41), No. 1, pp. 52–70, No. 2, pp. 53–79, No. 4, pp. 64–101, No. 5, pp. 41–105. The destructive effects of the flood of American gold on Spain has been documented in detail by Earl H. Hamilton in such works as "American Treasure and the Rise of Capitalism," *Economica,* No. 27 (1929), pp. 338–57, *American Treasure and the Price Revolution in Spain, 1501–1650* ("Harvard Economic Studies," Vol. XLII [1934]), and "The Decline of Spain," *Economic Historical Review,* VIII (1938), 168–79. These and other essays have been collected, in Spanish translation, in a volume entitled *El florecimiento del capitalismo y otros ensayos de historia económica* ("Biblioteca de la Ciencia Económica," Vol. VIII [Madrid: Revista del Occidente, 1948]).

Americo Castro has written vividly on imperialism, messianism, and Erasmian influence in *Aspectos de vivir hispánico: espiritualismo, mesianismo, actitud personal en los siglos XIV al XVI* (Santiago de Chile: Editorial Cruz del Sur, 1949). Especially relevant to our thesis are pp. 21–54 and 125–49. See also the very excellent paper by Richard M. Morse, "Toward a Theory of Spanish American Government," *Journal of the History of Ideas,* XV (1954), 71–93, and Ramón Menéndez Pidal, "La idea imperial de Carlos V," *Revista Cubana,* X (1937), 5–31. Lewis Hanke illuminates the utopian side of the judicial process and labor policy in *The Spanish Struggle for Justice in the Conquest of America* (Philadelphia: University of Pennsylvania Press, 1949). Silvio Zavala has contributed a volume on *Filosofía política en la Conquista de América* (Colección Tierra Firme 27 [Mexico, D.F.: Fondo de Cultura Económica, 1947]). Marcel Bataillon's *Erasme et l'Espagne* (Paris: E. Droz, 1937) is a classic of its kind. José Miranda has written on "Renovación cristiana y erasmismo en México," HM, XI (1951), 22–47; John L. Phelan on *The Millennial Kingdom of the Franciscans in the New World* (Berkeley: University of California Press, 1956); Silvio Zavala on *Ideario de Vasco de Quiroga* (Mexico, D.F.: El Colegio de México, 1941) and *La 'Utopia' de Tomás Moro en la*

Nueva España (Mexico, D.F.: Antigua Librería Robredo, 1937). George Kubler furnishes excellent data on the utopian background of the Spanish friars, as on the utopian impulse in New World city planning, in his remarkable *Mexican Architecture in the 16th Century* ("Yale Historical Publications, History of Art," Vol. V [2 vols.; New Haven: Yale University Press, 1948]). Town planning is also discussed by Dan Stanislawski, "Early Spanish Town Planning in the New World," GR, XXXVII (1947), 94–105, and in "The Origin and the Spread of the Grid-Pattern Town," GR, XXXVI (1946), 105–20.

The process of cultural restriction which produced the "culture of the Conquest" was first recognized and formulated by George M. Foster, "Aspectos antropológicos de la conquista española de América," *Estudios Americanos*, VIII (1954), 155–71. Eliseo Vivas comments on the Spanish desire for personal autarchy in "The Spanish Heritage," ASR, X (1945), 184–91; and Salvador de Madariaga contrasts Spaniards and Englishmen in *The Rise of the Spanish Empire* (London: Hollis & Carter, 1947), p. 125. The colonies were a social frontier where commoners as well as poor nobles could hope for wealth and station. The resultant upward mobility and its consequences are well described in José Durand, *La transformación social del conquistador* ("México y lo Mexicano," No. 16 [Mexico, D.F.: Porrua y Obregón, 1953]) and in his "El ambiente social de la conquista y sus proyecciones en la Colonia," HM, III (1954), 497–515. Richard Konetzke deals with the same problem in his "La formación de la nobleza en Indias," *Estudios Americanos*, III (1951), 329–57. Durand has written on the conspicuous consumption of the colonists in "El lujo indiano," HM, VI (1956), 59–74.

The role of the Indian nobility in conversion is amply documented: see especially Fray Gerónimo de Mendieta, *Historia eclesiástica indiana* (1st ed. 1596; Mexico, D.F.: S. Chávez Hayhoe, 1945), Parts II, XX, XXXII; Charles Gibson, *Tlaxcala in the Sixteenth Century*, chap. 2. The best general account of the "conquest of souls" is Robert Ricard, *La "Conquête Spirituelle" du Mexique* (IETM, Vol. XX [1933]). The quote from Frank Tannenbaum on how the church made for religious continuity through its use of syncretism can be found in his *Peace by Revolution* (New York: Columbia University Press, 1933).

CHAPTER IX

José Miranda has written an excellent analysis of the Spanish entrepreneur in "La función económica del encomendero en los orígenes del régimen colonial de Nueva España, 1525–1531," INAH-A, II (1947), 421–62. J. Rey Pastor is the author of a general treatise on Spanish technology in *La ciencia y la técnica en el descubrimiento de América* (Buenos Aires: Espasa Calpe, 1942). Modesto Bargalló has written a book on colonial mining, *La minería y la metalurgia en la América española durante la época colonial* (Mexico, D.F.: Fondo de Cultura Económica, 1955). Mendizábal's long study on "La minería y la metalurgia Mexicanas, 1520–1943," appears in MOC, V, 25–72. Robert C. West has dealt with one mining area in *The Mining Community in Northern New Spain: The Parral Mining District* (IA, No. 30 [1949]). Henrie Hawks's comment of 1572 on the miners of New Spain appears in Richard Hakluyt, *The Principal Navigations, Voyages, Traffiques and Discoveries of the English Nation* (8 vols.; London: Everyman's Library, Dent, 1926), VI, 289.

François Chevalier, *La formation des grands domaines au Mexique: terre et société aux XVIe–XVIIe siècles* (IETM, Vol. LVI [1952]) will be the fundamental work on the origin of the Mexican hacienda for some time to come. Richard J. Morissey has dealt with "Colonial Agriculture in New Spain," in AgH, XXXI (1957), 24–29. George W. Hendry has covered "The Source Literature of Early Plant Introduction into Spanish America," AgH, VIII (1934), 64–71. James A. Robertson offers us "Some Notes on the Transfer by Spain of Plants and Animals to Its Colonies Overseas," in *Studies in Hispanic-American History*, edited by W. W. Pierson, Jr. ("James Sprunt Historical Studies," Vol. XIX [Chapel Hill: University of North Carolina, 1927]), pp. 7–21. All sorts of data on plants and animals may also be gleaned from Mariano Cárcer y Disdier's study of acculturation in food and food habits, *Apuntes para la historia de la transculturación Indo-española* (Mexico, D.F.: Instituto de Historia, 1953). Fernando B. Sandoval has dealt with sugar production in *La industria del azúcar en Nueva España* (Mexico, D.F.: Instituto de Historia, Universidad Nacional Autónoma de México, 1951); Alberto Ruíz y Sandoval with cotton in *El algodón en México* (Mexico, D.F.: Oficina Tipográfica de la Secretaría de Fomento, 1884), especially in Part 2; William F. Leggett with cochineal and indigo in *Ancient and Medieval Dyes* (Brooklyn, N.Y.: Chemical Publishing Co., 1944). Woodrow Borah has dealt with the problems of New Spanish sericulture in his *Silk Raising in Colonial Mexico* (IA, No. 20 [1943]).

Livestock-keeping in Middle America still needs its historian. Charles J. Bishko's "The Peninsular Background of Latin American Cattle Ranching," HAHR, XXXII (1952), 491–515, is indispensable background reading. See also Ramón Carande, "Der Wanderhirt und die überseeische Ausbreitung Spaniens," *Saeculum*, III (1952), 373–87. Chevalier's book contains much information on the topic. José Miranda has discussed the organization of the great cattle-keepers in "Notas sobre la introducción de la Mesta en la Nueva España," *Revista de historia de Américas,* XVII (1944), 1–26. Types of cattle introduced are discussed in Bishko's paper and in J. Frank Dobie's *The Longhorns* (Boston: Little, Brown & Co., 1941); Spanish horses in Robert M. Denhardt, *The Horse of the Americas* (Norman: University of Oklahoma Press, 1947), in J. Frank Dobie, *The Mustangs* (Boston: Little, Brown & Co., 1952), in George G. Simpson, *Horses* (New York: Oxford University Press, 1951). Salvador Ortíz Vidales has written on mules and mule-skinners in *La arriería en México* (Mexico, D.F.: Museo Nacional de Arqueología, Historia, y Etnografía, 1929). Francisco del Barrio Lorenzot has collected New Spanish guild charters in his *El trabajo en México durante la época colonial* (Genaro Estrada ed.; Mexico: Dirección de talleres gráficos, 1920). Richard Konetzke discusses guild charters in his "Las ordenanzas de gremios como documentos para la historia social de Hispanoamérica durante la época colonial," *Estudios de historia social de Epaña,* I (1949), 481–524. A recent study of guilds is Manuel Carerra Stampa, *Los gremios mexicanos* ("Colección de estudios histórico-económicos Mexicanos de la Cámara Nacional de Industria de Transformación," Vol. I [Mexico: Edición Iberoamericana de Publicaciones, S.A., 1954]). R. S. Smith has written on "The Institution of the Consulado in New Spain," HAHR, XXIV (1944), 61–83. Manuel Romero de Terrero y Vicent, *Las artes industriales en la Nueva España* (Mexico, D.F.: Pedro Robredo, 1923) discusses the products of craft skill.

Mendizábal covers "Las artes textiles indígenas y la industria textil Mexicana," MOC, VI, 257–496. Luis Chávez Orozco has edited a series of documents on the history of the *obraje* in *El obraje: embrión de la fábrica* (SEN-D, Vol. XI [1936]) and interpreted them in chapter 2 of his insightful *Historia económica y social de México* (Mexico, D.F.: Ediciones Botas, 1938).

The literature on the encomienda is large and growing. The leading works in the field are undoubtedly Silvio Zavala, *La encomienda indiana* (Madrid: Imprenta Helénica, 1935) and Lesley Byrd Simpson, *The Encomienda in New Spain* (Berkeley: University of California Press, 1950). Zavala has also dealt with Indian slavery in his *New Viewpoints on the Spanish Colonization of America,* chaps. 5 and 6; with Indian slavery in New Spain in "Los esclavos indios en Nueva España," HAC, pp. 427–40; and with slavery, encomiendas, and personal servitude in Guatemala in *Contribución a la historia de las instituciones coloniales en Guatemala* ("Jornadas," No. 36 [Mexico, D.F.: El Colegio de México, 1945]).

Philip W. Powell has written the best general study of Spanish penetration into the Gran Chichimeca: *Soldiers, Indians, and Silver: The Northward Advance of*

New Spain, 1550–1600 (Berkeley: University of California Press, 1952). Richard J. Morissey has dealt with "The Northward Advance of Cattle Ranching in New Spain, 1550–1600," AgH, XXV (1951), 115–21. Silvio Zavala has discussed the northern frontier of New Spain in his "The Frontiers of Hispanic America,". in *The Frontier in Perspective*, edited by Walker D. Wyman and Clifton B. Kroeber (Madison: University of Wisconsin Press, 1957), pp. 35–59, while Richard J. Morissey has compared the northern frontier of New Spain with the advancing western frontier of the United States in "The Shaping of Two Frontiers," *Américas*, III (1951), 3–6, 41–42. I have emphasized certain aspects of this northern periphery in my *The Mexican Bajio in the Eighteenth Century* (MARI-P, No. 17 [1955]), pp. 177–200.

On Spanish trade, see Charles Verlinden, "Modalités et méthodes du commerce colonial dans l'Empire espagnol au XVI siècle," *Revista de Indias*, XII (1952), 249–76. On the New Spanish fairs, Manuel Carrera Stampa, "Las ferias novo-hispanas," HM, II (1953), 319–42. See also W. Schurz, *The Manila Galleon* (New York: E. P. Dutton, 1939).

The diseases imported into the New World are discussed most satisfactorily in Horacio Figueroa Marroquín, *Enfermedades de los Conquistadores* (San Salvador: Ministerio de Cultura, 1957). Sherburne F. Cook has dealt with pre-Conquest conditions in "The Incidence and Significance of Disease among the Aztecs and Related Tribes," HAHR, XXXVI (1946), 320–35. The most comprehensive work on the New World origins of syphilis is Herbert U. Williams, "The Origin and Antiquity of Syphilis," *Archives of Pathology*, XIII (1932), 779–814, 931–83. Some doubts have been thrown on Williams' findings, but they stand confirmed by new evidence: see Charles Weer Goff, "New Evidence of Pre-Columbian Bone Syphilis in Guatemala," in *The Ruins of Zaculeu, Guatemala*, edited by Richard B. Woodbury and Aubrey S. Trik (Richmond, Va.: William Byrd Press, 1953), pp. 312–19. See also the remarks on yellow fever and malaria by Marston Bates, "Man as an Agent in the Spread of Organisms" in *Man's Role in Changing the Face of the Earth*, pp. 788–804.

The contrast between societies based on intensive cultivation of land with a heavy input of labor and societies that farm extensively with tools that save labor has been recognized long ago. See, for instance, Karl A. Wittfogel, "Die Theorie der orientalischen Gesellschaft," *Zeitschrift für Sozialforschung*, VII (1938), 90–122. Recently W. Frederick Cottrell gave an especially elegant formulation to this contrast in his *Energy and Society* (New York: McGraw-Hill Book Co., 1955). Lesley Byrd Simpson's *Exploitation of Land in Central Mexico in the Sixteenth*

Century (IA, No. 36 [1956]) documents the replacement of men by sheep. The contrast between hoe and plow cultivation has been treated by Oscar Lewis in his model study of agricultural systems in *Life in a Mexican Village* (Urbana: University of Illinois Press, 1951), chap. 7. Cottrell has used Lewis' figures to illustrate his own discussion.

CHAPTER X

Much of my basic argument derives from Woodrow Borah's basic *New Spain's Century of Depression* (IA, No. 35 [1951]). Borah has interpreted the decline of mining and the drop in food production as the result of depopulation, a point already made in his previous study of *Silk Raising in Colonial Mexico*. Cook and Simpson have documented the decline in population in detail. François Chevalier has shown clearly how the hacienda developed as a response to shrunken markets and downward economic trends. Silvio Zavala has written an excellent essay on the origins of peonage, "Orígenes coloniales del peonaje en México," TE, X (1944), 711–48. See also Lesley Byrd Simpson's "Mexico's Forgotten Century," *Pacific Historical Review*, XXII (1953), 113–21.

Frank Tannenbaum has pioneered the social scientific study of the Middle American hacienda in *The Mexican Agrarian Revolution* (Washington, D.C.: Brookings Institution, 1929). Jan Bazant has offered illuminating comments on the capitalist character of the hacienda in "Feudalismo y capitalismo en la historia económica de México," TE, XVII (1950), 81–98. Sidney W. Mintz and I have discussed the hacienda as an institution in "Haciendas and Plantations in Middle America and the Antilles," SES, VI (1957), 380–412. The paper contains a bibliography. Much of what I have here written on the hacienda is based on it as well as on a paper I gave at the Seminar on Plantation Systems of the New World, in San Juan, Puerto Rico, November 17–23, 1957.

Silvio Zavala and José Miranda have written an excellent summary of colonial Indian policy, "Instituciones indígenas en la Colonia," in Alfonso Caso *et al.*, *Métodos y resultados de la política indigenista en México* (INI-M, Vol. VI [1954]), pp. 29–112. On the sixteenth-century Spanish efforts to maintain the pre-Conquest culture of the conquered see the books of Fray Bernardino de Sahagún, available in many editions, and Francis B. Steck and Robert H. Barlow, *El primer colegio de América: Santa Cruz de Tlatelolco* (Mexico, D.F.: Centro de Estudios Franciscanos, 1944). I have yet to find a statement on the deculturation and reduction in social complexity of the Indians after the Conquest as clear as Paul Kirchhoff's comments in HC, pp. 253–54.

Oliver La Farge has given us a time scale of deculturation and reintegration in the Guatemalan highlands in his "Maya Ethnology: The Sequences of Cultures," in MN, pp. 281–91. Ralph L. Beals has done the same for Mexico in "The History of Acculturation in Mexico," in HAC, pp. 73–82, and again in HC, pp. 225–32. Charles Gibson has written the only synthesis to date of the development of Indian communities in his "The Transformation of the Indian Community in New Spain, 1500–1810," *Journal of World History*, II (1955), 581–607. Aspects of this development are treated in Luis Chávez Orozco, *Las instituciones democráticas de los indígenas Mexicanos en la época colonial* (Mexico, D.F.: Instituto Indigenista Interamericano, 1943) and in François Chevalier, "Les municipalités indiennes en Nouvelle Espagne, 1520–1620," *Anuario de historia del derecho Español*, XV (1944), 352–68; Luis Chávez Orozco, *Las cajas de comunidades indígenas de la Nueva España* (SEN-D, Vol. V [1934]).

My discussion of the Indian community as a type obviously neglects important variants. These may be ascertained by consulting the works cited in Howard C. Cline, "Mexican Community Studies," HAHR, XXXII (1952), 212–42, and in Robert H. Ewald, *Bibliografía comentada sobre antropología social Guatemalteca, 1900–1955* (Guatemala City: Seminario de Integración Social Guatemalteca, 1956). Yet there is also a unity in diversity, which Robert Redfield and Sol Tax characterize in "General Characteristics of Present-Day Mesoamerican Indian Society," HC, pp. 31–39.

A number of studies have been specifically helpful to me in my generalizations. Fernando Cámara Barbachano has discussed the relationship between politics and religion in the Indian community in his "Religious and Political Organization," HC, pp. 142–64, a topic also illuminated in an excellent paper by Manning Nash, "Political Relations in Guatemala," SES, VII (1958), 65–75. For the pre-Hispanic roots of religious redistributions, see Fray Toribio de Paredes (Motolinía), *Motolinía's History of the Indians of New Spain*, translated and edited by F. B. Steck, O.F.M. ("Documentary Series," Vol. I [Washington, D.C.: Academy of American Franciscan History, 1951]), I, 106–7. I find very persuasive John Gillin's analysis of Indian values in his "Ethos and Cultural Aspects of Personality," HC, pp. 193–212. Sol Tax has discussed "World View and Social Relations in Guatemala," AA, XXXIX (1937), 423–44. See also Antonio Goubaud Carrera, "Some Aspects of the Character Structure of the Guatemalan Indians," AI, VIII (1948), 95–104. The economic features of the Middle American Indian community emerge with great clarity from a paper by Pedro Carrasco which compares "Some Aspects of Peasant Society in Middle America and India," KAS-P, No. 16

(1957), pp. 17–27. See also Sol Tax, *Penny Capitalism: A Guatemalan Indian Economy* (SI-ISA, Vol. XVI [1953]).

Indian markets are analyzed in "The Folk Economy of Rural Mexico with Special Reference to Marketing" by George M. Foster in the *Journal of Marketing*, XII (1948), 153–62 and by Alejandro Marroquín in two interesting papers: "Introducción al mercado indígena Mexicano" (Mexico: INI, 1955, mimeographed) and "Consideraciones sobre el problema económico de la región Tzeltal-Tzotzil," AI, XVI (1956), 191–203. All scholars interested in Middle America will wish to read Bronislaw Malinowski and Julio de la Fuente, *La economía de un sistema de mercados en México* ("Acta Anthropologica," Época 2, Vol. I, No. 2 [Mexico, D.F., 1957]).

The notion of "life-risks" as an explanatory concept can be found in one of my papers, "Closed Corporate Peasant Communities in Mesoamerica and Central Java," SWJA, XIII (1957), 1–18. This paper is a further development of another which discussed the Indian community as a sociocultural type, "Types of Latin American Peasantry," AA, LVII (1955), 452–71.

CHAPTER XI

C. E. Marshall has traced "The Birth of the Mestizo in New Spain," in HAHR, XIX (1939), 161–84. Nicolás León describes the social position of the mestizo during the colonial period in *Las castas del México Colonial o Nueva España* (Mexico, D.F.: Museo Nacional de Arqueología, Historia, y Etnografía, 1924).

Racial prejudice is one thing, social prejudice another. See on this point such works as Eric Williams' magnificent *Capitalism and Slavery* (Chapel Hill: University of North Carolina Press, 1944); Oliver Cromwell Cox, *Caste, Class, and Race* (Garden City: Doubleday & Co., 1948). Frank Tannenbaum has written on slavery and race prejudice in Latin America in *Slave and Citizen: The Negro in the Americas* (New York: Alfred A. Knopf, 1947). On legal parallels to Latin American slavery in the American colonies, see Wilbert E. Moore, "Slave Law and the Social Structure," JNH, XXVI (1941), 188–90.

The social and political dynamism of the mestizo was recognized clearly by the Mexican sociologist Andres Molina Enríquez in his epoch-making book *Los grandes problemas nacionales* (Mexico, D.F.: Imprenta de A. Carranza e Hijos, 1909). I have followed some of his leads in my paper on "La formación de la nación," CS, IV (1953), 50–62, 98–111, 146–71, and again in *The Mexican Bajío in the 18th Century*. Eusebio Dávalos Hurtado, "La morfología social de Nueva España, móvil de su independencia" in EAMG, pp. 593–603, has taken a similar point of view.

Various social and cultural categories have been proposed by anthropologists for the study of mestizo social groups. John Gillin has spoken of "Modern Latin American Culture" as synonymous with "Mestizo Culture" or "Ladino Culture" in "Mestizo America," in *Most of the World*, edited by Ralph Linton (New York: Columbia University Press, 1949), pp. 156–211, and in "Modern Latin American Culture," *Social Forces*, XXV (1947), 243–48. William Davidson has discussed the rural mestizo components in "Rural Latin American Culture," in the same journal, pp. 249–52. Charles Wagley and Marvin Harris have used the terms "peasant," "plantation worker," "town," "metropolitan middle class," "urban proletariat" to dissect the phenomenon more finely in "A Typology of Latin American Subcultures," AA, LVII (1955), 428–51. I dealt with the rural mestizo under the rubric "open peasant community," in "Types of Latin American Peasantry," AA, LVII (1955), 452–71. A sophisticated treatment of the variables involved marks Richard N. Adams, "Cultural components of Central America," AA, LVIII (1956), 881–907. He has also contributed a detailed study of mestizo culture in Guatemala in his *Cultural Surveys of Panama—Nicaragua—Guatemala —El Salvador—Honduras* (Washington, D.C.: Pan American Sanitary Bureau, 1957).

I have emphasized the danger of equating the emerging mestizo with the emerging European middle classes of the incipient Industrial Revolution. The problems posed by the phenomenon of the middle class in various parts of Latin America are described and analyzed in Theo Crevenna (ed.), *Materiales para el estudio de la clase media en la América Latina* (6 vols.; Washington, D.C.: Social Science Office, Pan American Union, 1950–51). Ralph L. Beals has provided an interesting synthesis of this and other relevant material in "Social Stratification in Latin America," *American Journal of Sociology*, LVIII (1953), 327–39. He has made use of the term "middle class," but has wrestled valiantly with its unintended implications. John Gillin has used the term "middle mass" in "Cultura emergente," *Integración social en Guatemala,* edited by Jorge Luis Arriola (Guatemala City: Seminario de Integración Social Guatemalteca, 1956), pp. 435–57, in which he has been followed by Manning Nash, "The Multiple Society in Economic Development: Mexico and Guatemala," AA, LIX (1957), 825–33. On problems of historical development see Miguel O. de Mendizábal, MOC, II, 559–71; Angel Palerm, "Notas sobre la clase media en México," CS, III (1952), 18–27, 129–35; Nathan L. Whetten, "The Rise of a Middle Class in Mexico," in Theo Crevenna (ed.), *Materiales para el estudio de la clase media en la América Latina,* II (1950), 1–29. José E. Iturriaga, *La estructura social y cultural de México* (Mexico, D.F.: Fondo de Cultura Económica, 1951), furnishes excellent quantified data on the development of social classes in Mexico: see pp. 24–89.

I have based many of my comments on the mestizo character on a growing Middle American literature striving to define the "essence" of the Mexican national character. This literature is reviewed by Gordon W. Hewes in "Mexicans in Search of the 'Mexican': Notes on Mexican National Character Studies," *American Journal of Economics and Sociology*, XIII (1954), 219–23, and by José E. Iturriaga in his *La estructura social y cultural de México*, pp. 225–44. The pioneer work in this regard is Samuel Ramos, *El perfil del hombre y de la cultura en México* (Mexico, D.F.: Pedro Robredo, 1938), the most perceptive is without doubt Octavio Paz, *El laberinto de la soledad* (Mexico, D.F.: Ediciónes Cuadernos Americanos, 1950). John Gillin's "Ethos and Cultural Aspects of Personality," in HC, pp. 193–212, and Melvin Tumin's provocative "Culture, Genuine and Spurious: A Re-Evaluation," ASR, X (1945), 199–207, have offered me Guatemalan parallels. María Elvira Bermúdez' *La vida familiar del Mexicano* ("México y lo Mexicano," No. 20 [Mexico: Antigua Librería Robredo, 1955]) is hopeful evidence of a growing interest in family studies, and Emanuel K. Schwartz, "Psychotherapy in Mexico," *Progress in Psychotherapy* (New York: Grune & Stratton, 1957), pp. 216–23, offers an overview of the growing psychiatric literature on Mexico. For a perceptive treatment on mestizo political behavior see Richard M. Morse's "Toward a Theory of Spanish American Government," *Journal of the History of Ideas*, XV (1954), 71–93, and the provocative remarks of Rodolfo Usigli in "Rostros y máscaras," *México: realización y esperanza* (Mexico, D.F.: Editorial Superación, 1952), pp. 47–55, on the politician as the "real" Mexican.

Nathan Whetten's *Rural Mexico* remains the most comprehensive study of land reform in Mexico. Sanford Mosk has surveyed *The Industrial Revolution in Mexico* (Berkeley: University of California Press, 1950). Luis Yañez-Pérez deals with the industrialization of agriculture in his able *Mecanización de la agricultura Mexicana* (Mexico, D.F.: Instituto Mexicano de Investigaciones Económicas, 1957). Sanford Mosk has also written on "The Coffee Economy of Guatemala, 1850–1918," *Interamerican Economic Affairs*, IX (1955), 6–20, and on "Indigenous Economy in Latin America," *Interamerican Economic Affairs*, VIII (1954), 3–25. Charles M. Wilson has dealt with the history of the banana trade and the United Fruit Company in his *Empire in Green and Gold* (New York: Henry Holt, 1947). Leo Suslow has covered *Aspects of Social Reform in Guatemala, 1944–49* (Latin American Seminar Report 1 [Hamilton: Colgate University Area Studies, 1949, mimeographed]); K. H. Silvert's *A Study in Government: Guatemala*

(MARI-P 21, 1954) deals with developments thereafter. Nathan Whetten has discussed aspects of the revolutionary land reform in "Land Reform in a Modern World," *Rural Sociology*, XIX (1954), 329–36. Among the controversial discussions of revolution and counter-revolution in Guatemala I should like to cite Philip B. Taylor's "The Guatemalan Affair: A Critique of United States Foreign Policy," *American Political Science Review*, L (1956), 787–806, and "Ambiguities in Guatemala" by John Gillin and K. H. Silvert in *Foreign Affairs*, XXXIV (1956), 469–82.

The social and cultural concomitants of these economic and political developments in Mexico are ably treated in José E. Iturriaga's *La estructura social y cultural de México*. Oscar Lewis has recently given us "Mexico desde 1940," *Investigación Económica*, XVIII (1958), 185–256. For Guatemala we possess the series of essays by different contributors edited by Jorge Luis Arriola, *Integración social en Guatemala* (Guatemala: Seminario de Integración Social Guatemalteca, 1956) and Jorge del Valle Matheu's *Sociología Guatemalteca* (Guatemala: Editorial Universitaria, 1950). Luis Villoro's *Los grandes momentos del indigenismo en México* (Mexico, D.F.: El Colegio de México, 1950) is an interesting history of Indianism by a philosopher; the ideology of Indianism receives critical review in Beate Salz, "Indianismo," *Social Research*, XI (1944), 441–69. Julio de la Fuente has described the spread of *pocho* culture in his most interesting *Cambios socioculturales en México* ("Acta Anthropologica," Vol. III, No. 4 [Mexico, D.F., 1948]), a subject also discussed in Lewis' paper on Mexico since 1940. Attempts to generalize about the course of development are Manning Nash, "The Multiple Society in Economic Development: Mexico and Guatemala," AA, LXIX (1957), 825–33, and my "Aspects of Group Relations in a Complex Society: Mexico," AA, LVIII (1956), 1065–78. An excellent discussion of the characteristics and implications of mass society appears in Melvin M. Tumin, "Some Unapplauded Consequences of Social Mobility in a Mass Society," *Social Forces*, XXXVI (1957), 32–37.

The literature on Indian acculturation to mestizo patterns is enormous; much of it is very good indeed. However, I shall cite here only those studies which I have found especially profitable. Of the studies dealing with Mexico, I should like to mention Wilbert E. Moore's *Industrialization and Labor* (Ithaca: Cornell University Press, 1951), especially for the discussion of the data on Atlixco contributed by Ricardo Pozas; Pedro Carrasco's *Tarascan Folk Religion: An Analysis of Economic, Social, and Religious Interactions* (MARI-P, No. 17 [1952]); and Paul W. Friedrich's "A Tarascan Cacicazgo: Structure and Function," in

Bibliographical Notes

Systems of Political Control and Bureaucracy in Human Societies (Proceedings of the 1958 Spring Meeting of the American Ethnological Society, Seattle, 1958), pp. 23–29. Of the studies dealing with Guatemala, I have found especially useful Richard Adams' *Cultural Survey* and the volume issued under his editorship, *Political Changes in Guatemalan Indian Communities* (MARI-P, No. 24 [1957]), as well as Manning Nash, *Machine Age Maya: The Industrialization of a Guatemalan Community* (AAA-M, No. 87 [1958]). Among studies holding great promise for future anthropological inquiry I would single out Oscar Lewis' "Urbanization without Breakdown: A Case Study," *Scientific Monthly*. LXXV (1952), 31–41, which traces the transition of a group of families from rural Tepoztlán to Mexico City.

Index

Acalán, upper Candelaria River, 109
Acamapichtli, 124, 136
Acapulco, Guerrero, 186, 187, 188
Acatlán, Oaxaca, 40
Achiutla, Oaxaca, 121
Acolhua, 124, 127, 148
Acosta, Jorge R., 112, 275
Acosta Saignés, Miguel, 82, 272, 277
Adams, Richard N., 287, 290
Africans, 262–63; cultural influence of, 238; numbers of, imported, 29; origins of, 29–30; physical characteristics of, 30; as slaves, 185, 193, 233, 236; spread of, in Middle America, 29
Agricultural systems, 58–62, 74–78, 178–79, 197–99, 251, 270–71, 288
Aguirre Beltrán, Gonzalo, 29, 261, 262–63, 269
Alanís Patiño, Emilio, 44, 267
Alonso, Amado, 266
Altitude, effects of, on physique, 26–27
Altschuler, Milton, 273
Amanteca, 83, 272
Amaranth, 53–54, 178
American Indians, 21; differentiation of, in Middle America, 26–27, 262; entry of, into New World, 21–22, 48; origins of, 22–23; spread and differentiation of, 23–26
Amurians, 22
Andalusia, 29
Anderson, Edgar T., 269
Andes, 1
Andrews, E. Wyllys, 273
Aniline dyes, 180
Antigua, Guatemala, 11
Antilles, 188
Apoala, Oaxaca, 121
Arana Osnaya, Evangelina, 265
Arizona, 77, 194
Armillas, Pedro, vii, 267, 270, 271, 272, 273, 274, 275, 276
Arriola, Jorge Luis, 289
Art styles, 70–71, 90–93, 99, 231, 248–50, 256, 272–73
Atetelco, Teotihuacán, Mexico, 102, 273
Atlantic, 15, 56, 180, 182
Atlixco, Puebla, valley of, 9, 10, 289
Atoyac River, 10
Atzcapotzalco, Mexico, D.F., 83, 102, 122, 123, 132, 134, 137, 146

291

Ceremonial centers, 70, 74, 77, 78, 83, 272
Cerro de la Malinche, Tula, 113
Cerro de las Mesas, Veracruz, 27, 71
Chalchihuites, Zacatecas, 114, 116
Chalma, State of Mexico, Black Christ of, 10, 170
Ch'ao-ting Chi, 261
Chapala Lagoon, Jalisco, 8
Chapman, Anne, 277
Charnay, Desiré, 111, 113
Chávez, Carlos, 248
Chávez, Cristóbal de, 275
Chávez Orozco, Luis, 282, 285
Chenopodium, 54
Chevalier, François, 281, 284, 285
Chiapas, 11, 13, 27, 63, 100, 109, 220
Chibchan, 37, 265
Chichén Itzá, Yucatán, 101, 124–25
Chichimec, 9, 114, 119, 124, 126–29, 130, 131, 151, 192–93, 276
Chichimeca, the Great, 9, 16, 114, 191–95, 282
Chickens, 183
Chihuahua, 114
Childe, V. Gordon, 50, 268
Chili pepper, 65, 66
Chimalpahin Cuauhtlehuanitzin, Domingo de San Antón Muñón, 95, 276
Chinampa agriculture, 74–76, 78, 132, 271
Chinantec, 26, 44
Chocho-Popoloca, 95
Chocolate, 181
Cholula, Puebla, 6, 18, 90, 94–95, 96, 105, 106. 121, 125, 168, 273. 274
Chontal, 34, 41, 124
Cisneros, Ximénez de, 166
Citlaltepetl (Pico de Orizaba), 3
Cline, Howard C., 285
Coatlícue. See Lady with the Serpent Skirt
Coatzacoalcos River, 13
Cobá, Yucatán, 101, 105
Cochineal dye, 180, 181–82, 187, 281
Cocucho, Michoacán, 226
Coe, Michael D., 268, 270, 272, 273
Coffee-growing, 8, 247, 288
Cofradía pattern, 216
Colhua Mexica. See Mexica

Colhuacán, Mexico, D.F., 124, 130
Colima, 82
Collins, Henry B., 265
Colombia, 37, 52
Colonial society, integration of, 201, 211–14, 230–32
Columbus, Christopher, 65, 130, 152
Comas, Juan, 262
Compostela, Jalisco, 177
Conklin, Harold C., viii
Cook, Orator F., 273
Cook, Sherburne F., 104, 263, 264, 268, 273, 278, 283, 284
Cooke, C. Whyte, 273
Coon, Carleton S., 262
Copán, Honduras, 82, 86, 100–101, 104, 105, 111, 273
Copán River, 100
Copper work, 227
Corbeled vault, 99
Core areas, 3, 15, 18–20, 194, 261; and hinterland, 3, 108–9, 116–17, 119, 129, 191, 194, 234, 274
Cortés, Hernán, 140, 152, 154, 161, 177, 249–50
Costa Rica, 71
Cotton, 55, 56, 81, 180, 227, 281
Cottrell, W. Frederick, 283
Council of Trent, 165
Counter-Reformation, 231
Covarrubias, Miguel, 270, 271, 272
Cox, Oliver Cromwell, 286
Coyote motif, 102
Crafts, 54–58, 81–82, 184–86, 213, 226–27, 238
Crevenna, Theo, 287
Cross, symbol, 172
Cuba, 188
Cuchumatán Mountains, 11
Cuernavaca, Morelos, 9
Cuicuilco, Mexico, D.F., 77, 90
Cuitzeo, lagoon of, Michoacán, 8
Culiacán, Sinaloa, 194
Cultivation: divergent traditions of, 51–52; origins of, in Middle America, 50–53; spread of, toward north, 117, 269, 275
Cultural creativity, 230–32, 256
"Culture of the Conquest," 45, 160, 238

293

Index

Mazahua, 44
Mazápan pottery, 104
Mazatec, 26, 44
Mazateco-Popoloca, 122
Measles, 196
Mecapayan, 41
Medina, Bartolomé de, 177
Mediterranean whites, 21, 23, 28
Meggers, Betty J., 273
Mendieta, F. Gerónimo de, 173, 280
Mendizábal, Miguel Othón de, 263, 264, 269, 274, 281, 282, 287
Menéndez Pidal, Ramón, 279
Merchant guild (consulado), 184, 187
Mérida, Yucatán, 13, 101
Mestizos, 185, 207; behavior patterns, 238–41, 288; compared to Indians, 238–40; as a cultural group, 230, 233–56, 286–88; physical type, 31, 32, 264
Metztitlán, Hidalgo, 116, 151
Mexica, 6, 8, 9, 73, 76, 83, 88, 89, 112, 117, 120, 121, 124, 127, 129, 130–51, 154, 168, 171, 179, 192, 249, 276–78
Mexico, 1, 3, 8, 9, 10, 18, 19, 31, 34, 37, 43, 121, 130, 224, 235, 247, 248, 250, 252, 253, 254, 266, 267, 288–89; State of, 7; valley of, 3, 6, 9, 18, 40, 48, 49, 55, 63, 65, 66, 70, 71, 73, 74, 75, 105, 106, 113–14, 123, 124, 127, 129, 131, 132, 135, 191, 197, 220, 268, 275
Mexico City, 6, 19, 56, 75, 93, 132, 179, 188, 234, 249, 290
Michoacán, 8, 129, 166
Middle class, 241–43, 247, 287–88
Miles, Suzanne W., 261, 278
Militaristic period, 79, 82, 86, 102–29, 130, 273–76
Millon, René F., 271, 277
Mining, 8, 176–78, 192, 194, 201, 205, 238, 247, 281, 284
Mintz, Sidney W., viii, 284
Miranda, José, 280, 281–82, 284
Mixcoatl, 121
Mixtec, 40, 41, 42, 44, 84, 88, 95, 111, 121, 122, 149, 151, 180, 265, 273
Mixtecan, 37, 40, 265
Moctezuma, 155, 203
Moctezuma, Carlos, 200

Molina Enríquez, Andrés, 263, 286
Mongoloid characteristics, 22, 23, 27
Monte Albán, Oaxaca, 10, 79, 83, 88, 89, 90, 92, 93, 96–97, 104, 266, 272
Monzón, Arturo, 277
Moore, Wilbert E., 286, 289
Moors, 157, 158, 162, 165
More, Thomas, 165, 166
Morelos, valley of, 9, 18, 40, 56, 58, 81, 111, 121, 133, 146
Morissey, Richard J., 281, 283
Morley, Sylvanus Griswold, 267, 271, 273, 274
Morse, Richard M., 266, 279, 288
Mosk, Sanford A., 288
Motagua River, 11
Mourant, A. E., 262
Mules, 183–84, 192, 282
Mullers, 54
Murals, 79, 93, 97, 102, 271, 272
Mutations, 24

Nahua, 37, 40, 41, 42, 127, 171, 265, 266
Nahua names for other language groups, 41
Nahuat, 41, 129
Nahuatl, 34, 35, 41, 42, 84, 88, 95, 122, 133, 267
Nahuatzen, Michoacán, 227
Narváez, Pánfilo de, 154
Nash, Manning, 285, 287, 289, 290
Nationalism, 244, 252, 256
Natural selection, 25–26, 262
Nayarit, 116
Nebrija, Antonio de, 43
Negro. See Africans
Neo-Realists, 248
Nevado de Toluca, State of Mexico, 40
New Mexico, 51, 63, 192, 194
New Spain, 166, 178, 182, 184, 186, 187, 188, 189, 190, 194, 195, 201, 203, 205, 211, 231, 234, 235, 237, 238
Newman, Marshall T., 26, 262
Newman, Stanley, 265
Nexapa River, 10
Nicaragua, 121
Nicarao, 121
Nichols, Madeline W., 266
Nicoya, Costa Rica, Gulf of, 12
Noguera, Eduardo, 273, 274

Population, 11, 13, 263–64, 273; aboriginal, 31; decline after Conquest, 195–201, 284; of different language groups, 44; influence of, on genetic makeup, 24–25; mestizo, 235; occupation breakdown of, in 1895, 246; racial composition of, 30; of Teotihuacán, 74; of Tikal, 98

Positivism, Comtean, 231

Pottery, 69, 79, 82, 104, 109, 184, 186, 226, 274

Powdermaker, Hortense, vii

Powell, Philip W., 282

Pozas, Ricardo, 289

Prejudice, 236–37, 286

Priests, 70, 78–90, 106, 147–48, 169, 213, 245, 271, 273, 277

Progreso, Yucatán, 13

Projectile points, 48, 49, 55, 268

Proletariat, 242, 247

Proskouriakoff, Tatiana, 271, 272

Protestant ethic, 162

Protestantism and Reformation, 156, 161–62, 165

Protopopoloca, 40

Puebla: City of, 5; State of, 3, 82, 121, 146, 266; valley of, 6, 9, 18, 40, 94, 125, 127, 180

Puerto Ángel, Oaxaca, 276

Puerto Limón, Costa Rica, 12

Pulque, 63, 66, 206, 208, 269

Pumpkins, 65

Puritanism, 161

Querétaro, Querétaro, 122

Querns, 52, 54

Quetzal bird, 78, 81, 84

Quetzaltenango, Guatemala, 11

Quiché, 44, 84, 111, 125–26

Quimby, George I., 265

Quinoa, 54

Quintana Roo, 104

Quirigua, Guatemala, 11

Quiroga, Vasco de, 166

Radin, Paul, 147, 277

Railroads, 247

Ramos, Samuel, 287

Rands, Robert L., 271

Ratzel, Friedrich, 261

Raymond, Joseph, 260

Recinos, Adrián, 274

Redfield, Robert, 207, 285

Religion: buildings for, Hispanic, 6–7, 166, 231; buildings for, pre-Hispanic, 83, 90–91, 94–101, 105, 112, 124–25, 272; conversion to Christianity, 167–75, 199–200, 213, 280; of early village cultures, 56–58; on haciendas, 206; in Indian communities, 215–18, 219, 220, 224, 285; Mexica, 131, 145–49, 199, 276–77, 278; Militaristic, 160–7, 124–25; reformism in, 165–67, 279; of Spain, 164–65; syncretism in, 146–47, 167, 168–72; Theocratic, 70, 81, 83–89, 271, 272

Rendón, Silvia, 271, 275

Revolution, 247–52, 289

Rey Pastor, J., 280

Ricard, Robert, 280

Ricketson, Oliver G., 260

Ritchie, Ruth, viii

Rivera, Diego, 250

Rivers, 12

Robelo, Cecilio A., 267

Robertson, James A., 281

Rock temple, Malinalco, 10

Rocky Mountains, 1

Rodríguez Prampolini, Ida, 278

Roman Catholic Church, organization of, 171, 173–74

Romano, Arturo, 51

Romero, Javier, 268

Romero de Terreros y Vincent, Manuel, 282

Roys, Ralph L., 274, 277, 278

Rubber, 81

Ruíz y Sandoval, Alberto, 281

Ruppert, Karl, 271

Ruz Lhuillier, Alberto, 274

Sahagún, F. Bernardino de, 93, 213, 284

Salamanca, Spain, 140

Salas, Mario Alberto, 278

Salinas River (Chixoy), 11

Salt, 56, 65–66, 269

Salz, Beate, 289

San Juan de Ulua, Veracruz, 152

Spanish merchants, 8, 187–88, 234, 245
Spanish society, characteristics of, 156–58, 278–80
Spear-throwers, 48
Squash, 54, 65
Squier, Robert J., 270
Stanislawski, Dan, 261, 280
Starr, Betty, 261
Steam-driven machinery, 185
Steck, Francis Borgia, 284
Steggerda, Morris, 264
Stelae, 80, 106, 110–11, 271, 272
Steward, Julian, vii, 261, 270
Stewart, T. Dale, 268
Stirling, Matthew W., 272
Stock-raising, 182–83, 192, 194, 197–98, 201, 226, 238, 281
Storage, 54, 81
"Sublimis Deus," papal bull, 175
Sugar-growing, 10, 179, 187, 281
Sultepec, State of Mexico, 177
Surplus: and division of labor, 20, 69, 73, 81, 108; redistribution of, in Indian communities, 215–16, 228, 254; uncertain, 204–5
Suslow, Leo, 288
Swadesh, Morris, 35, 44, 264, 265
Sweat bath, 200
Sweet potato, 52
Syphilis, 196, 283

Tabasco, 19, 71, 124
Tacuba, Mexico City, 132
Tajín, Veracruz, viii, 93, 96, 127
Tallow, 182, 187
Tamaulipas, 51, 63, 64, 65, 116
Tamayo, Jorge L., 260
Tanaco, Michoacán, 226
Tannenbaum, Frank, 171, 280, 284, 286
Tarahumara, 26
Tarascans, 8, 44, 60, 129, 151, 191, 226, 276
Tawney, Richard, 161–62
Tax, Sol, 224, 261, 285, 286
Taxco, Guerrero, 177
Taylor, Philip B., 289
Tehuacán, Puebla, 40, 266
Tehuantepec, Isthmus of, 10, 29, 35
Temalscatepec, Michoacán, 177

Tenancingo, State of Mexico, valley of, 9
Tenoch, 130
Tenochca. *See* Mexica
Tenochtitlán, 6, 19, 83, 130–51, 154, 168, 192, 275
Teotihuacán, State of Mexico, viii, 19, 74, 77, 79, 80, 81, 82, 83, 84, 86, 88, 89, 90, 93–94, 95, 96, 97, 102, 105, 106, 109, 111, 112, 113, 114, 122, 123, 271, 272, 273, 274, 275
Teotlálpan, 113–14, 117
Tepanec, 123, 132, 136, 138
Tepexpan, State of Mexico, 49
Tepexpan Man, 49, 268
Tepoztlán, Morelos, 58, 198, 290
Tequixquiac, State of Mexico, 48
Termer, Franz, 260
Terra, Helmut de, 51, 268
Terracing, 74, 116
Tertiary, 10
Texcoco, State of Mexico, 42, 127, 132–33, 134, 148, 155, 200, 276
Textile production, 55, 141, 180, 185–86, 188, 227, 247, 252, 282
Thatch-and-pole construction, 54
Theocratic period, 69–109, 270–73
Theocratic rule, characteristics of, 78–80, 106, 122
Thomas (Apostle), 168, 172
Thomism, 231
Thompson, J. Eric, 100, 268, 270, 271, 274, 275
Tikal, Guatemala, 97–98, 104, 106
Time concepts, 86–88, 218
Tlacopan (Tacuba, Mexico City), 132, 133–34
Tlaloc. *See* He Who Makes the Plants Spring Up
Tlatelolco, Mexico City, 131–32, 141
Tlatilco, Mexico, D.F., 71
Tlaxcala, Tlaxcala, 18, 127–28, 151, 155, 173, 193, 276
Tloque Nahuaque, 148
Tobacco, 188
Todos Santos Cuchumatán, Guatemala, 148
Tollán, 111–12, 119–20, 126, 275
Toltec, 119–26, 127, 128, 129, 137, 145, 168, 191, 275. *See also* Epigonal Toltec; Pioneer Toltec; Tollán; Tula
Tolteca-Chichimeca, 119, 125

PRINTED IN U.S.A.

PHOENIX BOOKS

PHOENIX BOOKS

PHOENIX BOOKS

 PHOENIX SCIENCE SERIES